Foreign Sounds
or
Sounds Foreign

John Yau

MadHat Press
Cheshire, Massachusetts

MadHat Press
Cheshire, Massachusetts

Copyright © 2020 John Yau
All rights reserved

The Library of Congress has assigned
this edition a Control Number of
2020935421

ISBN 978-1-952335-01-3 (paperback)

Cover art and design by Marc Vincenz
Book design by MadHat Press
Author photo by Eve Aschheim

www.madhat-press.com

First Printing

For Thomas Micchelli, Albert Mobilio, and Hrag Vartanian

Also by John Yau

Poetry

Crossing Canal Street (1975)
The Reading of an Ever-Changing Tale (1977)
Sometimes (1979)
Broken Off by the Music (1981)
Corpse and Mirror (1983)
Radiant Silhouette: New & Selected Work 1974-1988 (1989)
Big City Primer (1991), with photographs by Bill Barrette
Edificio Sayonara (1992)
Berlin Diptychon (1995), with photographs by Bill Barrette
Forbidden Entries (1996)
I Was a Poet in the House of Frankenstein (2000)
Borrowed Love Poems (2002)
Ing Grish (2005), with Thomas Nozkowski
Paradiso Diaspora (2006)
Exhibits (2010)
Further Adventures in Monochrome (2012)
Egyptian Sonnets (2012)
Bijoux in the Dark (2018)
Annals of a Gumshoe (2019), with Trevor Winkfield

Fiction

The Sleepless Night of Eugene Delacroix (1980)
Hawaiian Cowboys (1995)
My Symptoms (1996)
My Heart Is That Eternal Rose Tattoo (2001)

Criticism

The Passionate Spectator: Essays on Art and Poetry (2006)
The Wild Children of William Blake (2017)

Collaborations

100 More Jokes from the Book of the Dead (2001), with Archie Rand
The Autumn Fields of a Young Art Handler (2019), with Tom Burckhardt

Monographs

In The Realm of Appearances: The Art of Andy Warhol (1993)
A. R. Penck (1993)
Ed Moses: A Retrospective of Paintings and Drawings, 1951–1996 (1996)
The United States of Jasper Johns (1996)
Joan Mitchell: Works on Paper 1956–1992 (2007)
A Thing Among Things: The Art of Jasper Johns (2008)
William Tillyer: Watercolours (2010)
Jay DeFeo: Chiaroscuro (2013)
Mernet Larsen (2013)
Sam Francis (2014)
Richard Artschwager: Into the Desert (2015)
Catherine Murphy (2016)
Al Taylor: Early Paintings (2017)
Thomas Nozkowski (2017)
Philip Taaffe (2018)

Editor:

The Collected Poems of Fairfield Porter (1985), with David Kermani
Fetish (1998)

Table of Contents

I.
What Is a Poet? — 3

II.
Rudy Burckhardt and Edwin Denby, Flâneurs of Astoria — 9
The Flickering Grace of Rudy Burckhardt — 13
Frank O'Hara and the Practice of Everyday Life — 19
Kanemitsu in California in the 1960s and '70s — 29
On the Poems of John Godfrey — 33
Stranded with Rick Snyder — 37

III.
Asians in Hollywood — 43
Patty Chang: *The Product of Love* — 47
What Happens After Eric Baus's Pharmacy Fills with Sand? — 51
In Death, Licked by a Dog — 55
On *Haute Surveillance* by Johannes Göransson — 59
Staying Up with Suzanne Buffam's *Pillow Book* — 63
When a Poet Becomes Invisible — 67
Nicolas Hundley's Heretical Machinery — 71
Will Alexander's Celebration of the Possible — 73

IV.
China's Buried Past and Submerged Future — 77
The Five-Star Delight of Driving Across America with Ron Padgett — 81
At Play in The Fields of Language: The Poetry of Cathy Park Hong — 87
Donna Stonecipher, Global Flâneur — 97
Ai Weiwei: *New York Photographs 1983–1993* — 103
John Ashbery—A Prince of the Clouds — 107

An Artist Conjures the Ghosts of Displacement ... 113
The Earth Before the End of the Earth ... 117

V.

The Great Kenward ... 133
Language Is Not Colorless: The Amazing Writing of Sawako Nakayasu ... 139
Introduction to *New Generation: Poems from China Today* ... 147
The Need for Opaque Identities ... 157

VI.

Trevor Winkfield's Undomesticated Imagination ... 165
An Arcadian Moment in New York's Lower East Side, circa 1969 ... 169
George Schneeman, Quietly Radical ... 173
Why I Am a Member of the Ron Padgett Fan Club ... 177

VII.

Ian Hamilton Finlay's Philosophical Gardening ... 185
When Capri Was the Place to Be ... 191
How Frederic Tuten Became a Writer ... 195
Wallace Berman's Magical World ... 199

VIII.

"Purity" and the "Avant-Garde" ... 205
Marilyn Chin: Poet, Translator, Provocateur ... 209
Foreign Sounds or Sounds Foreign ... 215
The Meme After the Fall of The Tower of Babel ... 219

IX.

Nicholas Moore, Touched by Poetic Genius ... 227
Why I Am a Member of the Christopher Middleton Fan Club ... 235
Christopher Middleton's Prose ... 249
One More Thing I Want to Say about Christopher Middleton ... 253
Why I Am a Member of the Lee Harwood Fan Club ... 257

X.

Digging into Time and Memory with John Koethe	265
Douglas Crase, Literary Subversive	273
Charles North Shows Us How to Read without Relying on Theories	279
The Many Pleasures of Reading Donald Britton's Poems	285
Killed by the State	291
A Forensic Poet for Our Time	297
The Confessional Poem Made New	313
A Thriver in the Muck	307
Jennifer Reeves, Writer and Artist	311
Ann Lauterbach Expands the Possibilities of Poetry	315
The Rise and Fall of Three Actresses	321
Dissolving the Boundaries of Asian American Fiction	325
Acknowledgments	329
About the Author	333

I.

What Is a Poet?

In 1967, Clark Coolidge moved from Cambridge, Mass., where he was living with Aram Saroyan and others, to San Francisco to join David Meltzer's band, Serpent Power. In 1970, Clark and his wife, Susan—whom he met in San Francisco—moved to the Berkshires in western Massachusetts, where they lived on a hill at the end of a dirt road for 27 years. In 1997, they moved to Petaluma, California. Back in California, Clark saw more of David. They often gave readings together.

Poet is Coolidge's response to a poem, "When I Was a Poet" by Meltzer, which he heard his friend read many times. I think of the two works—Meltzer's "When I Was a Poet" and Coolidge's *Poet*—as a call-and-response between two old friends and musicians who played together on many occasions, talked into the wee hours of the night, enjoyed each other's company, and read and respected each other's work. As William Blake wrote: "I cannot think that real poets have any competition."

Each line of Meltzer's poem begins, "When I was a poet ..." before going in different directions. At one point in the poem, Willie Nelson and Paul Celan show up. At other times, it moves forward through sound and funny, self-mocking rhymes. Its structure enabled Meltzer to bring together all his interests: sound, metaphysics, Jewish mysticism, nature, humor, music, and much, much more. (I highly recommend watching him read it on YouTube).

Poet, Coolidge's response, is a 310-page serial poem, with many of the untitled poems being 14 lines long. The dedication reads: "Thanks to David." As one might expect with a Coolidge poem, all sorts of funny, bewildering things happen in every poem. One poem begins:

> The poem of eyedrops on the ashen warrior
> the poem of sea light on chopsticks
> the poem of Father Deal and his zephyr trail
> a poem from the Stuff and Nonsense board
> poem for putting things on top of other things

This is one of Coolidge's many writing techniques: he stretches the possibility of a word beyond any of its conventional definitions (or restrictions). At the same time, the precision of the first two lines explodes surrealism's collision of opposites. In the third line, you feel him shifting the focus from the lyric ("The poem of eyedrops on the ashen warrior / poem of sea light on chopsticks") to the epic ("Father Deal and his zephyr trail"). And then he shifts again ("a poem from the Stuff and Nonsense board") and again ("poem for putting things on top of other things"). By this time you begin wondering: what is a poem, anyway? It is something we have never agreed upon because any definition becomes a restriction, which Coolidge is against.

All of these shifts of attention and context happen in the first five lines of a 14-line poem: a list of open-ended phrases whose fuller context is never given to us. We are pulled into a realm of conjecture. Sixty or so pages later, a poem begins:

> I saw poets in rubbers
> I knew poets as brothers
> I saw poets entangled
> I saw poets in baubles and bangles
> I saw poets on tuesday
> I even met them on thursday

Are the "rubbers" galoshes or condoms, or some other kind of item? What starts out as a memory undoes the sentiment that is often intrinsic to this kind of Whitmanic declaration.

On the next page, Coolidge "kissed the poem and made a wish." A few lines later, "a poet picked up a used tortoise," which is one of many incongruous pairings that makes this reader, at least, both marvel and wonder: what is a "used tortoise"?

Throughout *Poet* Coolidge presents all sorts of surprises, for example, in "The Collected Poems of William Windex," as well as with allusions he does not comment on, preferring to stay in the present tense of writing his "poems written on long marches." It is as if Coolidge set out to imagine and document every kind of poet and poem, and the way they have been thought about:

>poems built on your father's spine
>poet who's a shelf reader
>poet who went dark
>poet still on the clock

At times, he is addressing the poet and the poem. Other times, they are addressing him. Sometimes, he seems to be responding to other poets: "the Ed Sanders classic Jackbatty Fructate." Does this have to do with the pleasure of masturbating? Other times, he plays with names: "The name is Pally Harmer fuzz poet." Science fiction makes an entrance as well:

>The apes had all left for another planet
>where they could chew in peace
>practicing a sort of naked mercy.

And the poem answers Coolidge's foray into this territory: "planet of whatever the hell you're talking about." Detective novels, cowboy movies, music, a love of lists and made up names—all of this comes into play in *Poet*.

Whenever Coolidge sets off in one direction, the reader had better be prepared to be startled by an unexpected shift, a sudden stop that vaults you into another dimension. His 310-page serial poem is about the poet, the poem, and poetry, without a trace of nostalgia or sappy romantic idealism. He names poems that have not been written, leaving us to imagine what they would be: "the poem about Camp Climax for girls." He wonders about what we will never read: "how many volumes of Corso have been lost?" All sorts of people make an appearance: "the poem where Jack Palance smiles." Lines turn in on themselves:

> The poet ought to cut down
> a kidney-shaped cloud precedes his exit from the car
> An ugly noise in the moist skull

People for whom poetry is a necessary part of their lives should love this book. They know all the tricks and tropes poets use to manipulate the reader. Instead of going down well-trodden paths—all of which he seems to know—Coolidge is interested in showing how the magician pulls the rabbit out of the hat, which he does with affection. Deeply suspicion of anything that smacks of self-importance, of making a blanket statement or pronouncement, he resists nailing down what the poet and poem are. He wants to do something bigger, which is to liberate the terms "poet" and "poem" from all the restrictions they have been saddled with. The humor running through this book is cool and tender, pointed and generous.

II.

Rudy Burckhardt and Edwin Denby, Flâneurs of Astoria

They took many walks in New York City and often looked down while others were looking up. One was a photographer who was born and educated in Switzerland. He took photographs of the legs and shoes he saw. The other, his friend, was born in China shortly after the start of the 20th century. He got viewers to think about legs, feet, and torsos from another perspective: dance. The two men met in Basel in 1934. A year later, they came to New York and rented a fifth-floor walk-up in a building on West 21st Street, between 6th and 7th Avenue, which has not yet been replaced by a tower. Willem de Kooning lived in the building next door. The rest, as they say, is history.

The two men are, of course, Rudy Burckhardt and Edwin Denby. Although neither of them has ever been regarded as a major figure, they are perhaps more than that because they are indispensable. Remove all the photographs of de Kooning taken by Burckhardt and what would we have left? This is not just true of de Kooning. Erase all the dance criticism Denby published and what would we know about Martha Graham and George Balanchine, not to mention the many dancers and dances he wrote about? For these and innumerable other reasons, they are central figures in New York's cultural history, even though they are not as well known as others who gave less, and I don't mean just in a public way.

I remember seeing Denby at a rehearsal in Merce Cunningham's Westbeth studio in the late 1970s, long after he had stopped writing dance criticism. When offered a chair, he refused because he wanted to sit on the floor. He was in his mid-70s and still spry. Later, he told me that he sat on the floor because that was closest to the view he would have had if the dance was being performed on a stage and he was seated in the audience. I also remember bumping into Burckhardt some years later, in Soho. One part of our conversation from that afternoon remains strong in my mind: he said that if you were old and did not know anyone young, you might as well be dead. Although I did not know either man particularly well, both of them got me to think a lot about the kind of attention one ought to pay to the everyday world one lives in.

The exhibition, *A Walk through Astoria and Other Places in Queens, 1943 by Rudy Burckhardt & Edwin Denby* at the Bruce Silverstein Gallery, represents the third collaboration between these two men, a photographer and a poet, resulting in a unique album of sequenced photographs and typewritten sonnets. In 1939, Burckhardt and Denby compiled their first album, *New York, N. Why?*, which is in the collection of the Metropolitan Museum of Art. In 1940, the two men went to Queens and made another album of photographs and poems, *An Afternoon in Astoria* (1940), which is in the collection of the Museum of Modern Art. In 1943, Burckhardt and Denby collaborated on their third album, *A Walk through Astoria and Other Places in Queens,* or what the poet calls, in the first sonnet, a "backyard of exploitation and refuse."

The photographs document an industrial zone that is empty of people under a gray, cloudless sky. America is at war and a mood of quiet gloom pervades the work, from the empty streets to the page design, in which Burckhardt has grouped four photographs of pairs of people: in each image, the two people are neither looking at nor talking with each other. They have sunk into themselves because there is nowhere else to go. Through all of this, Burckhardt manages to take in the gloominess while keeping it at a distance. He never gets that close to his subjects and they probably did not know he was photographing them. He was incognito.

In one picture, there is a simple church and unremarkable house rising up from behind an embankment of stones and gravel. Beyond them, in the distance, a vast cemetery full of gravestones stretches across the horizon, framed above by an elevated highway blocking the way to heaven. The thick, dark elevated track feels poised to crush the already dead even further, pushing even the stones back into the earth.

In another photograph, three buildings—one of them a tavern—stand in the middle distance, looking like something that you would see in a John Ford Western. Burckhardt's photographs are full of jolts that you catch only after looking for a while. If bleakness can be understated, then he is the only photographer I know who can get us to that place. The album comes across as vulnerable, like the poems typed on thin paper. In one sonnet, Denby has typed, "A truck is dead for the day." Above the word "dead," which is crossed out, he has penciled in the word "home." The truck is home for a day. "Dead" must have been too dramatic for Denby, which is why he crossed it out.

Burckhardt and Denby's three albums should be brought together and published in a facsimile format in chronological order. According to an essay authored by Christopher Sweet and published on the gallery website, "The form, of the composed, arranged, and sequenced unique photographic album as a work of art in and of itself, is original to Burckhardt." And yet, no one has reproduced them as a single book. Perhaps this will be rectified in the future.

The Flickering Grace of Rudy Burckhardt

When it comes to the artistic community of New York City, especially from the late 1930s to the end of the 20th century, I can think of many writers, photographers, and artists who readily qualify as *flâneurs,* but there is only one who matches Charles Baudelaire's description of the "passionate spectator," someone who could be called "a kaleidoscope gifted with consciousness, responding to each one of its movements and reproducing the multiplicity of life and the flickering grace of all the elements of life."

In his films and photographs, which seem particulary suited for his way of seeing, Rudy Burckhardt captured the "flickering grace" of New York, particularly in the resolute movement and idle hanging out of its citizens. However, in contrast to Baudelaire's mordant wit, Burckhardt imbued his work with an infectious innocence and gentle delight that, paradoxically, also infuses it with a quiet melancholy and gravitational tug that is not immediately apparent.

If, like me, you are at all curious about how different the landscape of New York, as well as its inhabitants in their fashions and tastes, look since the 20th century ended, then you should make your way to the exhibition, *Rudy Burckhardt: Subterranean Monuments: Photographs, Paintings and Films: A Centenary Celebration,* at Tibor de Nagy. Burckhardt, who was never interested in focusing on his career, or calling attention to himself as a professional artist, worked across different mediums long before it became fashionable. In addition to a selection of his photographs, paintings and films, this exhibition includes books, collage postcards, a typed poem, and two paintings done on mushrooms.

Aside from the films, the exhibition concentrates largely on two genres, still-life and landscape, whether of the city or of the woods near his house in Maine, where he went each summer from 1956 to 1999, the year that he decided to leave his body behind. Many of the views tend to be either close-ups of storefronts or trees, or vistas looking out over rooftops, as if the city were a mountainous landscape, which it is.

The few exceptions, such as the black-and-white photograph, *Crossing* (1948), in which we see a row of people crossing the street in the foreground, with a cavern of tall buildings serving as a backdrop, hint at the range of what caught his eye. In this photograph, one is likely to recall the oft-quoted lines from William Shakespeare's comedy, *As You Like It:* "All the world's a stage, / And all the men and women merely players; / They have their exits and their entrances...." As evidenced in the early film *The Climate of New York* (1935), which is being shown along with other films, Burckhardt is empathetic to human purposefulness and vanity, from striding pedestrians to children digging in the mud with sticks to two women of vastly different proportions comparing their new hairdos.

In all of the work, one senses Burckhardt's interest in the chaotic order of everyday life and throwaway things. One senses his melancholic awareness of just how fleeting and enchanting, everything is. There is an emotional depth and complexity to the work that we have yet to fully plumb, perhaps because what comes across first is Burckhardt's droll humor.

Burckhardt was born in Basel, Switzerland, in 1914. He went to London to study medicine, but gave it up when he discovered photography. He came to New York in 1935 with the poet Edwin Denby, who went on to become a great and influential dance critic. Both Denby and Burckhardt were interested in movement, but for very different reasons. Denby was interested in the gymnastic beauty a dancer could achieve, while Burckhardt was inspired by people going determinedly to and fro, as if something great awaited their arrival.

Although Burckhardt studied painting briefly with Amédeé Ozenfant, he rightfully considered himself a primitive. In his essay, "How I Think I Made Some of My Photos and Paintings," he describes a primitive painting:

A painting done without much skill; the finished picture is visualized beforehand, and the subject is more important than how it is painted, brought to a degree of completion, clear without ambiguity, without loose ends, as if it were the only painting ever made, outside of trends or history.

This is the conundrum animating all of Burckhardt's work. Born into a well-to-do Swiss family, he received a classical education that included, as he said, "many years of Latin and Greek." As an artist, he is self-taught and at home in different mediums. He made crisp, sharply focused, close-up photographs of storefronts and newsstands, because that is what the subject demanded, while in his views from rooftops, he was as sensitive to the city's haze and air as to the buildings in the distance. In the paintings done in Maine, he often focused on the bark of a tree and the lichen growing on it. Whatever he looked at became a subject of intense and loving scrutiny. In addition to close-ups and long views, he would juxtapose the two in a single photograph or painting without making the image seem contrived.

In the photograph *Willem de Kooning Studio I* (1950), the view is of a cabinet whose top is cluttered with coffee cans full of paintbrushes by a window, where, across the street, a man and woman are walking in opposite directions. Burckhardt has collapsed the near and far, making both a point of interest. Together, they evoke the viewer's experience of de Kooning's paintings–standing back and moving in close.

In the still-life painting *Purple Band* (1946), Burckhardt has arranged a nail, a bolt, a striped bowl, a snail shell and a tourist replica of the Statue of Liberty on a table with a prominent knothole. A pair of pliers stands upright on the table, resting against the dirty plaster wall right behind the table, beside a colored postcard of an ocean liner with three smokestacks, and on the far right, a nail hole. Everything in the painting is given its own space, and one senses from the postcard and Statue of Liberty replica that there is an autobiographical current running through his choices.

In *38th Street South* (1987), done more than forty years after *Purple Band,* he is still a primitive paying close attention to what is in front of him. The painting is an aerial view of a gray, nondescript office building seen in the distance, wedged in by other buildings. It is the homeliest of the bunch, which is perhaps why Burckhardt gave it so much space in the painting. Within the grid of windows, he has been attentive to the overhead yellow fluorescent lights glowing in each little rectangle, each pair of them depicted at a slightly different angle. In his attention to such details, one senses that nothing else existed during the time he worked on this painting but the inconsequential things he was looking at.

Burckhardt wasn't interested in the decisive moment or in overt social commentary. And yet, I would not call him an aesthete either. As someone who has passed the iconic New York building known as the Flatiron countless times, and seen innumerable people photographing it, Burckhardt's vintage photograph, *Flatiron Building, Winter* (1947/48) presents a view that remains fresh.

Seen from the air, it also underscores the resolve of New York real estate moguls to buy and build on whatever plot of land is available, including a triangular block bordered by the crisscrossing of Broadway and Fifth Avenue. It is when you get a sense of how narrow the building is—and this is because Burckhardt shows just the building's prow-like front and the Broadway side that you realize how a combination of greed, ingenuity and vision (in this case, that of the architect Daniel Burnham) can result in something magical.

For me, one of the revelations of the exhibition was the inclusion of Burckhardt's painted mushrooms, including a self-portrait, as well as collage postcards and a typed poem, which are indicative of how many different things he did throughout his life. In this museum-quality exhibition, it is quickly apparent that Burckhardt is essentially uncategorizable. To say that he is a photographer, filmmaker and painter seems almost meaningless because the work does and, more importantly, doesn't fit together. What about the collages or the poem? Are there more of them? What are they like? What about a complete volume of his writings?

In the photograph *Snail and Can Opener* (1945), while looking at the way Burckhardt places a snail shell, its eye-like form, in the center of the objects he has arranged on table top, with a postcard of the Empire State Building on the wall behind, I was reminded of what Baudelaire wrote about "the perfect *flâneur:*" "[T]o see the world, to be at the center of the world, and yet to remain hidden from the world … "

Frank O'Hara and the Practice of Everyday Life

Frank O'Hara's relationship to art and artists manifested itself in a multitude of ways. In 1958, he and Larry Rivers worked on a suite of lithographs, *Stones,* which combined his improvisatory poems with the artist's fragmented drawings. In 1960, he collaborated with Norman Bluhm on poem-paintings, a series of 27 works done in watercolor and gouache on paper. In 1963, he and the Italian artist Mario Schifano collaborated on a series of poem-drawings, *Words & Drawings.* In 1964, he wrote the subtitles for Alfred Leslie's 42-minute black-and-white film, *The Last Clean Shirt,* which follows two characters, a black man and white woman, as they drive around Manhattan in a convertible. According to Olivier Brossard, in his essay, "The film *The Last Clean Shirt* by Alfred Leslie and Frank O'Hara":

> *The Last Clean Shirt* is a true collaboration between a film maker and a poet since Frank O'Hara wrote the subtitles to the dialogue or rather the monologue: the woman is indeed the only character who speaks and she furthermore expresses herself in Finnish gibberish, which demanded that subtitles be added.

In addition to collaborating with artists, O'Hara also wrote about their work. He was an editorial associate at ARTnews for two years (1953–54). In 1959, he wrote the first monograph on Jackson Pollock. As the art editor for the little magazine *Kulchur* in 1962 and '63, he wrote three "Art Chronicles" in which he reviewed a wide range of exhibitions. He also wrote introductions for the catalogues of exhibitions that he organized for the Museum of Modern Art in New

York, where he worked for more than a decade, initially as an assistant in the International Program (1955–60). In 1960, he was appointed Assistant (later Associate Curator) in the Department of Painting and Sculpture, where he organized a number of exhibitions until his tragic death in 1966, at the age of forty. These include *Franz Kline* (1963), *Robert Motherwell* (1965), *Reuben Nakian* (1966) and *David Smith* (1966). And, of course, there are the numerous poems that take painters and paintings as their subject, which include his poem to Pollock, "DIGRESSION ON NUMBER 1, 1948"; his diary-like assessment of the difference between being a painter and a poet, "Why I Am Not a Painter"; and his ekphrastic poem, "On Seeing Larry Rivers' *Washington Crossing the Delaware* at the Museum of Modern Art." At O'Hara's funeral in 1966, Philip Guston told Joseph LeSueur: "He was our Apollinaire" (Gooch 11). In his eulogy, Larry Rivers said: "Frank O'Hara was my best friend. There are at least sixty people in New York who thought Frank O'Hara was their best friend."

O'Hara's involvement with painters and art helps explain why one of the recurring paradigms used to characterize his writing process derives from the attributes of an "Action Painter," a term coined by Harold Rosenberg in his essay "The American Action Painters." This is how Rosenberg described the change that had taken place in painting in Manhattan between the late 1940s and early '50s, around the time that O'Hara moved to New York in the fall of 1951:

> At a certain moment the canvas began to appear to one American painter after another as an arena in which to act—rather than as a space in which to reproduce, re-design, analyze or "express" an object, actual or imagined. What was to go on the canvas was not a picture but an event.
>
> The painter no longer approached his easel with an image in his mind; he went up to it with material in his hand to do something to that other piece of material in front of him. The image would be the result of this encounter. (22)

Inspired by existentialism, Rosenberg emphasizes an encounter (or process), which culminates in a painting (or "an event"). Painting was no longer a space in which to "reproduce ... an object, actual or imagined." And the artist no longer began "with an image in mind." Or, to put it another way, the painter, open to the prospect of unexpected possibilities, discovered the painting as it emerged through the process of painting.

In her essay "Frank O'Hara and the Aesthetics of Attention" (1976), Marjorie Perloff wrote: "In [the poem] 'Music,' I would posit, O'Hara removes objects from the 'automatism of perception' by adapting the techniques of film and action painting—perhaps his two favorite art forms—to a verbal medium" (160). Later, in the same essay, she wrote:

> "Music" has no paraphraseable theme; its aim is to quite simply defamiliarize a scene all too familiar to any New Yorker, indeed to any city dweller. The poem captures the sense of magic, urgency, and confusion of the modern cityscape during this particular "season of distress and clarity." Like an action painting, it presents the poet's act of coming to awareness rather than the results of that act. (162)

Perloff's description of the poem as "as an act of coming to awareness" echoes an observation that John Ashbery made five years earlier, in his "Introduction" to *The Collected Poems of Frank O'Hara* (1971):

> Frank O'Hara's concept of the poem as a chronicle of the creative act that produces it was strengthened by his intimate experience of Pollock's, Kline's and de Kooning's great paintings of the late forties and early fifties, and of the imaginative realism of painters like Jane Freilicher and Larry Rivers. (viii–ix)

Certainly, this sense of discovery is in his poem, "On the Way to the San Remo," which is dated 1954 in his book *Lunch Poems,* where we read the following lines:

> The 6th Avenue bus trunk-lumbers sideways
> it is full of fat people who cough as at a movie
> they eat each other's dandruff in the flickering glare (11)

At the same time, as compressed and shifting as these perceptions are, with "cough" being the operative word that transports the "fat people" from sitting on a bus to being at movie, paralleling film editing techniques, one can also make the case that O'Hara's stanza seems to be aligned with the goals outlined in William Wordsworth's "Preface" to *Lyrical Ballads* (1800):

> The principal object, then, proposed in these Poems was to choose incidents and situations from common life, and to relate or describe them, throughout, as far as was possible in a selection of language really used by men, and, at the same time, to throw over them a certain colouring of imagination, whereby ordinary things should be presented to the mind in an unusual aspect; and, further, and above all, to make these incidents and situations interesting by tracing in them, truly though not ostentatiously, the primary laws of our nature: chiefly, as far as regards the manner in which we associate ideas in a state of excitement.

By Wordsworth's standards, O'Hara's lines come from "common life" and the situation he "describe[s]" (people sitting on a bus) is related in "a selection of language really used by men." "[A]t the same time, [he] throw[s] over them a certain colouring of the imagination, whereby ordinary things should be presented to the mind in an unusual aspect...."

It is also in the "Preface" that Wordsworth famously writes: "Poetry is the spontaneous oveflow of powerful feelings: it takes its origin from emotion recollected in tranquility." Here is where Wordsworth and Rosenberg part company. For Wordsworth, poetry, however spontaneous it is, comes after the event; the poem is recollected (or written) in tranquility. Rosenberg, on the other hand, thinks of painting as an encounter between the artist and the materials—someone with a loaded paintbrush facing an empty canvas. Rosenberg believed that the act of painting (or in O'Hara's case, poetry) is synonymous with the event (or experience).

While there is much to commend in Perloff's and Ashbery's writings about O'Hara, I want to shift the focus away from writing and painting to writing and walking, which, in O'Hara's poems can be synonymous acts ("I walk through the luminous humidity...," "Personal Poem," *LP* 32). I see these entangled acts in light of an observation made by the French writer Michel de Certeau in his essay, "Walking in the City":

> The act of walking is to the urban system what the speech act is to language or to the statements uttered. At the most elementary level, it has a triple "enunciative" function: it is a process of *appropriation* of the topographical system on the part of the pedestrian (just as the speaker appropriates and takes on the language); it is a spatial acting-out of the place (just as the speech act is an acoustic acting out of language); and it implies *relations* among the differentiated positions, that is, among pragmatic "contracts" in the form of movements (just as verbal enunciation is an "allocution," "posits another opposite" the speaker and puts contracts between interlocutors into action). It thus seems possible to give a preliminary definition of walking as a space of enunciation. (97–8)

In poems such as "A Step Away from Them," "The Day Lady Died," "Personal Poem," and "Poem (Lana Turner has collapsed!)"—all of which are included in his slim volume *Lunch Poems*—O'Hara defines walking and enunciating as a single, inseparable act unfolding in the present tense. A good example would be "A Step Away from Them" (*LP* 15–17), which opens:

> It's my lunch hour, so I go
> for a walk among the hum-colored
> cabs. First, down the sidewalk
> where laborers feed their dirty
> glistening torsos sandwiches
> and Coca-Cola, with yellow helmets
> on. They protect them from falling
> bricks, I guess. Then onto the
> avenue where skirts are flipping
> above heels and blow up over
> grates. The sun is hot, but the

> cabs stir up the air. I look
> at bargains in wristwatches. There
> are cats playing in sawdust.

The time of the poem is identical with the poet's "lunch hour," during which he goes "for a walk." It is when he can leave his job and routine behind, and go in whatever direction he pleases. The poem marks his movement through the topography ("down the sidewalk" leads "onto the avenue") as it records his speech ("It's my lunch hour, so I go"). Movement and language are identical. The poet is thinking out loud, telling the reader in conversational speech what he is doing, seeing, tasting, hearing and, at the end of the poem, touching and being touched by.

Following de Certeau's lead, the poet, during his journey through streets, "takes on the language," transforming it as he moves ("so I go / for a walk among the hum-colored / cabs ..."). In the second of his enunciative functions, de Certeau equates the spatial acting out of walking with the acoustic acting out of language. Later, in "A Step Away from Them," O'Hara writes:

> I stop for a cheeseburger at JULIET'S
> CORNER. Guilietta Masina, wife of
> Federico Fellini, *è bell' attrice.* (*LP* 16)

The name of the diner ("JULIET'S / CORNER") brings him to "Guiletta Masina, wife of / Federico Fellini, *è bell' attrice*." It is an acoustical passage in which the sound of one name leads him to the actress and wife of the Italian fillm director and star of his film *La Strada* (1956), which received an Academy Award for Best Foreign Film. Elsewhere in the poem, O'Hara uses sound to connect two strangers, one eyeing the other ("A Negro" with "a toothpick" and "A blonde chorus girl clicks").

In his essay "Frank O'Hara," James E. B. Breslin wrote:

> More concerned with the *activity* of creation than with *fetishizing* its products, O'Hara eluded the stability of any theoretical position, any style. "To move is to love," he wrote (*CP,* p. 256), reversing the usual

sense of love as a permanent commitment. His imagination remains uncommitted—mobile, protean, contradictory and alive. (254)

"A Step Away from Them" is a performative poem in which the poet walks about the city, with one perception following another, full of displacements ("hum-colored / cabs") that combine sight and sound, gay desire and eroticism ("where laborers feed their dirty / glistening torsos sandwiches / and Coca-Cola"), and constantly shifting and free "floating sensations ("I look / at bargains in wristwatches. There / are cats playing in sawdust"), with one line spilling over into the next, endowing a fluidity upon the discrete and isolated perceptions. The other striking fact of this poem is O'Hara's non-hierarchical approach to class and race ("laborers" with "dirty / glistening torsos," "a blonde chorus girl" and "A lady in / foxes" with her "poodle," as well as "A Negro" and "Puerto Ricans"). They are all the beneficiaries of the poet's precise and darting attention.

Learning from the French poet, Pierre Reverdy, a few of whose poems he translated, and whose book he carries in his pocket, O'Hara writes:

> And one has eaten and one walks,
> past the magazines with nudes
> and posters for BULLFIGHT and
> the Manhattan Storage Warehouse,
> which they'll soon tear down

His use of a gender-neutral, indefinite pronoun—which is common in French, but rarely used in English, particularly in a poem, enables the poet to pull back from the unanswerable question he asks at the end of the previous lines:

> First Bunny died, then John Latouche,
> then Jackson Pollock. But is the
> earth as full as life was full, of them? (*LP* 16)

By using "one," O'Hara acknowledges that all of us—not just the poet/speaker of the poem—are only a step away from mortality, that our proximity to death is a constant and common condition. For

O'Hara, walking—the act of moving and experiencing the visceral pleasures the city has to offer, its sights, sounds, and tastes—is tantamount to being alive and to writing. According to de Certeau: "Walking affirms, suspects, tries out, transgresses, respects, etc., the trajectories it 'speaks'" (99). O'Hara's speaking affirms cabs, construction workers' sweaty torsos, skirts lifting up, wristwatches for sale, cats, billboards, sounds, time, eating and drinking, movies, friends' deaths, urban renewal, as it documents his unplanned movement through the streets. "A Step Away from Them" is—to use Breslin's words—"mobile, protean, contradictory and alive." It is a walk, not a quest. The poet has no destination, all he knows is that he is alive and on his lunch hour, whereas some of his friends are dead, and that he is just a

> step away
> from them.

As the ending of "A Step Away from Them" makes clear, one of the things that helps O'Hara stay alive and open to the chaotic world, even as it makes him more conscious of death's proximity, is poetry:

> "My heart is in my / pocket, it is *Poems* by Pierre Reverdy."

Along with Reverdy, he cites Walt Whitman, Hart Crane and William Carlos Williams as his models in his anti-manifesto, "Personism: A Manifesto." He also states why he admires them: "And after all, only Whitman and Crane and Williams, of the American poets, are better than the movies" (498).

Rather than retreat from popular culture and mass media, particularly movies, O'Hara wanted to write something that was at least the equal of the cinema—a poem which unfolds in the present tense and is full of cuts and dissolves, techniques the poet would adapt to his poems, and which were likely to have been inspired by his reading of Reverdy's poems, with their cubist shifts from line to line in spare, non-poetic language.

O'Hara's poem "An Image of Leda" opens: "The cinema is cruel / like a miracle." If we substitute "Life" for "The cinema," we get a sense of the poet's view of reality, which, for the moviegoer, includes the unreal pleasure of "loving / a shadow and caress- / ing a disguise" (*CP* 35–36). While the moviegoer might not achieve real intimacy, the poet/walker in the city becomes increasingly aware of his fundamental solitude from others, but he steps back and does not dwell on it ("A glass of papaya juice / and back to work"). Both his life force ("My heart") and sense of intimacy ("in my pocket") is entangled with the book of another poet ("*Poems* by Pierre Reverdy"). Reverdy's book of poems has touched O'Hara, literally and metaphorically. It is what keeps him going.

Works Cited

Ashbery, John. "Introduction." *The Collected Poems of Frank O'Hara*. 1971. Ed. Donald Allen. Berkeley: U. of California P., 1995.

Breslin, James E. B. "Frank O'Hara." *Modern to Contemporary American Poetry 1945–1965* (Chicago: University of Chicago Press, 1984): 210–49. Rpt. in *Frank O'Hara: To Be True to a City*. Ed. Jim Elledge. Ann Arbor: U. of Michigan P., 1990.

Brossard, Olivier. "*The Last Clean Shirt* by Alfred Leslie & Frank O'Hara." *Jacket* 23 (Aug. 2003): np. Web.

de Certeau, Michel. "Walking in the City." *The Practice of Everyday Life*. Trans. Steven Rendall. Berkeley: U. of California P., 1984.

Gooch Brad. *City Poet: The Life and Times of Frank O'Hara*. New York: Knopf, 1993.

O'Hara, Frank. "The Day Lady Died." *Lunch Poems*. San Francisco: City Lights, 1964. 25–26. Print. Pocket Poets Series.

O'Hara, Frank. "An Image of Leda." *The Collected Poems of Frank O'Hara*. 1971. Ed. Donald Allen. Berkeley: U. of California P., 1995. 35–36. Print.

O'Hara, Frank. "On the Way to the San Remo." *Lunch Poems*. 11–12.

O'Hara, Frank. "Personal Poem." *Lunch Poems*. 32–33.

O'Hara, Frank. "Personism: A Manifesto." *The Collected Poems of Frank O'Hara*. 498–499.

O' Hara, Frank. "Poem (Lana Turner has collapsed!)." *Lunch Poems*. 78.

O'Hara, Frank. "A Step Away from Them." *Lunch Poems*. 15–17.

Perloff, Marjorie. "Frank O'Hara and the Aesthetics of Attention." *Boundary* 24 (1976): 779–806. Rpt. in *Frank O'Hara: To Be True to a City*. Ed. Jim Elledge. Ann Arbor: U. of Michigan P., 1990.

Rivers, Larry. "Speech Read at Springs." *Homage to Frank O'Hara*. Ed. Bill Berkson and Joe LeSuer. 1980. Bolinas, Big Sky, 1988. P. 138.

Rosenberg, Harold. "The American Action Painters." *ARTnews* 51.8 (Dec. 1952): 22.

Wordsworth, William. *The Prose Works of William Wordsworth*. 3 vols. Ed. W. B. Owen and Jane Smyser Oxford: Clarendon Press, 1974.

Kanemitsu in California in the 1960s and '70s

The small selection of lithographs and works on paper by Matsumi "Mike" Kanemitsu (1922–1992) offered a tantalizing glimpse into the work of an artist who has largely been bypassed by history. The first time I came across his name was in "Personal Poem" by Frank O'Hara, which I read in 1971: "Now when I walk around at lunchtime / I have only two charms in my pocket / an old Roman coin Mike Kanemitsu gave me …" At the time I didn't know that this man with a Japanese name was an artist, and it wasn't until the early 1980s that I learned he was a friend of Norman Bluhm (1921–1999) and Michael Goldberg (1924–2007), both of whom I met around this time. They spoke about him with great affection and told me that it was Jackson Pollock who gave him his nickname, "Mike."

Clearly, Kanemitsu hung around the Cedar Bar, and was embraced by, as well as belonged to, what has come to be called the "Second Generation of Abstract-Expressionists." In 1956, his work was included in a Whitney Annual, and in 1962, he participated in a group show at the Tanager Gallery, a Tenth Street cooperative, and was one of the *14 Americans* at the Museum of Modern Art. And yet, his name remains largely absent from most histories of the New York art world in the fifties.

I thought about all this when I went to the Los Angeles County Museum, where I asked for the location of the exhibition—which had been listed in a local magazine—and was directed to the Japanese Pavilion. The docent at the Pavilion brought my two friends and me by elevator to the second floor, saying that his work might be among the prints by Hiroshige and others, but that there was no show of Kanemitsu at the museum and she didn't know whom I was talking about.

After returning to the ticket office and asking a number of people who tried to get me to become a member of the museum, I was directed to a small room segregated among large rooms of period furniture. There were no signs along the way to guide us. While there was a wall text, there wasn't even a modest brochure explaining who Kanemitsu was to someone who might have accidentally stumbled into the exhibition. Despite the fact that the exhibition felt like an afterthought, I was able to learn more about an artist whose name piqued my curiosity more than twenty-five years ago.

Kanemitsu was born in Ogden, Utah in 1922. In 1925, at the age of three, he was sent to Japan, where he grew up in a suburb of Hiroshima. In 1940, he returned to the United States and in 1941 enlisted in the United States Army. After the Japanese attack at Pearl Harbor, he (like other Japanese) was arrested and sent to a series of internment camps. It is during this time that he began devoting his time to drawing and working in pastels, with materials given to him by the American Red Cross. Towards the end of the war, he was released from internment and served in the army as a hospital assistant in Europe.

In his autobiographical lithograph, "Santa Anita Yesterday & Today," which was from the suite of nine prints, *Illustrations of Southern California* (1970), Kanemitsu vertically stacks three images: at the top, a cameraman filming from behind bars, under a black cloth; in the middle, a jockey astride a horse; and, near the bottom, a family of internees staring out from behind barbed wire (They were first brought to the racetrack before being shipped to their various destinations). Black rain (tears, blood?) splatters across the surface. Understandably, the history of the racetrack that is covered over, hidden, or unspoken is one of Kanemitsu's recurring preoccupations.

After the war, Kanemitsu studied with Fernand Leger in Paris and then came to New York to study with the early American modernist, Yasuo Kuniyoshi, at the Art Students Leaque. (Kuniyoshi is perhaps best known in New York for having his work deaccessioned by the Museum of Modern Art). Kanemitsu, who worked in Japanese sumi ink and brushes his entire life, was able to transfer the effect of wetness and gesture into lithography. (One wonders what conversations on this subject he might have had with his friends at the Cedar Bar).

While Kanemitsu is best known for his formal innovations in lithography, I think what is more important is his synthesis of suggestive pop imagery with abstract shapes, which he began doing as early as 1961 with "Oxnard Madame," a subject whose imagery morphed into the eighteen lithographs of his *Mickey Mouse Suite* (1970), in which the rounded buttocks of the "Oxnard Madame" became Mickey's ears. (I suspect that Kanemitsu was aware of the anti-Japanese cartoons Walt Disney produced during World War II.) My feeling is that Kanemitsu did his best prints between 1961, when June Wayne invited him to work at the Tamarind Lithography Workshop in Los Angeles, and 1970, when he completed *Mickey Mouse Suite.*

In his synthesis of pop imagery (Mickey Mouse's ears), abstraction, autobiography (the artist as "Mikey Mouse"), and sexual adventures (the Oxnard Madame was a black transvestite who hung around an army base), Kanemitsu anticipates the work of the well-known Japanese artist, Takashi Murakami, the underknown Peter Williams, whose depictions of an African American boy wearing Mickey Mouse ears says something about one segment of the population's relationship to the supposed innocence of cartoon figures, the cult figure, Masami Teriaoka (it may be that Kanemitsu directly influenced Teraoka, since the latter was a student in Los Angeles when the older artist was becoming celebrated for his prints), and, more distantly, Joyce Pensato whose work is finally beginning to get the attention it deserves.

Born in the twentieth century, before the rise of globalization, what Kanemitsu, Teraoka, and Williams share is the experience of knowing that—even when one dons the surface apparel of mainstream culture—it remains impossible to assimilate. However, instead of developing a nostalgic alternative or trying to step outside of that complicated entangled history to an idealized moment, Kanemitsu tried to live in the present with all its contradictions. He may be a minor artist, but his accomplishment doesn't deserve to be thrown out with yesterday's news. And until a more comprehensive view takes place, particularly of the suites of prints I mentioned, I am happy to have been able to see this small selection of work by an artist whose name I came across in a poem by Frank O'Hara years ago.

On the Poems of John Godfrey

There are poets who wander around a city—from determined to aimlessly—and write about their experience. Charles Baudelaire trudged down the new broad avenues of Paris, feeling alone among the window-shoppers. Edwin Denby and Rudy Burckhardt went to Astoria, Queens. While working at the Museum of Modern Art, New York, Frank O'Hara liked to walk around midtown on his lunch hour. David Schubert and Paul Blackburn descended the concrete stairs and rode the subway to Coney Island and other stops along the way.

More recently, John Godfrey eagerly goes "outside on / early summer dawn," ready to traverse Manhattan's East Village and Lower East Side. What distinguishes his work from that of his forebears is his refusal to tell stories. His kaleidoscopic poems and prose poems seldom seem to be generated by a single incident.

For many years Godfrey has watched his neighborhood stumble, crash and rise, from ethnic and bohemian enclave to burned-out buildings and shooting galleries to co-ops, condos and hip restaurants. Small presses have published all his books and chapbooks. His first books—*26 Poems* (1971) and *The Music of the Curbs* (1976)—were done on a mimeograph machine at the Poetry Project, St. Mark's Church In-the-Bowery, New York.

I was reminded of the latter title when, in his most recent collection, *Tiny Gold Dress* (Lunar Chandelier Press, 2012), I read the poem "Off the Curb," which begins:

> Overwhelmed by adequacy
> Lower lip salient
> Body language

>   of apostrophes
>   The hard head
>   buttress against
>   the ooze of
>   plenitude

The hardheaded poet buttressed against the ooze of plenitude—no heroics, no self-mythologizing; that is Godfrey in a nutshell.

This is how Charles Baudelaire—the original walker in the city—would have described his heir:

> And so away he goes, hurrying, searching. But searching for what? Be very sure that this man, such as I have depicted him—this solitary, gifted with an active imagination, ceaselessly journeying across the great human desert—has an aim loftier than that of the *flâneur*, an aim more general, something other than the fugitive pleasure of circumstance. He is looking for that quality which you must allow me to call 'modernity'; for I know of no better word to express the idea I have in mind. He makes it his business to extract from fashion whatever element it may contain of poetry within history, to distil the eternal from the transitory. (From "The Painter of Modern Life," translated by Jonathan Mayne)

Neither "the fugitive pleasure of circumstance" nor William Stafford's well-known line "I thought hard for us all" (from his best-known poem, "Traveling through the Dark") propels Godfrey's poems forward. He doesn't center his work around the "I," doesn't claim that his life is special, blessed or anything other than ordinary. Rather than constructing a narrative which culminates in a revelation, Godfrey remains open to the minute particularities and imaginative wanderings of everyday life—the multitude of wayward thoughts, musings and associations, the erogenous zone of thinking and looking.

"Tiny Gold Dress," the book's title poem, opens the volume with these lines:

>   Days so fleet you have to've

> seen unruly ones
> I do all the time

Godfrey accepts and celebrates rowdy urban living, "loath to exercise / standard sense / Out of order suits [him]." His poems teem with bits and pieces of city life, but they don't necessarily add up and they are not anecdotal. There are myriad incidents rather than quick stories. His compressions of perception slow down the reader, open up spaces of reflection for poems about movement—the fragments of consciousness that come from one's constantly changing attention, the necessity of staying alive to what the city throws at you.

Godfrey understands how people look at each other, as well as how they want to be seen:

> Her eyes offer room to sleep.

Later in "Room to Sleep", he writes:

> I invent her radiance
> Exaggeration is slight
> Identify her straight side
> Sun at her back
> A world away

One of the things that I marvel at in Godfrey's poems is the ease with which he moves between density and expansion, as in the following two lines in the poem "Overhang":

> Hubbub stars taxi man
> Five year old girl of angelic ebony

A staccato cluster of sounds slows down as the words (or worlds) open up. Godfrey's sudden animating shifts—like stepping off the curb—compel readers to constantly refocus their attention. They have to stay attuned to word after word, line after line, which echo what it's like to walk in a city. There is little room for relaxing, for pulling back as if you are omniscient, and Godfrey knows this and stays true to it. This is what differentiates Godfrey from those who write a story or recast an encounter into an anecdote. It is the opposite of narrative,

John Yau

which, in many contemporary poems, can practically lull you to sleep with its incantatory slowness (a cheap substitute for sincerity). Do people—especially poets—really think as slowly as turtles creeping across the sand?

Nothing spectacular has to happen to catch the poet's keen attention.

> So many buzzers
> without names
> Doors without
> distinguishing marks

Not only is Godfrey a poet of the streets, for many years he was a RN Clinician in HIV/AIDS, which brought him up close to people who remain largely invisible. In "Silhouette," which is "*for Heaven C. (1995–1995)*", the poet writes:

> Economical casket
> An infant aflame and
> then off with if not
> off to your name

"Ultimate Word" ends this way:

> Grave won't stay clean
> Rusted foliage of pine\
> Incised markings stained
> by weathers and resin
> Beloved the ultimate word

In his cinematic poems—brimming with close-ups, collisions and dissolves—Godfrey writes tenderly of his beloved city and all his beloveds. From the outset he knew that he would "walk away with/a direction but no/visible means/of destination."

Amidst the cacophony and chaos the poet quietly tells us: "I hear and am healed." Perhaps we too should slow down and hear what he has to say.

Stranded with Rick Snyder

In his seminal essay, "The Painter of Modern Life," Charles Baudelaire defined the modern artist, or *flâneur,* as a "solitary individual endowed with an active imagination." This figure was a detached but passionate individual walking through the city, carried along by its tumultuous crowds, observing but unobserved. There have been many *flâneurs* and derivative wannabes since then, but only the best of them have added something new to Baudelaire's original conception. In his quietly charged, laconic poems, Rick Snyder adds something solid and useful to the long rich history of the poet walking alone in the city. And by some measure, he is just hitting his stride.

Although Snyder published his first chapbook in 1999, *Escape from Combray* is his first full-length book. In it, he not only assumes the mantle of the *flâneur*—a seductive position fraught with pitfalls—but he doesn't settle for any of the familiar, often trivializing moves that so many urban dwelling poets end up publishing. There's no nostalgia, bursts of easy outrage, teary laments, self-pitying cries, or transcendence in Snyder's poems. Alienation isn't touted as an affliction that is endured or understood only by the poet, but recognized as a condition that we all inhabit.

Understanding just how detached and passionate one must be to register what the world and we have become, Snyder doesn't try (as Baudelaire did) to "distil the eternal from the transitory" because to do so now would be an escapist response to the post-9/11 world we inhabit. (The interested reader should download Snyder's e-book, *Forecast Memorial* (2002) from www.durationpress.com—three longish poems written two months after 9/11 and made of lines and fragments carefully spliced together from the constant barrage of mass media "facts" and fictions that filled up our lives in the aftermath.) Instead, he is "stranded/between the steel buildings/and stainless sky … surrounded by strangers/in putty and bone … none of whom/is Dante Alighieri." The 14th-century poet who journeyed through the Inferno until he reached Paradise can't help the one who is living in 21st-century America with no promised land in sight.

The "I" in Snyder's poems comes across as muted and self-reflective, always aware that sanctuary is at best an illusion. At the end of "Walking Home," which on the surface is about passing by:

> the relief of Jesus
>
> staggering under
> the weight of his cross

The poem ends with

> while Simon (I think)
> stands at his side
> keeping one hand
> still on the cross
>
> not knowing
> what he should do
>
> now that they've walked
> to Calvary.

Snyder is a religious poet who, while he hasn't lost faith, hasn't found any answers.

He registers the connections and disconnections in a world full of cheaply-made consumer products which, as Merleau-Ponty writing about Cézanne pointed out, "[w]e become used to thinking that all of this exists necessarily and unshakably." Like Cézanne, Snyder "suspends these habits of thought and reveals the base of inhuman nature upon which man has installed himself," as well as acknowledges two very different and opposing trajectories without reaching a resolution in his poem, "HOW ARE YOU DOING"

> As much as you deserve it,
> I wouldn't wish this
> Sunday night on you—
> not the Osco at closing,
> not its two tired women
> and shaky security guard,
> not its bin of flip-flops
> and Tasmanian Devil
> baseball caps,
> not its freshly mopped floors
> and fluorescent lights,
> not its endless James Taylor
> song on the intercom,
> and not its last pint of
> chocolate mint ice cream,
> which I carried
> down Milwaukee Ave.
> past a man in an unbuttoned
> baseball shirt, who stepped
> out of a shadow to whisper,
> How are you doing?

In "POEM FOR AN AUNT," Snyder describes the possessions of his deceased aunt with a precise, understated acuity in two stanzas:

> On the massive couch that sticks to
> my skin, in the rocking chair
> with two ribs missing,
> I study her broken cuckoo clock.
>
> Then the ashtray like a big beige ear.
> The bleached-out soap opera
> on the 27-inch tv: our portraits
> arranged carefully on top.

John Yau

And then after a perceptual shift that Snyder scores with a stanza break, the poem seamlessly turns and opens out:

> For a second I think I remember her.
> Then that apartment building
> built over its own parking garage.
> Yellow brick. Standing water.

Line by line, the poet goes from a hesitation ("For a second I think I remember her.") to the inhuman, everyday world ("Yellow brick. Standing water.") without veering into any of the false solaces society eagerly offers. Effusiveness or even terseness—any human utterance, in fact—feels forbidden, not to mention self-dramatizing. Palpably evoking the cold, indifferent silence that envelops us all, no matter where we are and what we are doing, Snyder conveys how far we have traveled since Baudelaire's time.

Escape from Combray is a powerful first book by a poet-translator from Catullus, and essayist, who has resisted aligning himself with any coterie or theory (check out his evenhanded, insightful essay, "The New Pandemonium: A Brief Overview of Flarf" in the invaluable online magazine *Jacket:* http://jacketmagazine.com/31/snyder-flarf.html). Based on what I've read of his works, Snyder's detachment and passion appears to extend to all of his endeavors, which is a very rare and increasingly necessary feat to achieve in this day and age.

III.

Asians in Hollywood

In her *New York Times* review (September 7, 2007), of the Museum of Modern Art's film program, *Sessue Hayakawa: East and West, When Twain Met* (September 5–16, 2007), Rachel Saltz wrote:

> [Hayakawa] played his share of bad guys and also his share of non-Japanese. In this series alone he is an Indian rebel leader, an Arab donkey tender, an American Indian, a Chinese Tong warrior and, in *The Cheat,* the 1915 film that made him a star, a Burmese ivory trader. Directed by Cecil B. DeMille and beautifully photographed by Alvin Wyckoff, *The Cheat* chugs right along, a model of streamlined silent storytelling. It has its racist elements, suggesting that the ivory trader's civilized veneer—his spiffy suits and suave ladykiller manners—hides a sadistic depravity: In the most eye-popping, sensationalist scene he burns a brand onto the white heroine's back. But it also shows off Hayakawa's intensity and skill as an actor.

In *The Cheat,* the sadistic, smirking, sensual Hayakawa forces the corrupt, embezzling stockbroker's wife face down on his desk before ripping off the sleeve of her dress and, with a hot iron, branding her—an audacious act which seared his way into the public imagination. For a few years after *The Cheat,* Hayakawa was a sought-after film star, who paved the way for Rudolph Valentino as an exotic Other. He lived an extravagant lifestyle, threw lavish parties and drove a gold-plated Pierce Arrow. White women were his biggest fans.

In 1919, he and his wife, Tsuru Aoki, starred in *The Dragon Painter.* Produced by Hayakawa's Haworth Pictures Corporation, the cast of the film was largely Japanese. The one exception was Edward Piel Sr., who played the painter Kando Indara. According to his filmography, Piel Sr. also starred as the Tong leader, Wong Chong, in *The Purple Dawn* (1923) and had an uncredited role as an old Chinese railroad worker in *The Iron Horse* (1924).

In 1921, for various reasons, Hayakawa had to leave Hollywood and work in Europe and Japan. His fortunes changed further in the 1930s, when anti-Japanese sentiment began growing stronger. The hatred of Asians in the U.S. dates back to at least the mid-19th century, embodied in the passing of the Naturalization Act of 1870, shortly after the end of the Civil War. The Naturalization Act of 1870 enabled people of African descent to become citizens, while declaring anyone of Asian descent to be a permanent alien.

In 1949, at the age of 60, Hayakawa, who was one of the highest-paid Hollywood actors in 1915, lamented, "My one ambition is to play a hero." Although Hayakawa never got to fulfill his ambition, because an Asian playing the part of a hero was inconceivable to Hollywood producers, he received considerable attention in 1957 for playing an honorable villain, Colonel Saito, in David Lean's film *The Bridge on the River Kwai* (1957). Being an honorable villain meant that you were nearly human, which is better than being considered part of the Yellow Peril (code for Asian and non-Christian).

Hayakawa, who was nearly 70, was nominated for an Academy Award for Best Supporting Actor for the role, but the members of the Academy gave the Oscar to Red Buttons, who played Airman Joe Kelly in *Sayonara* (1957), directed by Joshua Logan, because a man who dies for love—forbidden love, in fact—will almost always triumph over a villain, no matter how honorable he is: this is the Hollywood economy of good and evil. The cast of *Sayonara,* which is about interracial marriage, included Marlon Brando, James Garner, Patricia Owens and Ricardo Montalban, who played the Japanese character, Nakamura.

Kelly, who is stationed at the Itami Air Force Base near Kobe, Japan, is about to marry a Japanese woman, Katsumi (played by Miyoshi Umeki). He also introduces Major Lloyd "Ace" Gruver (played by Brando) to a Japanese woman, Hana-ogi (played by Miiko

Taka). *Sayonara* revolves around the fate of these two star-crossed two couples.

Chronologically speaking, Brando went from playing a wily Okinawan villager, Sakini, in the film comedy, *The Teahouse of the August Moon* (1956), to playing a decorated Air Force pilot named "Ace," who falls in love with a soft, compliant Japanese woman.

It took more than two hours every day for the makeup crew working on the set of *The Teahouse of the August Moon* to make Brando look Japanese. It has been claimed that Brando was so good at disappearing into his role that viewers wondered why they never see him in the film.

When the United States military orders Kelly to return to America, while refusing him permission to bring his pregnant wife, they commit double suicide, causing "Ace" to further overcome his own earlier opposition to interracial marriages and propose to Hana-ogi. Umeki also won an Academy Award for Best Supporting Actress for her role as the doomed Katsumi. Between 1929, when the first Academy Awards were handed out, and 2018, Umeki has been the only Asian woman to receive an Academy Award for acting.

By killing both herself and her unborn infant, Katsumi prevents a biracial child from staining the boundaries of America's segregated social order. A very early version of this Hollywood storyline is central to the silent film *Toll of the Sea* (1922), starring Anna May Wong, in her first leading role, as Lotus Flower. A variation of *Madama Butterfly*, the silent film *Toll of the Sea* is set in China rather than Japan. Following in the tradition of Giacomo Puccini's opera, *Madama Butterfly*, which premiered on February 17, 1904, at La Scala in Milan, Asian women have routinely committed suicide (or, in some cases, been conveniently killed) so that order can be restored to the universe, as envisioned by Hollywood and White America.

In this story of forbidden romance, Lotus Flower falls in love with the American, Allen Carver (played by Kenneth Harlan), who she finds floating in the water near her home and helps resuscitate. Even though Lotus became pregnant with Allen's child, he realizes their marriage can't succeed and returns to America without her. A few years later, when Allen returns to China, he is married to Barbara, also known as "Elsie" (played by Beatrice Bentley). Allen and "Elsie" convince Lotus to give them the child, as it would be better if he were raised in America. Ensuring that the child will not have to know of her existence, and can become white, Lotus walks into the ocean and drowns. This was the first time that Wong had to commit suicide in order to preserve the white race, but it would not be the last.

Patty Chang: *The Product of Love*

The slapstick performer, after skidding into a pratfall, always gives a wink to assure the audience that everything is okay. That wink comes in different forms, from Buster Keaton's granite impassivity to Charlie Chaplin's looking at the camera and connecting with the moviegoer.

For all the strangeness she packs into her work, the performance and video artist Patty Chang never winks, allowing a merciless and ultimately disquieting collision of hilarity, discomfort, and confusion to unfold. In early filmed performances, she seemed to be channeling Unica Zurn without the masochism, while adding a dark, unsettling combination of humor and embarrassment, always centered on the female body. She never focused on the fact that she is an Asian American woman, though she also never ignored it, which left some critics at a loss as what to say.

In *Melons (At a Loss)* (1999), after slicing open one side of her bra to reveal a cantaloupe, Chang methodically spoons out the fruit and eats it, while simultaneously balancing a dish on her head and telling a story about her aunt. In *Eels* (2001), she sits facing the camera, her face undergoing a gamut of emotions as wet eels squirm beneath her tight-fitting, parochial white blouse. As in all of Chang's work, the incongruity of elements and multiple viewpoints give the performance a chilling edge, while resisting reductive summations and overarching narratives. By recognizing identity as both a construction and imposition, Chang destabilizes its repressive, inhibiting forces in surprising ways.

By 2005, she had begun using the film medium to concentrate on exploring as well as choreographing collisions between East and

West. For her film *Shangri-La* (2005), Chang went to Zhongdian, a Chinese city near the Tibetan border. It had decided it could attract tourists by officially changing its name to Shangri-La (Xianggelila), the fictitious utopia dreamed up by James Hilton in his immensely popular escapist novel *Lost Horizon* (1933), which Hollywood quickly adapted into a movie and later into a musical remake that—in my opinion—deserves a Golden Turkey Award for serving dollops of pablum to the Depression-era public.

In both the book and film versions, the survivors of a plane crash are rescued by Tibetan monks and brought to the lamasery of Shangri-La, where peace, harmony, love, and long life reign supreme. In one part of *Shangri-La,* Chang hires local photographers—whose main source of income seems to derive from staging faux-Hollywood wedding videos for western tourists—to document her "marriage" to a Caucasian. In scene after scene, Chang finds a way to frame the odd slippages of meaning and interpretation that are central to Zhongdian's existence.

The springboard for her most recent work, *The Product of Love* (2008), a two-channel video projection, is the real-life meeting in Berlin of two iconic figures, the Hollywood film actress, Anna May Wong (1905–1961) and the German writer and translator, Walter Benjamin (1895–1942), whose essay "The Work of Art in The Age of Mechanical Reproduction" is required reading in nearly every art school.

Full of staged translations and mistranslations, Chang's film is a wild "porno"-inflected riff on Benjamin's interview with Wong, which he wrote up for *Die Literarische Welt* (think Luis Buñuel's *Viridiana* meets the Three Stooges).

Wong was truly exotic and "Other" when she arrived in Berlin in 1928 to appear in Peter Eichberg's film *Song* (1929). According to Graham Russell Gao Hodges, Wong's biographer, there were only thirty Chinese women in all of Berlin at the time, so it is more than likely the sophisticated Benjamin had never conversed or been alone with a Chinese woman when he met Wong and her sister, who accompanied her to Europe. Along with working on the film, Wong, who was preternaturally gifted in languages, studied German eight hours a day, so that by the time she met Benjamin a few months after her arrival, she was able to converse comfortably with him in German. As Hodges aptly puts it, Benjamin "searched the boundaries of his poetic imagination to describe her." It is clear from his text that he is totally smitten, particularly after Wong stretched out on a couch and rearranged her hair so that it resembled, in Benjamin's words, "a dragon romping on water."

Chang's staging of this meeting is presented in two forms, each of which "explains" the other: the first—a short projection of three people (one man and two women, one of whom is Asian) translating Benjamin's text into English (it is not included in his nearly 500-page *Selected Writings, Volume 2, part 1, 1927–1930*, published by Harvard University Press). The speakers are often flummoxed as they try to find the appropriate words, which can't have been all that easy, given the dauntingly poetic nature of the prose. They also offer interpretations of their own translations, referring directly to an archived copy of *Die Literarische Welt* that is pasted into a large portfolio. Language is slowed down, broken apart, but not necessarily put back together in some easily consumable manner. As far as I can tell, we did not get the whole text, only snippets at a time, as the film goes from one translator to another, each of whom is in a different locale. The forward motion of this section of the film is continuously interrupted, as if language and reality are never in sync.

Once the short projection ends, a longer one begins on the opposite wall. In a rundown beauty parlor in China, the beauticians make over a Chinese woman to resemble Anna May Wong (she actually doesn't, which is also part of Chang's point) and then do the same for a Chinese man, who emerges looking like Walter Benjamin, complete with a wig of unruly hair and a moustache. The film switches to a room in which the action between "Wong" and "Benjamin" takes place, intercut with a subtitled sequence in an office where two men, speaking in Chinese, talk about the film, which they have been working on. There is an especially awkward and funny moment when one of the men struggles to remember the right phrase for a woman's erogenous zone or, as he finally recalls (or so the subtitle tells us) after a number of tries, "G-spot."

The encounter between actress and actor playing Wong and Benjamin is a truly weird mélange of narratives and overlays of meaning that cannot be easily sorted out. Chang is at her best when she favors density, risking confusion. Her reversal, where an Asian male playing "whiteface," is made all the more grotesquely comic by Benjamin's unintentional hyperventilating as he clutches Wong, clumsily trying to unzip her dress and cop a feel. They are supposed to be acting, yet they seemed truly uncomfortable with what they were doing.

At one moment I felt like a voyeur watching two prim adults who had never dated anyone before suddenly being thrown into an erotic encounter. When they appeared to be improvising, actress and actor just seemed lost, but the "directed" moments were equally strange. After being instructed what to do by someone largely off-camera, the man kneels on the bed, and caressing the calf and kissing the foot of the woman who is pretending to be asleep or is simply so overcome with boredom that she refuses to acknowledge anything going on around her. Other incongruities include the man wearing a ridiculous pair of striped briefs while facing the camera, but buck naked when facing away.

After a while, the film supersedes its subject, like Charlie Parker does when he improvises his version of "Mary Had A Little Lamb." More than the mistranslations that have and will continue to occur between East and West, the film conveys the sense that all communication between individuals is prone to misunderstanding, and that the absence of a common language dooms us to bewilderment, particularly in the realm of Eros and intimacy. Rather than taking sides in the discourse about relationships and power, Chang examines it from a fresh, unsettling perspective. Her ability to be simultaneously straightforward and strange is unrivaled by others working in performance and video. She never winks, never letting us off the hook.

What Happens After Eric Baus's Pharmacy Fills with Sand?

The Tranquilized Tongue (City Lights Books, 2014), Eric Baus's fourth book, is his best yet. It consists of more than sixty compact prose poems, some of which are only one sentence long, and with none as long as the first one, "The Illuminated Egg," a single block of ten sentences. Each poem title begins with "The," followed by a two-word collage, collision, cosmos or conundrum that often animates dead matter. "The Statue's Saliva" is one example. "The Feral Film" is another.

Baus follows through on the title's declarations–its unlikely magnetic bonding–by beginning each sentence in each prose poem with "The." This grammatical application emphasizes that the noun immediately following "The" is particular (and therefore actual) rather than general. This is the one- sentence long prose poem, "The Posthumous Glass:"

> The window appeared between the ambulance and the ant's shadow.

This isn't a description so much as a proposal. *The Tranquilized Tongue* is a collection in which impossible particulars are stated as incontrovertible facts.

This is "The Illuminated Egg," the first prose poem in *The Tranquilized Tongue,* in its entirety:

> The word moon assembles its intestines inside the king's saliva. The letters cried. The birth of each letter contained one hundred films. The merged nerves dropped to the ground. The arrows were injured by what the speech spread. The microphone was looking

for an echo to explain. The picture of the burst tongue offended the crowd. The birth cloud reddened between rains. The city's moans drowned underneath the first growls. The voice atomized the line between the children's clinging hands.

The poem's title alludes to illuminated manuscripts, and to works that meld words and images, which the poet defines as a site of birth. With each proposal (sentence), Baus incrementally defines and redefines the perimeters in which his particulars will unfold. First, the word *moon* is regarded as a living and material body with an outside and inside ("intestines") that is an inherent part of the king's bodily fluids ("saliva"). It is in this place (the mouth) where the word "assembles its intestines," its guts. In the second line ("The letters cried."), Baus underscores that words are made of both graphic symbol (letters) and sounds ("cried"). The individual sounds ("birth of each letter") spawn "one hundred films" (multiple images). Sounds, the poet goes on to write, bounce back ("echo"), while leading to similar sounds.

Baus defines the poem as a chamber ("illuminated egg") whose boundaries have not yet been reached, as well as a bricolage constructed from different categories of things (saliva, films, and nerves, among them). Made as much of matter as of sound, the poem is an acoustical chamber where words, sounds, letters and images are constantly emerging, intermingling, echoing, and changing into other words, sounds, letters and images. And just as the mouth can be the illuminated egg or chamber where these possibilities are born, it can also dissolve ("atomized") the line or string of syllables. This is a world of unpredictable and miraculous change, a world that is simultaneously philosophical and alchemical, an inseparable mixture of factual propositions and flights of fancy.

In his insistent use of the declarative "The," Baus presents the reader with propositions, which is likely to bring to mind Ludwig Wittgenstein's book, *Tractatus Logico-Philosophicus* (1922). In that book of numbered propositions, the reader encounters the following three declarations:

> The world is everything that is the case.
> The logical picture of the facts is the thought.
> The thought is the significant proposition.

Baus has melded this language of propositions with the labyrinthine thinking of the 17th-century polymath and founder of Egyptology, Athanasius Kircher, who has been characterized by critics as Jorge Luis Borges before Borges because of his interest in the trivial and the miraculous.

Baus, a poet of Synesthesia, situates his work on porous borders between sound and image, echo and repetition. In his swiftly transforming world, one word is apt to molt into another. In "The Illuminated Egg," "The word moon" becomes "the city's moans." Out of the accretion of declarations Baus builds a multi-part, echo-filled room glittering with images that resist immediate apprehension. The one-sentence prose poem, "The Inverted Urn," is a good example:

> The parallel tenors trilled to atone for the séance's ellipses.

Throughout the book, Baus calls attention to sound and the means by which it is transmitted: microphone, frequency, voiceover; hooted, pitched, intoned, creaked, hummed; decoded, translated, asked, murmured, deciphered. "Phoneme" is another word that recurs in *The Tranquilized Tongue,* the smallest distinct particle of sound that distinguishes one word from another ("The glass arms swam into the branches of a swan.") Reading is slowed down, as all phenomena become miraculous, shot through with humming wonder.

Sound and thought (or the signifier and the signified), according to Ferdinand de Saussure, whose theories helped give birth to the field of semiotics (the study of signs), are inseparable. Focused on "sound-image" or "sound-pattern," Saussure believed that writing was a separate system that was secondary and dependent on the phonetic, on speech. He also believed the signified is a concept rather than the thing itself. While Baus surely knows a good deal about semiotics and is more than likely conversant with the latest developments and revisions of Saussurean principles, I sense that he has a fundamental disagreement with the founder of semiotics over the nature of words, which he makes clear in the very first line of "The Illuminated Egg:"

The word moon assembles its intestines inside the king's saliva.

Whereas Saussure believed that linguistic signs were immaterial, Baus posits that words are living beings. Otherwise, how could the "word moon assemble its intestines inside the king' saliva"? As I see it, Baus has aligned his work with Arthur Rimbaud and his sonnet "Voyelles" (Vowels). It is in this alchemical poem that Rimbaud equates the letter *A* with both a color ("black") and an animated presence (the "black velvety jacket of brilliant flies …"). This is how Baus extends Rimbaud in his single-sentence prose poem, "The Demolished Flock:"

The word moth followed the burning fleet home.

Signifier and signified are equals. The gap between word and thing does not exist in these prose poems. Baus is a charter member of a loose, unaffiliated group of acoustically attentive poets who focus on the different relationships that bind and unbind sound to printed word: Clark Coolidge, Nathaniel Mackey, Andrew Joron, Harryette Mullen and Cathy Park Hong.

Baus's domain—his illuminated egg, feral film, and marionette's casket—is populated by moths, bees, giraffes, swans, deer, pupae, ants, doves, sturgeon, pigeons, quail, hawks and pumas. This is the world Baus envisions after nature reclaims the cities ("The city's sickness nested in the mouth of the fountain") and animalistic powers overcome decorum ("The city's moan drowned underneath the first growls"). The territory Baus evokes is bordered by the "divine technologies" of Christopher Dewdney and the dystopian modernity of J. G. Ballard, but it is wholly his own.

Is our world one where "[t]he lost signal beacon[s] back" or is it one where [t]he tranquilized tongue rename[s] its aphasia?" Baus is on a journey to find out.

In Death, Licked by a Dog

Currently at The Drawing Center, *Unica Zürn: Dark Spring* is the first museum presentation in America of the drawings and paintings of Zürn (1916–1970), who is known in the English-speaking world as the author of two books, translated as *The Man of Jasmine & Other Texts* (1994) and *Dark Spring* (2000). That the mainstream art world has taken far longer to deal with Zürn's accomplishment is understandable; it needs to find a way to present the work in an appropriate and culturally established physical space, whereas, in publishing a book, a small press doesn't need or necessarily even want institutional approval. The frame most commonly applied to Zürn's art is psychoanalytical, with the salient questions being whether or not her life can be separated from her art, and how to explain what many regard as her "masochism," particularly in regard to her collaborations with her partner, Hans Bellmer.

As Renée Riese Herbert points out in *Magnifying Mirrors: Women, Surrealism, and Partnership* (1994), the "years spent as Bellmer's companion coincide almost exactly with the most productive period of her life." It is during this period that she moved from Berlin to Paris, met and fell in love with Henri Michaux, drew and painted, wrote anagrammatic poems as well as two books of autobiographical fiction. It is also during this period that she was diagnosed with schizophrenia and suffered the first of a number of breakdowns. In *Compulsive Beauty* (1993), writing about Bellmer and others, Hal Foster suggests "the surrealist image is patterned upon the symptom as an enigmatic signifier of a psychosexual trauma." If we accept this view, the Surrealists, as exemplified by Zürn, Bellmer, Magritte (think of *Le Viol,* 1934), and others, are wounded creatures reacting to childhood trauma, which amounts to an easy explication of the relationship between the artist's childhood and project (who among us hasn't been traumatized?), as well as a diminishment of its impact.

Admirably curated by João Ribas, and accompanied by a catalog with very different and insightful essays by Ribas and Mary Ann Caws, the exhibition consists of more than fifty drawings in ink and watercolor on paper, a handful of paintings, as well as letters, anagrammatic poems, and the infamous cover of *Le Surréalisme, Même* (1958), which makes clear that Surrealism had not, in a postwar world, lost any of its power to provoke and disturb, despite judgments to the contrary by numerous theorists and critics. If the few paintings scattered through the exhibition are any indication of what she did in that medium, it is evident that we need to see a much larger selection.

Zürn's drawings are of phantasmagorical creatures, whose bodies are made of varying, repeated patterns that suggest scales, feathers, and armor, something that is not skin. Inversely, one can also see the linear marks as cuts, scars, and tattoos. Many of the creatures have multiple heads and numerous eyes—a motif that has often been read as indicative of her schizophrenia. In some cases the bodies are heads within heads, and rows of eyes, like those you see in a Byzantine angel. Made of different parts, each sectioned off from the other, and often undulating and stretched out, with protrusions of all kinds, the figures resemble jellyfish-like creatures, transparent bodies full of exposed organs. The eyes stare at us, but we also see through these bodies. And when she leaves open spaces, we are being invited to fill them. Zürn has rendered intimacy and remoteness inseparable, which is why her work in different mediums is so disturbing.

Zürn was a religious ecstatic. During these states, whether she was collaborating with Bellmer or incarcerated in an institution, as she was on a number of occasions, the artist mentally left her body (it becomes an outer shell) to go inward where she ultimately found release. The drawings conflate receptivity and isolation. In their hypnotic concentration, the patterned lines and shapes go from mesmerizing to unsettling. Our experience of them is not purely aesthetic, which is exactly what the Surrealists wanted. If you have any doubt about this, consider the photograph of Zürn that appeared on the abovementioned cover of *Le Surréalisme, Même*. Headless and limbless, her body is seen from the back, with the vertebrae just barely visible. Tightly tied with thin string, causing her flesh to bunch up into mounds and folds, Zürn has become a piece of trussed meat ready for the oven—an association that she, as a German overcome at times with feelings of guilt, was no doubt fully aware.

In linking her "masochism" to her childhood, observers sidestep Zürn's attempt to absorb the Holocaust without seeking redemption. As a religious ecstatic or an inverse Sufi, where complete stillness rather than dancing was the only release, eroticism and death had become one. And yet, at the end of *Dark Spring,* after the nameless young girl jumps to her death, Zürn writes: "The first one to find her is the dog. He sticks his head between her legs and begins licking her. When she does not move, he begins whimpering quietly and lies down beside her on the grass."

Placing her corpse (or corpus) before us, her work resists all attempts to anesthetize it, render it neutral. In her eyes and those of her creatures, viewers and theorists who try to force her work into tidy paradigms are nothing more than necrophiliac animals.

On *Haute Surveillance* by Johannes Göransson

Before we settle into our plush faux-velvet seats, share bags of popcorn and watch the latest film about zombies who have managed to escape from Pittsburgh and its many parking lots, does anyone out there dream of making a movie about Jeffrey Dahmer, starring Brad Pitt or James Franco? No matter where you turn, post-9/11 America keeps upping the ante in the contradiction department. A typical day is apt to mean the press finds it necessary to document the three designer outfits the pregnant Kim Kardashian needed to wear in a span of less than twelve hours, while a photogenic newscaster with perfect teeth dutifully files a report about a baby that died of starvation, shrapnel or sexual abuse (take your pick) during the past twenty-four hours, registering shock and outrage. The appropriate music follows each of these segments. And then come the lavish commercials about the secret enhancing power of a facial cream or the perfect dessert to cap a romantic evening.

America is a site of narcissistic extravagance and extreme deprivation, with the gap widening between the two. It exists somewhere between Technicolor fantasy and black-and-white documentary. It is both a country at war (with itself and with others) and a tacky movie in which the hostages are always freed just before the audience gets restless.

What would Walt Whitman have done with these contradictions seems to be one of the questions that motivated Johannes Göransson to write *Haute Surveillance* (Tarpaulin Sky, 2013), a book that shares something with Whitman, Monique Wittig, J. G. Ballard and

Dostoevsky's "underground man." Göransson, who has previously published five books and translated the Swedish poet Aase Berg into English, is one of the few contemporary poets who bring disgust into his writing without cloaking it in irony or some other self-protective device.

In "Song of Myself"—which many consider Walt Whitman's quintessential poem in *Leaves of Grass*—the poet famously declares: "I am large, I contain multitudes." The speaker in Haute Surveillance is the bastard offspring of the gargantuan "I" animating Whitman's poem. Near the beginning of the book, Göransson declares:

> I write this for the mute actress and the dead girls and the Virgin Father who speaks in this mausoleum and Mother Machine Gun who carries my body through the tumultuous crowds. Sticky and stricken-out, I write this for people on posters. I write this for the breathers and bleeders. I write this with a geometry suggesting awkwardness. I write this as a punishment. I write this for those infested and luxurious and teeming.
>
> I write this for the people who are at war.
>
> I write this from hotel rooms and because I have a medical condition. The skin bleeds and pinches. It's a ridiculous death I am living and I live it ridiculously in an economy of trickle-down disease.
>
> Speaking of dead children: There is no place for immigrants in utopia and all film-makers must be renounced. I could never grow up in a house like that. Unless I was a dead child. An embalmed child. A child that never vandalized his own do-wop body with surveillance equipment.
>
> I vandalize my do-wop body due to my modest self-control.
>
> I call my line of work *haute surveillance*.

Is this what it means to be a poet with a social consciousness living in America? You are reduced to being in the business of fashionable observation. Or is all of America—where you can follow Justin Timberlake, the partially naked Rihanna, and countless others on Twitter—in the business of high-class voyeurism, which is one small step away from renting a pornographic road movie in your shabby motel room.

> This novel is written for breathing virgins. To help them understand the wonder that is their skin to help them perform admirably. To teach them about heroic and half-shot out buildings. To hurt them so correctly they will never doubt that they have been hurt in the kill. This is a novel about the black-and-white virginity of early cinema, the body tricked into doubles and contortions. Hello I am you.

In addition to the Virgin Father and Mother Machine Gun, Göransson has populated *Haute Surveillance* with the Starlet, Father Voice-Over, the Black Man, Sister Dark, the expresident, the Soldiers, the Genius Child Orchestra, abortionists and anti-abortionists. These and other archetypes keep reappearing in unexpected ways. Shelley Duvall, in *The Shining*, drops in from time to time. Various movies (*Hiroshima Mon Amour*) and books (*In the Penal Colony*) get mentioned.

What the poets associated with "Flarf" recognize—and the literary mainstream still ignores to a large degree—is that the Internet has flattened daily life into a constantly swirling, cacophonous mosaic. Instead of extending that jarring, two-dimensional world into poems, Göransson has absorbed Frank O'Hara's "intimate yell" and made it all his own. *Haute Surveillance* is a world of wounded voices.

> I have a nightmare about a girl covered with blood and when I wake up sweating my wife tells me a fairytale.

For all the disparate information that Göransson brings swiftly and confidently into play, *Haute Surveillance* is not a collage. None of it feels arbitrary, which is nothing short of miraculous. At the very least, the author's ambition was to write a new "Song of Myself" addressing these confusing, contradictory times in which we are at war, as well as to construct memorable situations without resorting to a plot or other familiar literary devices. He succeeded at both. His reasoning is simple and direct:

> Sometimes I want a room of my own, but mostly I just want a room without all these corpse-patterned wallpaper.

Göransson's fast-paced, present-tense writing critiques itself while moving forward, collapsing together all of discourses and vocabularies associated with the nightly news, feminism, sexual identity, Hollywood movies, science fiction, performance art, pornography, and poetry invested in the stable lyric "I." Bots from academia mix with bits of the street.

Haute Surveillance is written in blocks of prose, lists, and lines. The collapsing together of different discourses doesn't stop at the literal. Goransson turns it into a book that is unclassifiable—part epic poem, part science fiction, part pornographic film, and all literature. He writes sentences that the reader has to stop and think about. This is what I found so commanding about *Haute Surveillance*.

> In other words, I give you my childhood, you give me an odalisque with money in her snatch. I give you comfort from the scandalous world of fashion, you idealize me, placing a rose behind my ear. It's a deal for the radiantly impoverished.

Welcome to America, which prizes beauty above life. *Haute Surveillance* should be sold in every bookstore and newsstand in, on or about the premises of a bus station, train station, or airport.

Staying Up with Suzanne Buffam's
A Pillow Book

I tossed and turned, unable to sleep. I got up and went into the other room, so not to disturb my wife and dog, both of them sleeping soundly. I turned on the light and picked up a book from a tall pile that has been sitting on the floor by my cluttered desk, and which I have been working my way through, though not as steadily as I would like. I begin reading, secretly hoping (or not so secretly hoping) that it would help me go to sleep. Time goes by. More time goes by. I am not interested in going back to sleep. I want to finish the book I have in my hands. I am holding *A Pillow Book* (Canarium Books, 2016) by Suzanne Buffam. The irony is not lost on me.

Buffam's *A Pillow Book* is a smart, funny, provocative collection of lists, research into pillows and sleeplessness, and details about all kinds of people, including famous insomniacs (F. Scott Fitzgerald, Abraham Lincoln, Tallulah Bankhead, and, of course, Marcel Proust, make appearances). It is a book replete with interesting details, including Buffam's commentary on *The Pillow Book* by Sei Shōnagon, whose writing is woven into this book in imaginative and fanciful ways.

Dreams and anecdotes are recounted. Deadpan humor abounds throughout. Buffam channels Shōnagon as a way of commenting on the original and on her own book: "I now had a vast quantity of paper at my disposal, reports the nonchalant Shōnagon, and I set about filling the notebooks with odd facts, stories from the past, and all sorts of other things, often including the most trivial material."

Strange things happen, as when the screams and yelling of arguing neighbors intrude upon her and her husband as they're watching a zombie apocalypse film, resulting in the police showing up. At other times, the writing resists any context except that it is in this book that does not fit any genre: "Tonight my in-laws dropped by with a rolling suitcase full of silk. They are back from their fortieth medical school class reunion in Hyderabad, where they did a little shopping for Her Majesty." By the time you read "fortieth," you know you are in for a wild ride and Buffam does not disappoint. Within a short paragraph, she manages to mention "an ostensibly unintentional head butt" and such items as a "plastic King Tut Mask," a "salwar kameez," and an "itchy polyester medieval Scottish Disney princess vest." And yes, it all makes sense just the way a dream does.

Throughout the book, Buffam makes lists under such headings as "Jobs From Hell," "Questionable Gestures," "Extinct Languages A To Z," "Sounds I Don't Expect To Hear," and "Incongruous," which begins, "A vegan in Vegas." She has a wonderfully wry sense of everyday life, as when she includes under the list "Harder Than It Looks," "IKEA," and "Small talk with a psychoanalyst." Her sense of the commonplace is uncommon, fresh, original. She would probably point out things in a museum that you would never notice, and it would not be in the paintings or statues.

Buffam writes about herself as if she is closely observing someone else:

> I read a message last night from a woman I have yet to meet beyond the dim glow of a list-serv. She lives in Tampa, if memory serves, and won a juried prize last year for a mixed-media meditation on habitat loss across America, including charts, chants, photographs, oral histories, crowdfunded films, and salvaged trash.

This distance enables her to precisely recount all kinds of details: "The jade green pillow on which we sat, I recall, had been cut from coarse raw silk and embroidered with a vivid black pattern of stars inside a narrow band of chartreuse."

In some places, you experience a pleasant vertigo because it takes time to discern what is and isn't a dream. I did not dream this book up, however, Suzanne Buffam did. And I am happy to have spent a sleepless night reading it, knowing that I will open it up many more times, and savor the different pleasures it so generously offers.

When a Poet Becomes Invisible

The poems in Mary Ruefle's latest book, *Dunce* (Wave Books, 2019), are one or two pages long. Reading through them for the first time, I was struck by how often the words "tears," "death," and "dying" appeared.

Ruefle, however, doesn't emphasize these words over others in her poems; they are part of their fabric—part of everyday consciousness when you reach a certain age.

After I finished my first reading of *Dunce,* but before I went back to the beginning and started all over again, I decided to reread an interview that Ruefle did with Caitlin Youngquist for the *Paris Review* (December 12, 2016) when her collection *My Private Property* (2016) was published.

It is an unpretentious interview, which occurs only slightly more often than Halley's Comet appears in the night sky. Among other topics, Ruefle talked about what it means to be a woman whose age makes her invisible. Being two years older than Ruefle, who was born in 1952, I was particularly touched by this passage:

> Well, thematically, aging and death become one and the same for writers, and very often you lose young readership because you're no longer interested in the things young people are interested in. The time for exuberance, energy, endless curiosity, endless activity within a body of work, that drops away and everything becomes bittersweet. But this becoming invisible—all women talk about it. There's a period of transition that's so disorienting that you're confused and horrified by it, you can't get a grip on it, but it *does* pass. You endure it, and you are patient, and it falls away. And then you come into a new kind of autonomy that you simply didn't have when you were young. You didn't have it when your

parents were alive, you didn't have it back when you were once a woman to be seen. It's total autonomy and freedom, and you become a much stronger person. You're not answerable to anyone anymore. For me, it was a journey of shedding the sense of needing to please someone—parents, children, partners.

In her poetry, the ordinary becomes unsettling and magnetic. Ruefle shifts from one state of consciousness to another in less time than it takes to blink:

> Who won? I said.
> The game's tomorrow, he said.
> And I became the snail I always was,
> crossing the field in my helmet.

The shift that takes place between the second and third lines of this poem, "Super Bowl," from standing and talking in a public arena like supermarket checkout line, to inhabiting an isolated, inward space, happens frequently in *Dunce*. Often, after making the shift, Ruefle comes back to that public space, hearing and seeing everything around her differently.

Ruefle makes unexpected connections and associations that might initially strike the reader as outrageous, but come to possess a certain stubborn, opaque logic ("Words have no thoughts / just as you have no / lice."). She will then effortlessly pivot in another direction, which is one of the deep joys of reading Ruefle's poems. You never know what she is going to do next. And yet, when she does it, it is bound to hold your attention.

Ruefle is swimming ("I was swimming / with the taste of apple / in my mouth") and experiencing something unexpected. She goes for walks by herself and with a friend ("I am always up for a bog, said Mary. / I too, am always up for one, said I."). The repetition and odd diction animates the poem with delight. I am reminded of Matsuo Bashō's insight: "The journey itself is the home."

Ruefle is aware that the only destination that awaits her is death, and that turning away from that awareness doesn't alter the facts. She does not ask for pity or sympathy because death is democratic. "I am going to die" begins one poem. She recognizes her small, passing presence ("My face a thumbtack / in the earth.").

Recognizing that there is no permanent sanctuary from one's impending chaos, she consciously keeps moving forward ("I keep walking in the general direction."). The quest is for knowledge, pleasure, feeling, insight. ("I also saw a leaf-blower / and all the dead leaves / looked like they were having fun/jumping around as if they were alive again."). This feeling of inescapable isolation, of the attendant fears, surprises, and joys it brings, is at the heart of *Dunce*.

Ruefle writes list poems that make me gnash my teeth because I love them so much.

The poem "Little Stream" opens:

> My heart was bright and shining
> like a lobster in boiling water.
> And then I was just a child
> eating the leftover snow.
> I'd lost my mittens and my belly button
> was as good as gone, meaning
> I couldn't be born again, ever,
> So I sat by my a little stream
> with my eyes closed.

What follows is surprising, funny, captivating. The ordinary and mythic happen right next to each other. The lines move from objective witnessing ("I saw a woman carrying a child's coffin / on her head.") to fairytale whimsy ("I saw a rat so friendly / he shined my shoes with his tongue.") and do not stop.

Death is everywhere in these poems because it is everywhere in life ("with both ears I hear / the dainty popping / of bath bubbles— / and a light rain / falling on my mother's grave / comes back to me"). Ruefle will track the places her thinking takes her without pulling back or trying to turn it into a story, or imbue it with longing, or culminate in a revelation.

"A Morning Person" opens with "what a beautiful day for a wedding!" Less than 20 lines later it ends, "I hate my poems." What happens in between, all the places Ruefle takes us—her willing readers—is unrelenting attentiveness to everyday occurrences and imaginative flights, and the porous border between them. We need both to live.

Ruefle understands fragility. She has a wonderfully odd sense of reality. She knows that "At some age / the world begins to drift away," and she doesn't try to hold on. In her "journey of shedding," we are the lucky recipients of her indelible poems.

Nicolas Hundley's Heretical Machinery

Nicolas Hundley is a poet of pronouns. In many of his poems and prose poems, a pronoun—he, they, you, and we—is central to each line or sentence. This is how the prose poem, "The Blood You Let," begins:

> The blood you let coagulated into amber. You enlisted leeches, siphon, syringe—but still feel weak, foolish, transparent, bureaucratic, and, in the end, remained the infanta. You sought mirrors, gained mirrors, took on mirrors and the endless corridors.

Hundley's use of *you* becomes a distancing device, which later enables him introduce other pronouns, "we," "they," and "I." But the "you," who is lying in a hospital bed, is the center around which the other pronouns orbit. Given the circumstances, the reader should consider why the poem doesn't culminate so much as stop: "They went for tubes, for a length of tubing, and at this I had to intervene." For all the sparks generated by Hundley's juxtapositions, a lot of what goes on in his poems isn't immediately apparent.

When Hundley uses "I," the reader is apt to imagine that the author is seeing himself from a distance—that he has opened up a space between himself and the sentient voice in the poem, or that he has conjured a figure whose existence is bounded by the poem, or both. Imagine Frank O'Hara's "I do this, I do that" mixed with one of Samuel Beckett's miserable characters—a brew presided over by Louis Aragon, who announced "The marvelous is the eruption of contradiction within the real"—and you get a sense of the itemized, fractious temperament that distinguishes Hundley's debut collection, *The Revolver in the Hive* (New York: Fordham University Press, 2013), published in the Poets Out Loud series, edited by Elisabeth Frost.

Hundley, who lives in Austin, Texas, doesn't seem to be connected with any of the groups of poets currently jostling for attention. He is a loner who has absorbed and reconfigured aspects of Gertrude Stein and H. P. Lovecraft, concrete music and gothic science fiction. This is the opening of the prose poem "The Ecclesiastic Office of the Bible."

> Ever since I took the bicycle to the temple, wheeled it into the temple, ushered the bicycle down the aisle, past the pews frequented by rodent and fugitive, placed the bicycle at the altar, altered it with the bicycle, it has been the temple of the bicycle.

The quietly insistent music of this sentence lifts it out of the purely narrative movement we associate with prose poems—the shifts within the repetition seems more Philip Glass than Stein—as Hundley builds upon it, extends it, opens it up. It suggests that his poems are led as much by sound as by meaning, that he discovers where he is going by getting there.

Was it W. H. Auden who said that he wanted to find one good line in a poem by a young poet—a string of words that would tell him that something interesting and perhaps special was there? Hundley has written lots of terrific lines, not to mention poems. More importantly, the lines don't all work the same way, and don't fall within the same emotional register. He isn't predictable. He can go from the strange to the eccentric for a reason that refuses to spell itself out.

> Gouda is a cheese drunk on tantric reverie
> Gouda is the name of a bird I once owned

Did I say that Hundley assembles wonderful lists? Or that his writings are comparable to a constellation of distant stars: he holds their divergent presences together through the logic of the poem until a wondrous illumination emerges.

Will Alexander's Celebration of the Possible

In "A Note on the Text" for his latest collection of poetry, *Across the Vapour Gulf* (New Directions Poetry Pamphlet #22, 2017), Will Alexander writes:

> When I first laid eyes on the writing of Cioran, I was smitten by the form. The aphorism seemed cleansed of detritus. Unlike the sequential novel (so appropriately condemned by Breton) the aphorism in Cioran's hands seemed to spontaneously ignite. Poetry, history, philosophy, the essay, medicinally combined appearing on the other side of itself as insight.

M. Cioran, the misanthropic master of despair, seems like an unlikely choice for Will Alexander, the master of ecstatic language, which makes this encounter all the more engaging. Across more than fifty years, writing in Romanian and French, Cioran focused on despair and emptiness with the relentless determination of a bloodhound on the trail of a criminal, which, in this case, was life and all its illusions. Yet, despite the nihilistic gloom that pervaded every word he put to paper, Cioran was an alluring writer whose sentences pulled you in, holding you there, even if you could not reach the same dark conclusion. Another great stylist, the French poet St. John Perse, described Cioran as "one of the greatest French writers to honor our language since the death of Paul Valéry."

What Alexander shares with Cioran, Perse, and Valéry is that he is not averse to the obscure, as long as he can state it with an unparalleled clarity, such as he does in this sentence, which begins a section in *Across the Vapour Gulf:*

Walking around an orchard of riddles, a milky density of ants erupts, and the idea coalesces in my mind of mixtures of colour that emanate from the spectral beyond the constraint of consensus optical limit.

Surely, each of us have had a moment when it occurs to us that there are things we see that come from some place other than "consensus optical limit," be it dreams or visions or insight.

Alexander is to English as Valéry is to French: he honors the possibilities of language (reality) by making them real. One way he does this is by being nuanced in the domain of heightened language: "As a poet, I am a ghost in a village teeming with certitudes and hatchlings. My co-inhabitants always distracted by consensus fate, always kinetic with ideology and procreation."

As readers of Alexander's writing have come to expect, it is swarming with information from a vast library—like one lost in Alexandria—that the author has absorbed into his bloodstream: philosophy; science of all kinds, from color theory to the study of insects and lemurs; alchemy, geography; the Dogon; mining in Zimbabwe in 41,000 BC; science fiction; and the output of little-known writers. And really this is just the tip of the iceberg.

The question Alexander returns to throughout this book—I cannot think of it as a pamphlet, even though it is stapled together—is the nature of the individual consciousness; what does it mean to be awake and to see? Are your receptors open to receive what is there? As he tells us in his "Note," he came to the aphorism because he felt it was cleansed of detritus. This is also what he and Cioran have in common. For all the excess of Alexander's writing, it is extremely pared down. You cannot simplify what he says, as that would be an insult to the ignited inspiration and to the reader. What Alexander writes is not surrealist or lyric: It is one person's celebration of the senses, including, at last, the intellect and its roots in Eros.

IV.

China's Buried Past and Submerged Future

In the opening moments of the film *Flotsam Jetsam* (2007) by Patty Chang and David Kelley, currently playing at the Museum of Modern Art, New York, a bridge-like structure is seen in the distance, partially traversing what seems to be a wide river. It is a grey and overcast day, with a polluted-looking sky. The camera's cropped view, from the prow of a tour boat, frames three passengers sitting in the front row. A young woman in a pale blue uniform with a red and white scarf walks to the front, turns and welcomes them (and the audience) to the China Southern Airlines. She is a flight attendant and her instructions include how to blow air into a life preserver.

With this displacement, *Flotsam Jetsam* begins with decisively bent logic and does not let up. The flight attendant is one of a handful of anomalous characters populating this beguiling film, which brings together and mixes different forms, including documentary realism, fiction, television news, dream-like passages and a film-within-a film. In a sequence that comes shortly after the attendant appears, we see a man standing on a container in a shipyard, holding a sound boom. Just below him we see a man dressed in a tiger's outfit lying on the ground as workers pass by. As the camera zooms in on the tiger man, a voice instructs him to get up, run and hide in an enclosed area. His wife chases him around with a stick. By including the boom operator in the frame, while focusing on the wife chasing the tiger-man around, the audience knows it is watching a film-within-a-film.

Near the end of the sequence the couple's daughter enters the enclosed area (or stage set) and stops the mother. Once the filming is done, the workers walk away. What are we to make of this stand-alone sequence about a fractious Chinese family with a daughter? Is the tiger-father Chang's version of the Western stereotype, the Asian Tiger Mom? If so, what are we to make of the mom who beats the tiger-father away?

Out of an mélange of discrete sequences, such as the two I have briefly described, Chang and Kelley construct a complex, lyrical view of the impact of the Three Gorges Dam project on China's landscape and its people. Other moments tellingly include characters in and around a swimming pool; a group of men swim near the barge pulling life preservers behind them; two soldiers march along a pool's edge, the camera trailing them; a psychotherapy session takes place in a community pool; and the flight attendant walks alone near a swimming hole. In other sequences she sings to the tour boat passengers, and is framed in close-up, blinking.

In Chang and Kelly's film, which was made in 2007, before the Three Gorges Dam (1994–2012) was largely completed, one of the characters asks at two different points: "What is the imaginary?" According to *Flotsam Jetsam*, it is the beginning of loss, of no longer being able to return to actual places. In effect, the Three Gorges Dam project has turned a part of China and its history into a fairytale. The central sequence focuses on the construction of a one-sided wooden replica of a submarine, which is fitted together on a barge that is sailing toward an unspecified destination. A rectangular aperture cut into the submarine's side suggests a portal that will enable passengers to see what was submerged by the Three Gorges Dam, a project responsible for the displacement of more than a million people, the flooding of many important archaeological sites, and the extinction of the Baiji (Chinese River Dolphin) and other aquatic and terrestrial wildlife. While there are numerous allusions to the Three Gorges Dam, I heard its name cited only once in the film.

Flotsam Jetsam is not only about the irrevocable change that will take place in the riverbed's landscape, and its possible deleterious effect on China as a whole, but also, on a personal level, about the anxieties and preoccupations of individuals such as the father of the flight attendant, who encourages his daughter to study English. Both dream of a better life for her that may not be possible to attain.

China might be upwardly mobile as a nation, but that isn't the case for many of its hopeful, self-motivated citizens. Perhaps this is also the beginning of the imaginary for the flight attendant who is also an aspiring singer. And what will it mean for China if its citizens can't dream about a better life through their children?

Since 1999, Chang has expanded her practice from performance (and being in front of the camera) to filmmaking (and being behind the camera). After memorable and in some ways groundbreaking performances, such as *Melons (At a Loss)* (1999) and *Eels* (2001), Chang began making films and video projections—*Shangri-La* (2005) and *The Product of Love* (2008). In her mixing of documentary and fiction film techniques, she has transformed innovations by Abbas Kiarostami and Jean Luc-Godard into something all her own. With *Flotsam Jetsam,* I see the possibility of Chang making another move. Realizing that the film was made in 2007, I left MoMA wondering what this wonderful but still under-known artist is dreaming up now.

The Five-Star Delight of Driving across America with Ron Padgett

If you saw Jim Jarmusch's wonderful film, *Paterson* (2016), you know that Ron Padgett wrote four new poems for it. You also know that the film is the story of a bus-driver/poet named Paterson who lives in Paterson, New Jersey. If, in addition to seeing this movie, you have played Trivial Pursuit more than a handful of times, or taken a class in Modern American Poetry, you are likely to know that Paterson, the name of an unremarkable city on the Passaic River, is the title of William Carlos Williams' epic five-volume poem, and that Williams was Robert Smithson's doctor when he was growing up in Passaic.

What these preeminent individuals (Jarmusch, Padgett and Smithson) have in common is a love for the American vernacular. Like Williams, they recognize that the "pure products of America" have lost their marbles; flipped their wig; blown a gasket; hit the ceiling; gone off the deep end. As filmmaker, writer, and mover of rocks, Jarmusch, Padgett, and Smithson turn these banal products into dazzling flights of lyricism, with Padgett's looping passages of prose being the most zany of the four.

This is how Richard Brody's glowing *New Yorker* review (December 30, 2016) of Jarmusch's *Paterson* begins:

> Jim Jarmusch is among the rarest and most precious filmmakers of our time, because, at his best—as he is in his new film, *Paterson*—he conjures an entire world of his own imagination.

Brody's characterization of Jarmusch is equally true of Padgett: he is among the rarest and most precious poets of our time because he also conjures an entire world of his own imagination. And what an imagination it is.

After reading Padgett's recently published novella, *Motor Maids across the Continent*, the latest to come to us from Song Cave, one of the most exciting small presses around, you would likely agree that Brody's observation about Jarmusch's filmmaking style—"the loving precision of his documentary-rooted observations"—can be applied Padgett's madcap prose. But while Jarmusch's cinematic vision is rooted in the world at large, you cannot be sure what Padgett's weirdly actualized vision is rooted in—the everyday world, genre novels for adolescents, B-movies, Surrealism, fantastic tales, proper English novels, and Buster Keaton's unflappable demeanor are just some of the possibilities that crossed my mind.

What Padgett does can so seem easy—and in some sense it is—that it leaves the reader (this one, at least) astounded and delighted, smiling. His pyrotechnics never seem, well, pyrotechnical. In "Complete Works," an early poem that was written around the time he started working on *Motor Maids across the Continent*, the reader comes across this line: "Edgar divided the dainties among the fiends." By removing the "r" from "friends," Padgett causes the reader to do a double take. The thing is, what could easily become an annoying trick (or habit) resorted to once too many times, never happens in Padgett's writing, be it poetry or prose. He neither settles into habit, nor lets the reader read with one eye closed. His love of what is possible in language is evident in every sentence of this phenomenal book.

In a recent interview with Michael Silverblatt, the host of the nationally syndicated radio program, *Bookworm*, Padgett said that, in 1964, while he was a senior at Columbia University, he decided to read books that he would not have bothered with, partly in response to taking so many courses which "stuffed [him] with great literature." This is why he bought a used copy of *Motor Maids across the Continent* (1917), a sappy adventure novel written for teenage girls that tells the adventures of four young women, chaperoned by their matronly aunt, driving from Chicago to San Francisco.

Padgett originally intended to read the book, nothing more.

Luckily for us, he was carrying it when he went to see his teacher, Kenneth Koch, who took the book from Padgett and quickly crossed out a few words in the first paragraph and then wrote: "The End." For Padgett, this turned out to be the beginning. Started more than fifty years ago, and worked on at different points, it became a novella that bears little, if any resemblance to the original novel. Padgett's *Motor Maids across the Continent* is, on one level, a wacky adventure novel in which four young women (Nancy, Elinor, Mary, and Wilhemina AKA "Billie") and Miss Helen Campbell (their chaperone) drive a red car named The Comet across the western states, from Chicago to San Francisco.

Along the way, they keep encountering various characters, some of who seem to have stepped straight out of a silent movie. They are familiar types (the possessive father or the heartsick young woman, for example) seen from the oddest angle and becoming something altogether fresh and new. One of the characters is Blaise Cendrars, whose *Complete Poems* (University of California, 1992) Padgett translated. Although you do not have to know who Cendrars is to enjoy the novel, Padgett's research into this poet is unsurpassed. As he told Silverblatt, Cendrars was the first poet to incorporate found material into his poetry. In his groundbreaking book *Kodak* (1923), Cendrars got all the lines from Gustave Le Rouge's 18-volume, serialized science fiction novel, *The Mysterious Doctor Cornelius* (1912–13). Padgett wears his knowledge lightly so that the real delight of *Motor Maids across the Continent* comes from reading it, and not from knowing literary history or catching all the allusions.

Padgett's sentences mirror the trip, which is constantly being interrupted by inexplicable events that compel the intrepid travelers to take detours, or stop to help Cendrars, or free him, or enjoy a delicious repast, or choose a different route. These unexpected shifts—as if switching quickly and smoothly from one lane of the highway to another—begin happening right in the book's first paragraph ("… leaning back in her seat and folding her hands as if they were a letter of resignation."). A naturalist writer would have written: folding her hands as if in resignation. But Padgett is not a naturalist. The reality he describes is full of word substitutions, slippages, elisions, diversions, and unexpected jumps (… and we wished to show our appreciation by giving her a little membrane."), which always make sense within this fantastical place the author has created for our reading pleasure.

It is as if at any point in a sentence, Padgett follows the cues embodied in the words he uses ("She drew herself stiffer and straighter than a frozen broom and swept across the floor."). The cue could be sound or meaning or both. He could have stopped at "frozen broom," which certainly catches the reader's attention, but he does not; he goes from "broom" to "swept." You can call this kind of writing surrealist, but I think it is pure genius. And the real pleasure is that you do not know what kind of writing Padgett might use to describe something ordinary. At one moment the Motor Maids are driving through "these flat, monotonous wheat fields," and then, a moment later, he makes you shift your perceptual gears. ("To the right and left of them stretched a large green haircut yielding great waves of heat.") Are we supposed to think of "wheat" when we read "heat"? The descriptions are simultaneously particular and wobbly, which is difficult to pull off repeatedly, but Padgett does it without seeming to break into a sweat.

Reading *Motor Maids across the Continent* is like sitting in a car that has been commandeered by a driver who likes to exceed the speed limit. He does not want to scare you so much as enthrall you, and that is exactly what Padgett does, time and again throughout the book. As the story—if you can call it that—proceeds, things keep getting stranger. You find yourself wondering what he is going to pull off next and you are never disappointed when he does. *Motor Maids across the Continent* is a page-turner, which makes you not want to turn the page because you want to stop and marvel over all the different things that Padgett does in his crystalline prose.

One of many delights of this slim book is Padgett's ability to make all sorts of weird information and skewed perceptions seem perfectly logical. In one hotel where the travelers stop, they encounter diners who are going to take a stage coach "the next morning to a ranch that operated as a sanitarium." This leads them to notice that seated at "a nearby table were several trained patients." If you stop to wonder about the "travelers," and whether or not they are going to become "trained patents," you get happily sidetracked even while you try to follow one of the book's plots, which I won't give away.

On one hand, the book is a quick read, and yet what Padgett does with his sentences is to be savored. He neither falls into a predictable pattern nor comes across as arbitrary. That is what makes this book special. He offers a level of reading pleasure that we seldom encounter in novels these days. He takes a deep pleasure in the words, their sounds and variable meanings. There are the entertaining misadventures and there are the head-turning sentences. All of it is marked by the ease of Padgett's writing, his unrivaled directness.

At the heart of Padgett's writing is a knowing naivete: he sees everything—no matter how banal or how curious or strange—with the same attentive, innocent eye. "Glistening to the west, like a gem in December, is a beautiful lake, and from the very heart of the valley rises the city, nestled at the foot of a vast granite edifice that towers above the homes of its citizens." You get the feeling that what links "gem" and "December" is sound, and it is that sonic connection that motivated the writer to put them together, returning the mysteries of the world back to their proper place: everyday life.

I have deliberately not told you the bones (or plot) of this marvelous book because I want you to read it. *Motor Maids across the Continent* belongs on a shelf with Giorgio de Chirico's *Hebdomeros,* Kenward Elmslie's *Orchid Stories* (which was reissued by Song Cave in 2016, with a wonderfully illuminating introduction by Michael Silverblatt), Ted Berrigan's *Clear the Range,* Ishmael Reed's *Yellow Back Radio Broke Down,* and Mary Butts' *Ashe of Rings* (which was reissued by McPherson, along with additional writings, in 2015). It is luxuriantly bizarre in beautifully exact sentences. He moves from the frivolous to feeling with such smoothness it takes your breath away.

> The morning mists still clung to the citizens of Salt Lake City when The Comet flashed along the quiet back streets. How good it

seemed to settle back among his comfortable cushions and hasten to leave this stinking town. At the wheel, Billie looked straight in front of her. Her heart was unquiet and her gray eyes troubled.

Who would not want to go along for the ride?

At Play in The Fields of Language: The Poetry of Cathy Park Hong

> *The chances of overhearing a conversation in Vlashki, a variant of Istro-Romanian, are greater in Queens than in the remote mountain villages in Croatia that immigrants now living in New York left years ago.*
> —Sam Roberts, "Listening to (and Saving) the World's Languages," *The New York Times* (April 28, 2010)

The argument between lyric poetry (that is poetry that arises from the poet's voice (the "I") or what Robert Grenier characterized as "SPEECH") and text (the primacy of the written or printed word) is becoming an increasingly obsolete opposition. Globalism and immigration (or migration)—in the form of pidgin, mispronunciation, graffiti, and encoded signs—have overrun the various geographical boundaries as well as upended the rules defining areas of fixed vocabulary, grammar and spelling. The American language is a field in which decay and replenishment are ongoing, unpredictable ruptures. No one is sure what will happen next, what transformation some part of it will inevitably undergo. It is an inflicted and vulnerable body undergoing rapid change. Parts of it are blossoming while other parts are dying. It is this often volatile state of change and instability, slipperiness and unlikelihood, which Cathy Park Hong explores in her poetry.

Since her first book, *Translating Mo'um* (Hanging Loose Press, 2002), Hong has focused on developing different imaginary lingua franca (or bridge languages) that make communication possible between people who do not share a mother tongue. Her poetry posits a zone of uneven exchange that exists along borders and in boomtowns, resort cities and future worlds. She is the author of three books, all of which contain poems in which translation, pidgin, invented dialects, and made-up slang play a central role in a fabricated language that, in its treacherousness and slipperiness of sound and orthography, mirrors the turbulence that is central to our current state of affairs: the arguments over immigration and birthrights.

In "Zoo," the first poem in her first book, *Translating Mo'um* (Hanging Loose Press, 2002), Hong wrote:

> Piscine skin, unblinking eyes.
> Sideshow invites foreigner with the animal hide.
>
> Alveolar tt, sibilant ss, and glottal hh
>
> Shi: poem
> Kkatchi: magpie
> Ayi: child
>
> Words with an atavistic tail. History's thorax considerably cracked. The Hottentot click called undeveloped.
>
> Mother and father obsessed with hygiene:
> as if to rid themselves of their old third world smell.

On the left is a list of Korean words ("Shi," "Kkatchi,", and "Ayi"), while on the right is their English translation ("poem," "magpie," and "child"). Together, the words on the right hand side form a highly compressed, abstract version of an imagistic poem, which inevitably evokes—if somewhat distantly—Ezra Pound's misunderstanding of the Chinese ideogram via Ernest Fenellosa.

Hong exists between two languages, unable to speak one without being conscious of the other. She makes a connection between foreign language and the foreign body ("third-world smell"), which suggests that she believes language is visceral. The host country perceives the foreign body (or language) as a threat to its sovereignty, while the outsiders try their best to assimilate, to become less viral, to not smell. They want to cleanse themselves of their old language (the shame of it), which is something they can never do.

A note at the end of the book informs us that "[t]he standard Romanized spelling of *Mo'um* is *Mom*." Translating mom also means translating (and therefore both preserving and losing) the mother tongue.

In "During Bath," Hong writes:

> I am an old man in my fantasies, a darting pupil, a curious ghost.

In "All the Aphrodisiacs," she writes:

> What are the objects that turn me on: words—
> *han-gul:* the language first used by female entertainers, poets, prostitutes.

In contrast to Charles Baudelaire's *flâneur,* the "passionate spectator" who is a "lover of crowds and incognitos," Hong's figures—which include the original Siamese twins, Chang and Eng; the Hottentot Venus; and Tono Maria and the androgynous pronoun—cannot go incognito. Each of them is a quintessential outsider (or foreigner):

> As if I wrote myself
> to a sparkling erasure.
> or spoke with the wooden
> clack of a puppet's mouth,
> my palimpsest face haggard
> from revision

In 2006, Hong was selected by Adrienne Rich to receive the Barnard Women Poets Prize, and in 2007, her second book *Dance Dance Revolution* was published by W. W. Norton. In both *Dance Dance Revolution* and her most recent book, *Engine Empire* (W. W. Norton, 2012), the poet establishes a time and place—a space or setting—in which the poems are spoken and written. In *Dance Dance Revolution,* the place is the "Desert" and the time is after 2016, the near future. There are two author/speakers, "The Guide" who is interviewed by "The Historian".

"The Guide, who works at the "St. Petersburg Hotel"—which is modeled after the city—speaks a lingua franca or what she calls "Desert Creole," a cacophonous mishmash of puns, pidgin languages, malapropisms, neologisms, and portmanteaus. Reading and seeing is fractured and slowed down. According to "The Historian," "Desert Creole" is "an amalgam of some three hundred languages and dialects...." The book opens

> Opal o opus,
> behole, neon hibiscus bloom beacons!
> "Tan Lotion Tanya" billboard ... she
> your lucent Virgin, den's I taka ova
> as talky Virgin ... want some tea? Some Pelehuu

"Behole" can be read in so many different ways that it opens up a space in the book, inflecting a domain where we—as readers and listeners—are asked to reflect upon (Behold) the invisible other, the figure we don't want to see and try to bury or fill (Be hole), a figure who comments to itself (Be whole). Can we behold someone who is both erased and unable to overcome self-erasure? In the twists and turns of her invented, marginalized language, the poet is able to evoke a self that is both accused and accusing without becoming either didactic or ironic. It is one of Hong's singular achievements to create "The Guide" outside of these familiar territories.

"The Guide," as Adrienne Rich tells us in her citation, is "a former South Korean dissident from the Kwangju uprising of 1980 (comparable to Tiananmen Square, brutally repressed with the support of the U.S.). "The Historian" she goes to explain, is "a scholar raised in Sierra Leone, who annotates the Guide's commentaries in Standard English." (From 1991 to 2001 Sierra Leone was in a civil war that left more than fifty thousand dead and displaced over two million people.)

Dance Dance Revolution is a book of many layers and minglings. The poem is not synonymous with a lyric self because "The Guide" is made of many selves, languages, and public and private memories. At the same time, writing in an epoch where the author is dead, Hong does not replace the unified "I" (or lyric voice) with found text and collage, but with a weaving together of foreign languages and spin-offs of Standard English. What she holds up to the reader is language in a constant state of contention, change, and fecund decomposition.

In "Fadder"—"The Guide's" word for father—we hear fodder and fatter. The language is messy—both post-apocalyptic and primeval. This is "The Guide's" description of the day she was born:

> pop me out ... (me yeller fadder
> hid home, hidim from froth o birth's labot
> y labor o revolution).... I'se boomerang
> out, slip shod onto blood tile floor
> a squalim bile newborn.

In the "Desert," which resembles Las Vegas and Seoul (a rapidly expanding city), language (or the poem) isn't utterance, but excretion. There is no purity. One is always conscious of imperfection, the unattainable, and dirt.

At the same time, in counterpoint to "The Guide," there are seven prose "Excerpt[s] from the Historian's Memoir." "The Historian," who is from Sierra Leone, "hopped around an archipelago of boarding schools in London, Hong Kong, and Connecticut. School granted me an immunity from my foreign surroundings."

In another "Excerpt," we learn: "I was not allowed into the streets of Sierra Leone so I drew my own."

Although "The Historian" has a privileged life, she (like "The Guide") is isolated in the present, cut off from her past and drifting toward an unknown future. The difference is that "The Historian" received "immunity," while "The Guide" is a "double migrant" who has "ceded from Koryo, ceded from / 'Merikka, ceded y ceded…"

In addition to the two groups of separate but inseparable poems, Hong has included a third set in a section titled, "INTERMISSION: PORTRAIT OF THE DESERT." In the poems in this section, many of which are titled "Almanac," we learn that "Once, the Desert was actually a desert. / The guide, the only guide." Before the "a desert" became "the Desert"—a site of bloody conflict covered over by a resort area—it was filled with "buried mines, leftovers of war." The world and language are both minefields filled with hidden dangers. In order to deal with the fact that "[m]any locals had missing limbs":

> They adapted, created a caste system:
> The fully limbed down to the fully limbless.

Both iterations of Hong's desert are mirrors of language as it is currently used across the world, from artificial resorts (or the simulacrum) to border towns and boomtowns. Because language and setting mirror each other, the distortion becomes even more extensive, as in a funhouse hall of mirrors. Starting with the poem "Ontology of Chang and Eng, The Original Siamese Twins", which was the second poem in *Translating Mo'um,* Hong has repeatedly returned to the body as a site of deformation. "I am this chair/talking to him, the poet writes in "Elegy" (from *Dance Dance Revolution*).

Hong recognizes that language is a "caste system" that goes from the "fully limbed" (those in control) to the "fully limbless (those at the mercy of others). Lingua franca, slang and graffiti are among the various ways the limbless adjust to, as well as undermine, the limbed. By inventing a world in which the poems (or invented languages) mirror the dystopian setting, Hong establishes poetry's possibility in a realm bordered by science fiction and writers such as Gilles Deleuze, Donna Haraway, Samuel R. Delany, William Gibson, Ishmael Reed and Monique Wittig, clearing a path beyond the academic turf wars between text and speech, found text and soulful utterance. She writes from a terrain where language—already shattered and infected—is in continual collapse and metamorphosis.

Hong's most recent book, *Engine Empire* (2013), is divided into three discrete sections or, perhaps more accurately, three self-sustaining worlds, each with its own invented languages. In each section Hong utilizes radical forms and devices—a list, an abededarian, a lipogram— to propel her poems forward. The language is volatile, undergoing metamorphosis and extreme pressure. Tremors of discomfort suffuse throughout the music of Hong's poems:

> juddering slam of hammering jack,
> humming sussurations of catamarans,
> aerosol striations of welder's firecrack,
> then a caracas of fist cracks

The fact is—Hong doesn't repeat herself and she sounds like no one else. Chronologically speaking, the sections of *Engine Empire* are the Wild West ("BALLAD OF OUR JIM"); a contemporary Chinese boomtown ("SHANDU, MY ARTFUL BOOMTOWN"); and a near future world in which the Internet, in the form "smart snow," is being incorporated into everyone's mind ("THE WORLD CLOUD"):

> The snow is still beta.
> You feel the smart snow monitoring you,
> Uploading your mind so that anyone can access your content.

Despite being about the past, present and future, the three worlds mirror each other. Marginal characters grasping for security and material success populate all of them ("Jim," "Orright," and "an undersized girl with a tic"). At the same time, Hong's characters are neither ethnically pure nor at ease in their skin (their ethnicity). Beginning with ""BALLAD OF OUR JIM," the following lines are found in one of the book's three sections.

> Our Jim's a two-bit half-breed.

> I am covetous of you and curse your birth order.

> As if the ancient laws of miscegenation
> Are still in place

While the sections are discrete, Hong will make future and past intersect. "Quattrocento" is included in the last section. In the poem, whose title evokes the Italian Renaissance and the rise of perspective and humanism, Hong writes:

> That all towns now are rest stops
> to a vanishing point
> We're all going to the clouds,
> haunted by a gobbet
> of flesh marooned
> on the glass surface of image

If the vanishing point once indicated the world beyond (heaven or transcendence), it no longer does. Towns are rest stops on the way to our unavoidable disappearance. Hong is a materialist. She recognizes that words are things made up of distinct components (sounds), which can be detached and reassembled. She is working in a largely unpopulated area previously explored by the American poet and filmmaker, Frank Kuenstler, and the Italian poet, Amelia Rosselli, who called herself a "poet of research."

In "BALLAD OF OUR JIM," Hong writes "Abecedarian Western" (which employs an alphabetically arranged sequence) and uses a lipogram constraint (which sets a restriction on the letters the writer may use) in "Ballad in O," "Ballad in A," and "Ballad in I." In each of these poems, every word must have the letter indicated in the poem's title. The first stanza of "Ballad in A" reads thus:

> A Kansan plays cards, calls marshall
> a crawdad, that barb lands that rascal a slap;
> that Kansan jackass scats,
> camps back at caballada ranch.

The restraints underscore that language is trap and liberation, that there is no such thing as free expression. We live inside of language (or, in some cases, languages) and cannot step outside of its universe. Heaven and resurrection are not waiting for us. While the obvious precedents for "BALLAD OF OUR JIM" are Cormac McCarthy's *Blood Meridian* and Ed Dorn's *Gunslinger*, both of which are thoroughly masculine worlds, Hong has pulled them into Oulipian territory, infecting her lines with a racially conscious humor.

One thing that strikes me about Hong's work is her repeated refusal to mythologize her experience, while focusing, at the same time, on the very commonplace desire of various groups and individuals to explain their specialness. She is on the other end of the spectrum from Li Young-Lee, who never fails to mention in interviews that his father had been a personal physician to Mao Zedong, that he knew hundreds of Chinese poems by heart and read the King James Bible to his children. Lee is suggesting, of course, that these experiences have singled him out and made him special.

Even in her first book, *Translating Mo'um,* Hong rejected the option of the singled out "I" (both victim and hero), picking up instead on Theresa Hak Kyung Cha (1951–1982) and especially Cha's *Dictee* (1982) and its use of multiple languages. In Hong's first book, familiar types such as the mother or father never coalesce into a large-than-life presences or heroic figures. Instead, Hong writes:

> My mother said, "If you eat lying down, you'll grow hair on your / crotch.

In contrast to ethnic writers who use words to signify cultural difference, Hong employs them to evoke the linguistic mayhem that has become even more widespread with the advance of globalization. Her poems come from listening and reading. She hears words as a string of detachable sounds, recognizing that they could become more than one word. And it is out of this hearing, this acute sensitivity to the inevitable mutation of one word sounding almost like another, that she concocts poems. Rather than trying to assimilate and write in Standard English—which she can clearly do extremely well—she recognizes that to do so is a form of mimicry, and goes a step further in poems such as "Ballad in I".

> His grim instinct wilting
> Dispiriting Jim, climbing hill's hilt,
> Drifting Jim, sighing in this lilting,
> sinking light.

In *Engine Empire,* more so than in her previous two books, Hong brings in pop culture, increasing the scope of her references and allusions. I imagine that in addition to housing many books of poetry and fiction, Hong's library contains Baedekers and tour guides, lots of history books, and dictionaries to many languages. She gets us to consider things we might learn from. There is no standard pool of knowledge to draw from.

In "A Little Tête-à-tête," which is addressed to "Coleridge," her "affectionate friend," Hong mentions such media luminaries as Nick Faldo, Annika Sorenstam, and Tiger Woods. Working in different forms, she moves from what we might call a transparent language to a patois that is largely the poet's invention. In contrast to those who write as authorities or as witnesses, Hong invokes the poet as a ventriloquist.

Ventriloquism, we might want to remember, was originally a religious practice that had roots in the oracular tradition at Delphi. In *Translating Mo'um,* the poet wrote about a figure that "spoke with the wooden/clack of a puppet's mouth." In *Engine Empire,* that puppet has become so much more and so much else. It is a magnificent achievement. I have only one suggestion, which is that in order to move beyond the settings of her series of poems—and they ultimately become a kind of restraint—Hong will have to accept randomness. It is certainly within her power to do so.

Donna Stonecipher, Global Flâneur

In 2007, when I was asked to be one of judges of the National Poetry Series, I selected *The Cosmopolitan* by Donna Stonecipher. Coffee House Press published it the following year. Reviewing the book on his website, On The Seawall (October 23, 2008), Ron Slate wrote: "*The Cosmopolitan* is one of the most exciting and gratifying books of poems I've read this year." This is how he described the book:

> *The Cosmopolitan* is comprised of 22 "inlays"—Stonecipher's term for each multipart story. Each inlay has between eight and fourteen mini-stories, and each ministory has two or three sentences. "I was at the Met, looking at inlaid furniture, when the idea came to me to "inlay" a poem, she told [Camille] Guthrie. The inlay itself is a quotation from another author—Kafka, Ruskin, or Plato, but also Susan Sontag, Elaine Scarry, or Elfried Jelinek. "I wanted to very exaggeratedly and artificially call attention to the problem [of attribution] for myself by pacing a quote from another author squarely in the center of my text." The quotations lend themselves to aphorism—but Stonecipher uses them as fuel, not as maps, to travel further.

This is from "Inlay 4 (Susan Sontag)":

> Pity we who must corset our mental splendor into the whalebone of grammar, which laces us up so tight we have to remove a rib to breathe.

Stonecipher's ability to synthesize the visceral (corset), the ephemeral (splendor), and the abstract (grammar) into a self-sufficient sentence set her apart from her contemporaries: this was neither a style that could be picked up nor writing that could be taught. Whatever her sources or inspirations, she got here on her own.

Since my first encounter with Stonecipher's poems in a pile of anonymously submitted manuscripts, I have published her translation of the novella *Ascent* by Ludwig Hohl through my press, Black Square Editions, in 2012. Written in German, *Ascent* is about a mountain-climbing expedition that goes all wrong, a tragedy foreshadowed in the book's remarkable first paragraph. And yet, knowing that doom lies ahead, the reader keeps chugging along until reaching an end that is expected and unexpected. Stonecipher's deft translation revealed Hohl to be, as Susan Bernofsky wrote in a jacket blurb, "a great discovery, an unjustly neglected author."

In 2015, I wrote about her book of prose poems *Model City* (Shearsman, 2015) under the title: "This Is Not a Book Review of *Model City* by Donna Stonecipher." This is my description of *Model City*:

> The book consists of seventy-two consecutively numbered short prose poems collectively titled *Model City*. Each prose poem is divided into four sections, with each section being one sentence long. This adds up to 288 sections, each of which answers the question: What was it like? The antecedent becomes a dream, a memory, a fiction, or a perception, all of which are inflected by the fact that the poet's decision to begin every section begins with, "It was like … " Out this conceptual scaffolding, where the writing is always responding to an absent thing or event, Stonecipher opens up her "Model City" to admit all kinds of stuff, from a "real fox" to "a new opera house built in China by Zaha Hadid, and how it is beginning to crumble after having been open for six months."

However, just because I am not supposed to review a book by an author whose translation I have published does not mean I cannot plug a book she has neither finished nor found a publisher for, does it? Am I really supposed to curb my enthusiasm for an author whose work I was lucky enough to have discovered in a mountain of submissions?

By the time Stonecipher published *Model City*, it was apparent to a number of readers that she was renovating the prose poem in ways that opened it up, like a bursting star, enabling her to go in multiple directions and muse on just about anything. The prose poem in her hands can be a dream catcher, a travelogue, a report, an archive, a series of aphorisms, a contemplation of modernity, often simultaneously. As she titled three of the 24 chapters in her long essay *Prose Poetry and the City* (Parlor Press, 2017), it can embrace "Trivia," "Aphasia," and "The Sublime."

My feeling that Stonecipher has become a major poet, an innovator who writes in concise, sparkling language, was emphatically reinforced when I recently heard her read in Berlin from an unfinished manuscript, *The Ruins of Nostalgia,* which consists of more than 65 prose poems and does not yet have a publisher. The reading took place in a courtyard and the other readers were Barry Schwabsky, Matvei Yakelevich, and myself. In addition to publishing Stonecipher's translation, I have published books by Schwabsky and Yankelevich.

Siddartha Lokanandi organized the reading at his bookstore, Hopscotch Reading Room, where, in addition to encountering a wide range of books, whose haphazard arrangement makes for surprises and delights, you can also buy beer and other spirits long after the sun has departed. Although this was the first time I met Lokanandi, it was quickly apparent that he was interested in building connections and creating a borderless, multi-racial community, which isn't always the case among poets or the avant-garde.

Each of us read for 15 to 20 minutes as night slowly moved in. At the beginning of his segment, Yankelevich expressed amazement and happiness at the size of the audience, which was far larger than many of the readings he attended in New York.

By the time Stonecipher finished reading four poems from the unfinished manuscript, I knew that I wanted to write about them and that I did not want to wait until the book was published to do so, as this could take years and it clearly shouldn't. Also, at the time I did not know that Stonecipher had a book forthcoming, *Transaction Histories,* from the University of Iowa Press. I found it interesting that she neither announced her forthcoming book or read from it, perhaps because she had done a reading a few weeks earlier at Hopscotch Reading Room and resists repeating herself (which makes for an interesting contrast with her use of repetition in her poetry—just one of many things I find compelling about her work).

According to the publisher, *Transaction Histories* consists of "six series of poems that explore the disobedient incongruities of aesthetics and emotions." I don't think this description is going to lure a lot of readers. Like the "inlays" of *The Cosmopolitan,* the poems I have read from *Transaction Histories* are a series of mini-stories, each of which is numbered and made up of a half dozen sentences, at most. While each story is discrete, certain motifs reappear (plastic owls, photographs of boys in sailor suits, specimen boxes, and a clear plastic backpack) within a particular "Transaction History." Often, more than one motif will appear in different sections of the same poem. The sentences of each section stand on their own, suggesting a collage without being one.

This is the seventh section of "Transaction History 6," which appeared in issue # 11 of the online magazine *Wave Composition:*

> It was all too easy to swim in the lake that summer without thinking about the fish chasing smaller fish chasing smaller fish along the bottom, to glide along the surface with one's distorted limbs and feel that one was "deeply experiencing" the lake. He pulled out the tiniest cell phone she'd ever seen. Bitter Lemon was the drink of choice; then there was a craze for homemade seltzer; then suddenly everyone had to have absinthe.

This is what I love about Stonecipher's work. You never know what the next sentence is going to tell. The connections between the sentences feel both tenuous and tensile. You don't just read this paragraph; you reread it and take it apart, your curiosity driven by the desire to see what makes it tick.

In poem after poem, Stonecipher opens up a space in which readers can reflect upon what has been placed before them—a mosaic that is rigorous and elusive, a challenge to keep the whole in mind while remembering all the distinct elements, to recognize the different transactions or exchanges in the fluid world she evokes with preternatural precision. Stonecipher seems to be asking in this paragraph, what is the relationship between experience and folly, familiarity and escape?

At once detached and empathetic, Stonecipher observes, uncovers, and probes our present malaise, the recognition that the future and past are constantly colliding in our everyday lives, shadowed by the suspicion that such encounters may erase all evidence of our existence. The information explosion, with the vast access offered by the digital tentacles at our fingertips, has made us acutely aware of how truly insignificant we are as individuals in the grand scheme of things. Stonecipher's poems are located in cities undergoing relentless change, as all of them seem to be doing these days. The phrase "ruins of nostalgia" appears in each of the poems, usually at the beginning or at the end. If wistful affection for a golden age in our collective and personal past lies in ruins, how do we embrace the future that will eventually devour us? Can we continue to be open and compassionate? Here is the beginning of "The Ruins of Nostalgia":

> For a long time we had listened to the stories of those who had lived in countries that no longer existed, and the stories had been exciting—stories of privation, of deprivation, of limits, of lack. But after a time we had heard the same stories so many times that even the tellers grew weary of the telling. "Nobody had telephones—we just left messages on notepads attached to people's doors" (mm). "I wasn't allowed to go to university, because I did x (harmless thing)" (mm). "Everyone was having affairs, because the private life was the only realm in which you felt free" (mm).

That parenthetical interjection "(mm)" adds a note of humor as it exposes the need to distance ourselves from others in order to maintain our privileged status of voyeur, which we have become, whether we admit it or not. Stonecipher is in touch with the different ways we feel displaced and estranged in our everyday lives, the various states of incomprehension infiltrating all of our perceptions.

How do we adjust to the structural changes cities are undergoing due to gentrification and capitalism's demand for higher and higher profit margins, as if the importance of people is measured by how much they spend? Here is the beginning of "The Ruins of Nostalgia 20":

> Where there once had been a low-end stationery store minded by an elderly beauty queen, there was now a store for high-end espresso machines minded by nobody. Where once there had been an illegal beer garden in a weedy lot, there was now a complex of luxury lofts with Parisian-style ivory façades. Where once there had been a bookstore and a bike shop and a bakery, there was now a wax museum for tourists.

In his essay "The Painter of Modern Life" (1863), Charles Baudelaire recognized that the borders separating (and protecting) classes and individuals had broken down:

> The poet enjoys the incomparable privilege of being himself and someone else as he sees fit. Like a roving soul in search of a body, he enters another person whenever he wishes. For him alone, all is open; if certain places seem closed to him, it is because in his view they are not worth inspecting.

Stonecipher's renovation of the prose poem is inextricable from her sensitivity to how much further erosion has taken place since Baudelaire walked the streets of Paris. In this global economy, and the growing, insurmountable disparity between the privileged and vulnerable, she watches a world vanish and does not turn away from the particulars, "the obsolescence of queens," "a crippling housing shortage," "new families," and "the homeless lining the freeways."

Ai Weiwei:
New York Photographs 1983-1993

Ai Weiwei is the son of the important Chinese Modernist poet, Ai Qing, who believed in free expression and social criticism. In 1958, Ai Qing was sent to a labor camp because he openly criticized the Communist government for its treatment of the proto-feminist writer, Ding Ling. For the 16 years his father was in prison, Ai Weiwei experienced firsthand the severity of such a situation, where language is under constant pressure from the authorities, which possess the power to distort and twist whatever is said or written, and harshly punish writers and freethinkers such as Ai Qing and Ding Ling. In 1975, the "rehabilitated" Ai Qing returned with his family to Beijing, and Ai Weiwei enrolled in the Beijing Film Academy in 1978. His classmates included Chen Kaige and Zhang Yimou. He also helped found the "Stars," a group of radical, forward-thinking Chinese artists interested in performance and photography. In 1981, when Ai Weiwei was about to leave for America, he announced to his mother: "I am going home. And a few years later you will hear of me as another Picasso."

Ambitious from the beginning, Ai Weiwei studied English at the University of Pennsylvania and Berkeley before attending Parsons on a scholarship, which he soon lost after he failed an art history exam given in English. Over the next decade Ai Weiwei took more than 10,000 photographs, many of which weren't developed until recently. Together they form a diary/document of the education and self-discovery of Ai Weiwei. As much as the photographs tell you, I suspect the curators have downplayed or left out important pieces of information. There is only one photograph of Ai Weiwei's time in Atlantic City, for example, where he became well known in gambling circles for his skill at blackjack. His resourcefulness at surviving in America is a remarkable account, and his ability to win at blackjack—a game he learned while in America—is part of the story. Each photograph identifies its subject by name, place, and year. But not everyone is named. The activist poet and investigative researcher Ed Sanders, for example, is an unidentified figure engaged in an animated conversation with Allen Ginsberg.

By 1986, Ai Weiwei knew Ginsberg well enough to photograph the poet visiting him in his East Third Street apartment. There are at least eight other photographs of Ginsberg, the most images of any non-Chinese individual, with the latest from 1992. Ai Weiwei also photographed the poet Gu Cheng (1956–1993) wearing his signature stovepipe hat cut from a pant leg, arriving at Kennedy International Airport in 1988 (the year before Tiananmen Square). Like Ai Weiwei, Gu Cheng was the son of a prominent party member and poet, Gu Gong, who remained in favor until the Cultural Revolution. In 1967, Gu Gong and his family were sent into the countryside by the Red Guard to breed pigs and be "re-educated," effectively ending Gu Cheng's formal education. In 1993, Gu Cheng fatally wounded his wife, Xi Yie, before hanging himself.

Another photograph is labeled "Bei Dao 1988." The poet is sitting in Ai Weiwei's Third Street apartment, which seemed to function as a crash pad and meeting place for many Chinese émigré artists, musicians, filmmakers, and poets. Both Gu Cheng and Bei Dao were leading "Misty Poets" who were well received in America and Europe in the late 1980s, but, as with much in the West, attention soon moved onto other things, leaving some of the poets feeling stranded and even more isolated.

The exhibition consists of 227 sequenced photographs and filmstrips, which Ai Weiwei has selected, identified, digitized, and reproduced as silver gelatin prints. One filmstrip jumps from a view of the Chinese Consulate's carpet to a Lower East Side street corner at night. The earliest photographs are from 1983, while he was living in the Williamsburg neighborhood of Brooklyn. In 1985, he moved to Manhattan's Lower East Side, where he lived in two different apartments until he returned to China in 1993 to be with his ailing father.

Looking at the work in chronological order, one recognizes a cluster of recurring interests forming over time. One trope is that of homogeneous groups defining themselves within or against the larger mainstream culture (St. Patrick's Day Parade; the Hells Angels Club on East Third Street; the "Wigstock" concert; Chinese New Year's celebration in Chinatown; Ai Weiwei and his Chinese émigré friends). Another trope is of the power relationship between the state and opposition groups (Tompkins Square Park riot; Al Sharpton; Tawana Brawley protest). His interest in poets, particularly Ginsberg, is another focal point. Ginsberg defined the poet as the individual who stands up and speaks on behalf of the body politic ("I saw the best minds of my generation destroyed ..."). He also thoroughly documented his life in photographs.

Ginsberg is the one subject in Ai Weiwei's photographs who is identified with both countercultural groups ("the Beats" in the 1950s) and antiwar protest (the "Chicago 8" in the 1960s). The uproar over the publication of *Howl* and the government's early attempts to censor it for obscenity could not have been lost on Ai Weiwei. One particularly touching photograph is of Ginsberg and the artist sitting shoulder-to-shoulder on restaurant barstools, with their hands folded in identical lotus positions.

There are multiple narratives entwined within these photographs, and many of the individual views are just the tip of an iceberg. Critics have understandably tended to focus on Ai Weiwei's relationship to Marcel Duchamp, which is obviously there, and singled out his photographs of artworks by Duchamp, Warhol, and Jasper Johns, which often picture himself standing nearby. While it plays to the current market climate to stress Ai's conceptual bona fides, the more elusive aspects of his work remain just that, elusive. The old dictum that art comes only from art was rendered obsolete with the birth of abstraction, when sound poetry and poets such as Hugo Ball and

John Yau

Velimir Khlebnikov influenced artists such as Hans Arp and Kazimir Malevich. Ai Weiwei's long and involved relationship to poetry and language is equally apparent, but is seldom commented on, which is why it is important to draw attention to it. In ways both overt and—in the case of the academy—subtle, censorship of Ai Weiwei continues to manifest itself.

John Ashbery–A Prince of the Clouds

"Gleeful mischief" is how Gregory Cowles described John Ashbery's collages in *The New York Times* review of the book *THEY KNEW WHAT THEY WANTED: Poems & Collages* (Rizzoli Electa), edited by Mark Polizzotti. Cowles goes on to say, "The result is an entire oeuvre of fantasy landscapes [...]" Included in the book, as Cowles notes in his review, is an interview that I did with Ashbery, itself a collage made of excerpts from recorded conversations that we had over a ten-year period.

I mention Cowles's review because there are two exhibitions, which include nearly every collage that Ashbery made in his lifetime, that you can see in New York right now. If you prefer your exhibitions to be in chronological order, you might wish to first go to *John Ashbery: The Construction of Fiction* at Pratt Manhattan Gallery, curated by Antonio Sergio Bessa. Bessa's revelatory installation presents 120 of Ashbery's collages in groups, which largely coincide with the intermittent periods in which he worked on them. Fully illustrated and with an illuminating essay by Bessa, the catalog accompanying the show is a must.

Various items, including copies of his books, and sources he took images from, complement the exhibition. There is a vitrine that includes a chatty letter that Ashbery sent to the pianist Robert Fizdale, dated 1952, in which he mentions making collages with James Schuyler ("Jimmy" in the letter) after they had seen a Kurt Schwitters exhibition. A large Victorian collage that Ashbery bought and had by his desk is also included in the exhibition, just above the vitrine. If you don't know Ashbery collages, it is best to start with this exhibition, to begin at the beginning.

John Yau

The following day (or very soon after) you should go to *John Ashbery: Oh, What Fun!* at Tibor de Nagy, which includes 18 collages he made between 2015 and 2017, the year before his death. Bringing together nearly 140 works dating between 1948 and 2017, the two exhibitions amount to a comprehensive view of Ashbery's collages, as he probably made no more than 150. It will be a long time before this many of his works will be exhibited together again.

As I knew Ashbery for more than 40 years, studied with him at Brooklyn College in the mid-1970s, did the interview included in *THEY KNEW WHAT THEY WANTED: Poems & Collages,* and reviewed each of his collage shows, starting with his first in 2008, I am either qualified or disqualified to write about them. I will let the readers decide if they wish to keep reading or to stop here.

Knowing his works as well as I do, I started with the one at Tibor de Nagy. I wanted to see what I hadn't seen. Made when Ashbery was in his late 80s, many of the works evoke that moment of childhood innocence before it all comes crashing down, which it does for everyone. This state of innocence—it is also a state of grace—can be found in nearly all of the 18 collages on display.

One exception is *Dark Decollation* (2015), where a young man holds a decapitated head up by its thick black hair. Behind him we see part of an archway of a medieval city at night. Next to the young man is a cropped image, derived from a mail order catalogue, of a man wearing a green pullover shirt and beige chinos. The green in the shirt is echoed by the terre verte colors of the city, something that likely caught Ashbery's attention. What is also noticeable is the prominent bulge in the crotch area of the man wearing chinos.

Along the bottom of the collage, we read: "*RITRATTO DI BARTOLOMEO PANCIATTI.*" Ashbery has mischievously covered over a portrait of Bartolomeo Panciatichi (1507–1582) by Agnolo Bronzino (1503–1572) with the figures of Caravaggio's painting *David with the Head of Goliath* (c. 1607). There are so many ways that you can read this collage, starting with the fact that David is the name of Ashbery's longtime partner and husband and that Goliath is thought to be a self-portrait by Caravaggio. At the same time, a frank eroticism spreads throughout the work, from the bulging pants to David's mostly bare chest and exposed nipple. Ashbery came to the subject of the erotic male body late in his life, and mostly in his collages, where we see the lower part of young men dressed in casual wear, seemingly glimpsed in a crowd.

Ashbery's primary subject is an alternate world, what Cowles calls "fantasy landscapes," where nothing goes permanently wrong, and where disaster is nothing more than a prank. In *Wind Up Doll* (2017), a mechanical girl doll with long tresses and a metal crank protruding from her open back towers over the multi-level landscape of a fortress populated by men preparing for a siege. She has just let go of a single-propeller airplane. I think of many of the figures in the collages as Ashbery's alter ego—especially his images of young girls, infants, and Victorian women.

In his poem "The Albatross," Charles Baudelaire equates the poet with the albatross, a seabird that rules over the sky but is awkward and vulnerable on earth. In many collages, we see figures about to begin a journey. Often, but not always, there are two of them. They can be seated in a plane, as in *Vol de Nuit,* or be two children standing beside a rural road full of cars, as in *Oh, What Fun!* (2016). Nothing bad has befallen them yet.

Ashbery could take the most saccharine and sentimental images and with scissors and glue turn them into an innocent world in which disaster looms, an invisible presence that has not made its presence known. This tension enlivens the work as well as gives the collages their heart-rending edge. The journey his figures are about to undertake is drenched in hope, but, in all likelihood, will end in pain. They are Ashbery's paeans to innocence.

The two pairs of male legs we see in *Strawberry Stairs* (2015) evoke the furtiveness of gay life before the AIDs epidemic, which Ashbery witnessed, with many of his friends dying. In the right hand corner of the collage, we see a black-and-white image of a two-story wooden house with a family gathered on the porch. Both the men, whose upper bodies are obscured by leaved branches and three large strawberries, and the house are affixed to a background image taken from a Piranesi etching of a fictional "prison."

This state of innocence, which recurs throughout Ashbery's collages, is there at the beginning. In one of his earliest surviving collages, *Late for School* (1948), included in *John Ashbery: The Construction of Fiction*, we see images of two children standing in a doorway, with an older boy outside about to go to school. He has the head of a bird in one panel of this illustrated page, most likely inspired by Max Ernst's collages.

Ashbery, who is focused on the rarified world of childhood innocence, seemed capable of entering this world, easily and at will, like walking through a door to greet the morning sun. I think it is only when you see all the works that Bessa has brought together that you realize how he did it over and over without repeating himself—that he was able to assemble different visions of innocence tinged with a sweetness that never devolves into kitsch. Picking images of individuals at the beginning of a journey, Ashbery used the inherent dislocation of collage to hint at what awaited them.

The exhibition includes 35 collages, all done on postcards, dated 1972. They were made in Vermont at the house, where the poet and librettist Kenward Elmslie and the artist and writer Joe Brainard lived during the summer. After dinner, they would hang out at the dinner table making collages. I suspect that Brainard provided all the materials. While some of these collages have been previously exhibited, this is the first time that all the work from this year—which is really when Ashbery became a visual artist—has been exhibited together.

Aside from the fun of making them, Ashbery was evidently thinking of using the collages to generate a novel, partly inspired by his years of researching the idiosyncratic genius writer Raymond Roussel (1877–1933). In 1910, Roussel self-published a novel, *Impressions of Africa* (*Impressions d'Afrique*) (1910), that has, as one of its characters, a worm that can play a zither. There are dozens of other equally unique and unlikely characters filling the pages of this extravagant, carnivalesque novel about shipwrecked performers putting on a performance, as they wait for their ransom to be paid for their release from the clutches of the drag-clad Emperor Talou, ruler of Ponukele.

Roussel was obsessed with the metagram, and how the switching of one letter in a word could change the meaning of whatever sentence in which it was used. The other likely inspiration was Elmslie, who was working on a collection of fictions that would be published under the title *The Orchid Stories* (1973), later reprinted in 2016 with an introduction by Michael Silverblatt, host of KCRW's *Bookworm,* one of the most astute readers of innovative poetry and fiction. What distinguishes Ashbery is his uncanny ability to introduce just the right amount of gravitas into madcap weirdness so as to not elevate one over the other.

It is in these collages from 1972 that Ashbery starts bringing together all of his interests. He took material from comic strips, movies, early advertisements, high and low culture. The juxtapositions he gets are funny, odd, and—dare I say it?—Ashberyean. And yet, other than two collages he made in 1977, Ashbery stopped making collages until 2008, when he turned 80 years old. Isn't this remarkable—someone beginning a new body of work in what is ostensibly new material as he enters his ninth decade? The other change is that Ashbery begins using different things, such as game boards, pages from old magazines, and reproductions of well-known and little known works from art books and auction catalogues, as starting points. Formally speaking, he went from working on postcards to using larger formats, as well as adding more than one image to it.

As the master of juxtaposition in poetry, Ashbery knew how to pair images, as in *Salle d'Attente* (2016), where he superimposes Bronzino's 1545 portrait of Lucrezia Panciatichi in front of the interior of a railway station, such as ones he would have gone to during the years he lived in Paris. The combination of the woman's head and a receding space (underscored by the railroad tracks) enclosed within an architectural structure reminded me of that moment in film history when—in 1953—Cinemascope and other formats were used to compress a close-up and a panoramic view into the same scene.

In the collages that use game boards, it is like we are looking at a rebus that we will never be able to decipher. In *Promenade* (2011), Ashbery used a digitized printout of a gameboard, Rocket Dart-

Words, which was sold in the mid-1950s. He superimposed images (including one with the words "Mend All" on it) onto a grid of letters, five to a row. It does not appear as if any of the rows of letters adds up to a word. Since some of the letters are partially obscured by the collage elements, it is impossible to tell if any of the rows add up to a world. Meanwhile, one of the visual elements is a ring with a cluster of bands with numbers on them encircling it. Do the numbers function like those found in a safe? What are we to unlock with our looking?

While it would be easy to conclude that Ashbery's larger collages made from game boards are deliberately indecipherable and more abstract, I want to suggest that this is not the case, even if we are unable to do more than puzzle over them. In the lower left-hand corner of *Promenade,* we see an illustrated card divided horizontally into two images. In the upper half, we see the legs of a man wearing red breeches, while in the lower half, and partially obscured, we see the upper half a woman clasping her hands. Over this, Ashbery has laid a puzzle ring.

The man in red breeches is similar to other images of men in casual wear that Ashbery has put in his collages. The juxtaposition of his lower torso and a woman's upper body, partially covered by a puzzle ring, doesn't seem arbitrary or whimsical. And yet, even as I entertain various readings of this combination of images, I must also entertain that its coming together is random, even as the placement of an open archway over the letter *D* (an archway on its side) suggests otherwise.

This, I think, is Ashbery's genius, what he does that infuriates his detractors. He finds connections without making a big deal about it. He never claimed to have a message or be saying something that his audience needed to hear or see. He didn't mind wearing his enthusiasms on his sleeve, no matter how whimsical or silly they might be. He enjoyed himself when he wrote and that pleasure comes through. And through all of this a lamentation, sometimes just a few hints of it, is heard or seen, barely perhaps, but still there.

An Artist Conjures the Ghosts of Displacement

Yun-fei Ji, who was born in Beijing, China, in 1963, made an important body of work in Rome while on a Prix de Rome fellowship in 2006. He has made work in London; New York City; Beijing; and near Gambier, Ohio—where he currently has a studio. He is a Chinese artist who isn't just a Chinese artist, an American artist who isn't just an American artist. When a curator at an American museum told him he couldn't show his work because he is Chinese, he replied: "I am as American as Willem de Kooning."

I think the idea of identity is important to bring up, especially when there is a lot of heated discussion about it, from the Oval Office to dog park benches. It is a subject that Ji and I inevitably return to whenever we talk, which we first did in the winter of 2006 for an interview in *The Brooklyn Rail*. In the age of globalization and migration, both voluntary and forced, Ji is an artist who doesn't quite fit comfortably into China or America for more reasons than I can enumerate, and so I will focus on just one: his art. He can live in either place, and he has, but that does not necessarily mean he feels safe in either one.

The connection between Ji and classical Chinese art has been an obvious point of reference that many writers have noted. Less obvious is Ji's transformation of different strands of representation and calligraphic mark-making into something that is neither a nostalgic revival nor an unwieldy melding. Rather, what Ji has done is compose a space that weaves together aspects of Western and Eastern art in the service of his subject, which is the government-sanctioned displacement of a vast number of Chinese, as villages are erased from existence in the name of progress. He has braided together the caricatural drawing style of George Grosz, the grotesque realism of James Ensor, and the naturalist depictions of weird ghosts by Luo Ping, an unlikely gathering he has made into something all his own. By joining together divergent possibilities—such as Wifredo Lam had done before him—he has been able to respond to the particulars of China's desire to achieve economic dominance on the world stage.

In his exhibition *Yun-Fei Ji: Rumors, Ridicules and Retributions* at James Cohan, the artist brings a vast and deeply researched knowledge to bear on his longtime preoccupation with the direct effects of China's drive to supply sprawling megalopolises such as Beijing with an adequate supply of water. One way that China has done this is to force entire village populations to relocate. This means that neighbors are often separated and moved to different areas where they know no one.

At the same time, new cities are quickly being built, mostly to provide housing for workers in vast factories, such as those seen in the film *Manufactured Landscapes* (2007), directed by Jennifer Baichwal and starring Edward Burtynsky. If you take a bullet train across China, you will see clusters of high rises in the distance, which raise the question: who are the people living in these isolated enclaves and how did they get there? What purposes do these cities serve?

Ji works uses watercolor and ink to paint on paper. Should anybody ask, I would call him a painter. His subjects are the villagers displaced by Postmodern China's global ambition. Like many villagers throughout the world, they are superstitious, believing in ghosts and gossip, and distrustful of outsiders, which include the people living in a neighboring village. They are the country mice of Aesop's fable and its many variants and retellings.

In the tall, vertical work *Break Camp* (2017–18), two identical red trucks are partially visible near the top of the stacked composition. Beneath them, and spatially much closer to the viewer, the villagers' worldly goods—tables, chairs, pots, pans, barrels, baskets full of things wrapped in blankets, sheets, and quilts—are piled up. The slightly elevated view of this bric-a-brac-filled landscape is claustrophobic, since the horizon is not clearly defined. The people seem cut off from the rest of the world. This sense is underscored by the absence of modern conveniences: no televisions or radios are waiting to be put on the trucks. No one is on his or her cellphone.

Without emphasizing it, Ji shows the viewer a group of powerless, isolated people regarded by the government as obstacles to progress. The trucks are signs of the government's power, but we do not see the truck drivers or anyone enforcing the move. The attention paid to the villagers' meager possessions conveys the artist's sympathy and anger. As someone who grew up during the Cultural Revolution (1966–1976), and whose family suffered from it, as nearly everyone in China did, Ji knows that the tumult has not ceased but entered another phase. During the Cultural Revolution, Mao Zedong's perverse genius turned everyone into a spy or a victim, even within families; Jean-Paul Sartre's "Hell is other people" does not begin to describe that period of Chinese history when freedom of every sort was denied.

Who are the skeletons standing among the villagers? They are reminders that the past accompanies us wherever we go, but they are also more than that. The artist's depiction of ghosts, otherworldly creatures, and skeletons introduce us to a world where these beings are real, not just a figment of the imagination. There is no separation between the rational and irrational in his world, in which internally displaced refugees, carrying their worldly possessions, walk through a partially flooded terrain with no destination in sight. If, as the Japanese hermit poet Bashō said, "the journey itself is the home," then the people we see moving through this landscape are as at home as they will ever be.

That is why, in certain works, Ji's use of a scroll format seems particularly apt for his subjects: it is not because it is Chinese but because it evokes a journey that is endless and without sanctuary. Presented in a vitrine in the front gallery, *The Village Wen's Progress* (2017) is 19 ½ inches high and 132 ½ inches in length, while in the back room he placed *The Village and its Ghosts* (2014), which is 15 ¾ inches high by 684 ¼ inches wide. By making a monumental work that is impossible to see all at once, Ji reminds us that we can never know the entire truth of what these displaced people endured.

In *They Come Out Together* (2017–2018), nearly all the men and women are sticking out their tongues, a childish act of defiance. Others are wearing masks. It could be a Halloween party full of slightly inebriated revelers, but it is not: it is a group of powerless people angry about what is happening to them, which Ji never discloses. Rather than singling out the cause of their anger, as if it is only one thing, the artist is sympathetic to whatever acts of group insolence the villagers can muster. He knows that only in such childish behavior and concerted efforts can the individual feel relatively safe, even if that sense of security is at best an illusion.

In *The Underworld Petitioners* (2017–2018), three poorly dressed individuals are seated on the ground, imploring an unseen authority. By keeping the authorities offstage, Ji depicts a Kafkaesque world that has become irrevocable fact. The oversized, grimacing, distorted faces of the petitioners test our capacity for sympathy, which I think is part of the meaning that the artist is getting at. How do we feel about what happens to others who live largely invisible lives?

In *Tumbling* (2017–18), Ji depicts an upside-down horse and three men in their underwear sleeping on a straw mat as they plummet past tree branches, where wrapped bundles are snagged. A grinning skull is also visible. Are the men dreaming? If so, what does it mean for them to live in a world where three men must share one straw mat at night? Is it a collective nightmare?

Ji is a narrative artist who invites the viewer to complete the story he has depicted in muted colors. His mastery of painting in watercolors and inks is inimitable. It seems to me that the future of painting does not lie in parody, citation, or commentary. By using the kind of humble means—brush, paper, and colored water—that the villagers, who live without access to modern conveniences, would be familiar with, however educated or uneducated they might be, Ji aligns himself with his subjects. By being attentive to his subjects's ghost stories, insults, and reliance on rumors, Ji recognizes their irrepressible disobedience. For him, their defiance constitutes a small sign of hope.

The Earth Before the End of the Earth

At a poetry reading and talk that Ed Roberson gave at Northwestern on November 14, 2007, he pointed out that he is a Black poet who writes nature poems. Roberson didn't say, though he certainly could have, that his view of nature breaks as well as critiques the historical conventions of nature poetry, which is the picturesque view that enables the poet to believe there is a sanctuary outside of our social reality. In contrast to much nature poetry written in this vein, particularly as the subject was initially formulated in English Romantic poetry, Roberson's work does not view landscapes as sublime or transcendent, or as embodying proof of God's existence. He has consciously broken with a radical literary and artistic tradition that includes William Wordsworth and Vincent van Gogh.

While Roberson's statement at Northwestern might not initially seem sweeping or even unusual, it further gains in resonance once you place it in the historical context of what happened in American poetry after 1960, when Grove Press published the groundbreaking anthology *The New American Poetry 1945–1960,* edited by Donald Allen. The only Black poet in Allen's anthology was LeRoi Jones. (In 1967, Jones changed his name to Imamu Ameer Baraka, and later to Amiri Baraka.) It is within the violent decade of 1960–1970, and what happened both in America and in American poetry, that Roberson's self-definition must first be seen. The path he took was very different than the one taken by Jones.

As an undergraduate, Roberson won the grand prize in the *Atlantic Monthly*'s poetry contest in 1962. In 1970, the University of Pittsburgh Press published his first book of poetry, *When Thy King Is a Boy.* This means that he entered the literary scene during the 1960s, when the

Black Arts Movement, which Jones started in Harlem in 1965, after the assassination of Malcolm X, was ascendant. The Black Arts Movement and its institution, the Black Arts Repertory Theater, galvanized writers such as Ed Bullins, Nikki Giovanni, and Sonia Sanchez. According to Ishmael Reed—who, along with Jones and Lorenzo Thomas, was a member of the Umbra Poets Workshop (1962–1965), located on Manhattan's Lower East Side—the Black Arts Movement spawned multiculturalism and ethnic writing by Latinos and Asian Americans. Roberson was not part of the Black Arts Movement that brought many Black writers and artists to prominence.

More than 40 years after the publication of *When Thy King Is a Boy*, Roberson remains the only Black poet who can claim to be a nature poet without the slightest hint of irony. His position is at once isolated and—given the effects of climate change and the irreversible degrading of the planet—increasingly central. To go one step further, Roberson is a Black poet who writes nature poems unlike anyone else's.

I don't want to appear to be suggesting that Roberson is without champions. Joseph Donahue has written a long, marvelous essay, for the literary journal *Callaloo*, "Metaphysical Shivers Reading Ed Roberson," that explores the poet's relationship to gnosticism. Nathaniel Mackey has been a longtime supporter and has published many of Roberson's poems in his magazine, *Hambone*. In recent years, Roberson has been the recipient of the Lila Wallace Writers' Award, and the Poetry Society of America's Shelley Award. He may be "far outside that matrix of professional critics and reviewers where literary reputations are determined," as Ed Foster said in his 1996 review of Roberson's *Voices Cast Out to Talk Us In*, but he has not been neglected. Rather, what I want to press forward is the idea that the significance of Roberson's literary achievement has yet to be recognized by the mainstream literary establishment because it challenges accepted conventions regarding the task of both ethnic writers and nature poets.

Roberson is an anomaly, but this isn't why his achievement hasn't been more widely celebrated. It is because his poetry pushes back against a long-held belief that was given further credence by the Black Arts Movement, and is now accepted as a commonplace. The Black Arts Movement advanced the view that a Black poet's primary task is to produce an emotional lyric testimony of a personal experience that can be regarded as representative of Black culture—the "I" speaking for the "we." This tautological view of poetry is based on the use of "I" as the activating center of a discursive poem, the witness who lays out the evidence. Not only do many share this viewpoint, but it has also gone a long way in influencing how poetry written by ethnic writers has been received and celebrated in different quarters of the literary world.

From the outset of his career, Roberson did not subscribe to the widely accepted model of the ethnic poet. Instead of writing lyric poems in which he developed a comprehensive worldview based on personal experiences that were meant to be representative of Black culture, Roberson began his career writing poems about humankind's relationship to nature ("kenai lake alaska" is the title of one poem included in *When Thy King Is a Boy*). This and other poems in *When Thy King Is a Boy* were informed by the poet's experience in working as an undergraduate assistant in limnology, the study of inland bodies of fresh water, and in gathering and studying data in places as remote as Kodiak and Afognak Island, off the coast of Alaska.

> ... the one lake on the whole
>   peninsula that does not freeze
> is this one.

Later, in "kenai lake alaska," Roberson writes what Nathaniel Mackey characterizes as "labyrinthine, syntactically double-jointed lines ..." that open words up to multiple and even conflicting meanings:

> ships went down
> during the goldrush when the water was highway
> to what men dregged out of the earth

Roberson's "dregged" evokes "dragged," "dredged," and, mostly importantly, dregs now turned into a verb. His distorted word helps convey the violent relationship humans have to the earth when it comes to mining: nature is what can be exploited.

"News," another poem in *When Thy King Is a Boy,* opens with these lines:

> the news is covered
>
> today brought to you
> by the same coverage
>
> as smothered yesterday

Roberson's opening up of the word "covered" points to the double-consciousness that W. E. B. Dubois formulates in *The Souls of Black Folk* (1903), that "sense of always looking at one's self through the eyes of others." Roberson is never unaware of this double-consciousness, even when he is alone in a remote area of the world, far from others.

In addition to his experience in remote parts of Alaska, Roberson was a member of the Explorers Club of Pittsburgh, went on two expeditions to the Peruvian and Ecuadorian Andes, and explored the upper Amazon jungle. These and other experiences are the sources for many of the poems. Other sources I would mention include his motorcycling across the United States, travel in Caribbean, Mexico, Nigeria, and West Africa, sexual desire, growing older, his health, and life in Chicago. And yet for all the biography that gets into these poems, they are remarkably free of anecdote. They are informed by perception, memory, and study (forms of gathering data) rather than story (the retelling of an event). Whether camping in the Andes or walking down a street in Chicago, the poet's multipronged destabilizing of language mirrors the unpredictable, constantly threatened, provisional world he has inhabited.

Along with pushing back against long-held conventions about the subject matter that is appropriate to ethnic writing, Roberson's poetry challenges many received assumptions about our relationship to nature, particularly as invented by the English Romantic poets. It is this legacy and its widely accepted notions that lead the poet to state: "I'm not creating a new language. I'm just trying to un-White-Out the one we've got." Roberson uses a double negative, a common feature of Black vernacular English, to characterize his intention of uncovering what European (or White) culture's definitions of nature have covered over (or "smothered"), as well as the cover-ups that have routinely taken place since the early 19th century, particularly in regard to the relationship between America's understanding of nature as a bottomless cornucopia that can be exploited, and the history and ongoing bequest of the "Triangle Trade."

> As a boy there were no black boy
> scouts

Rather than filling the poet with intimations of immortality, nature enables him to gain a perspective on his mortality and the abyss into which he (like all of us) is falling:

> We look upon the world
> to see ourselves in the brief moment that we are of the earth
> *a small fern in a crevice of the cliff face*

Here, Roberson consciously confronts the English Romantic tradition, which believed that there was a supernatural or spirit world that existed beyond the physical one. He doesn't see nature as a separate entity in which he exists before going elsewhere, but scrutinizes it "in order to see [himself] in the brief moment that [he is] of the earth." As I shall underscore later in this essay, Roberson understands nature as a dynamic, self-regulating system involving the entirety of the earth's biosphere. In this system, which humans are a part, living matter and inorganic materials are in constant interaction.

Whereas William Wordsworth advanced that poetry is "the spontaneous overflow of powerful feelings" in response to an insight about the relationship between physical experience and traces of the supernatural, and William Blake famously witnessed "a world in a grain of sand," Roberson rejects a pantheistic view of nature. A scientific materialist who wants to observe what it means to be a bounded being orbiting in an unbounded reality, he recognizes that he is a vulnerable thing existing on the cusp of mortality and that, like a grain of sand, he is floating in infinity ("to see ourselves in the brief moment we are of the earth ...).

In poems such as "As at the Far Edge of Circling," Roberson expands upon a theme touched on by Hart Crane in his poem "Cape Hatteras." Addressed to Walt Whitman, Crane's poem meditates on our ability to recognize infinity while living in a modern industrial world, which alienates us from nature and thus reality.

> Walt, tell me, Walt Whitman, if infinity
>
> Be still the same as when you walked the beach
>
> Near Paumanok—your lone patrol—and heard the wraith
>
> Through surf, its bird note there a long time falling ...

Roberson's "As at the Far Edge of Circling" opens with these lines:

> As at the far edge of circling the country,
> facing suddenly the other ocean,
> the boundless edge of what I had wanted
> to know, I stepped
>   into my answer's shadow ocean,

For Roberson, the finite and the infinite are never so distinct and separate that he is able to forget that they are connected:

> I entered as a man enters
> a labyrinth,   seeing
> from hairline fracture to abyss
> the magnified whisper
> of memory   not finish its sentence

Roberson believes that nature (earth) is part of an immeasurable continuum, which human beings cannot exist outside of. The closest he comes to articulating his vision of our relationship to the earth is when he writes about being in a plane in his poem "Topoi":

> Gaia's gravity-swayed steps take on orbit,
> we in the tropic of balance, in a basket
> on her head, a blue wrap of sky, sun
> ripens the thin rind of the plane to home.

The poem ends:

> Sunk in time,
> the footprint of life is death, the grave
> there is no step out of, the compost earth.
> The earth is the footprint of life.

In 1979, the English environmentalist James Lovelock advanced a theory known as Gaia, which suggested that the earth's biosphere is shaped by the continuous, changing interactions of living organisms and inorganic materials. This perception of unity affirmed the implications of interconnectedness that Roberson evoked in his early poems. For him, there is no portal or sanctuary that enables the individual to transcend his physical existence and leave nature behind. We become part of "the compost earth." Even in death, we must contribute to the earth's material renewal.

Knowing that there is no vantage point to be gained, and that all of his experiences will be partial and contingent, the poet recognizes that "*the world / is mortality, the earth goes beyond us.*" The world will one day cease to exist, but the earth will continue to exist "beyond us." In Roberson's view, reality (nature) is "a labyrinth." Even though there is neither an escape from the labyrinth (or reality) nor a center to it, the fact that we are caught in it requires all of our attention.

While Roberson's assault on poetic tradition may not appear to be as overt as the ones mounted by the Language poets, particularly Charles Bernstein, Ron Silliman, and Leslie Scalapino, it certainly is as subversive and demanding. Although he has never socially aligned himself with an avant-garde tradition, such as the Black Arts Movement, Language poetry, Flarf, or, more recently, Conceptual poetry, he has become, in my mind, a central figure for at least four reasons:

1. He offers an alternative to ethnic writing that is conceptual, innovative, and quietly disobedient of mainstream tropes.
2. His view of nature as a continuous, dynamic interaction of living organisms and inorganic materials is necessary, urgent, and indispensable.
3. He has un-Whited-Out the poetry we got.
4. His dredging of sounds found in English language exposes the inherent prejudices and cover-ups that have become embedded in its usage over time.

Based on scientific observation, data, the study of history, and firsthand experiences, Roberson believes that nature (earth) and society (world) overlap and are inseparable, and that the relationship between them must be balanced. In *To See the Earth before the End of the World,* the poet's most recent book—and his most jarringly visionary and bracingly apocalyptic—the first, title poem opens with these lines:

> People are grabbing at the chance to see
> the earth before the end of the world,
> the world's death piece by piece each longer than we

As a passionate observer and dispassionate collector of data, Roberson wants to know what it means to live in a world where there is a business that provides well-heeled consumers with a rare view:

> *people chasing glaciers*
> in retreat up their valleys

Nature is a spectacle to exploit for financial gain, and the melting glacier is being billed as a performer whose once-in-a-lifetime act is a not-to-be-missed event for people who can afford to witness it. Based on an article that Roberson read in the *New York Times,* in which he learned about what is happening to a glacier he used to see daily when he was living in Alaska, the poem repeatedly finds ways to focus attention on a very troubling question: where and what have the pursuit of happiness (one of the three inalienable rights asserted by the Declaration of Independence) led us to? (Behind this implicit question is Roberson's understanding of the role that slavery played in both America and Europe's thinking). Additionally, isn't the viewing of the "world's death" a continuation of the picturesque, the idea of nature as something to witness, a form of entertaining sublime or sublime entertainment? This is the challenge to English literary tradition that Roberson's poetry embodies.

The poet wonders if we can ever break out of the habits and accepted ways of living that we have acquired through time. Can we reinvent ourselves before it is literally too late?

> All that once chased us and we
> chased to a balance chasing back, tooth for spear,
> knife for claw,
>   locks us in this grip
>   we just now see
>   our own lives taken by
> taking them out.   Hunting the bear,
> we hunt the glacier with the changes come
>   of that choice.

Earlier in our history we were able to negotiate a series of precarious imbalances between the natural world and ourselves, but now the imbalances have tilted past the point of no return, with disastrous consequences that we seem unable to collectively face.

> now—   it's days, and a few feet further away,
> a subtle collapse of time between large
> and our small human extinction.

The state of consciousness we must aspire to is one in which we see clearly what is in front of us as well as recognize our own mortality, which is always present and waiting. Collectively and individually, our existence is neither guaranteed nor absolute but conditional and interdependent, something we seem unable to recognize ("[a] communal instrument / with one note per player, / per person, per jar,"). The unknowable and mysterious parts of nature that we experience are not what the American naturalist John Muir called moments of "beauty-loving tenderness!" Roberson regards such humanist projections as a fictive state that exists outside of the physical universe. Rather, our life is punctuated by moments of disquieting awe that might make us all the more conscious of our brief time as mindful beings: "[t]he sight, a sci-fi alien view." Like "*a small fern*" determinedly growing in the inhospitable "rock face," human beings are both vulnerable and tenacious, always at the mercy of nature and time. No matter how substantial humans might believe they are, everyone in the end is materially insubstantial and, in that regard, inconsequential in the face of time: "Like wind, we have no / haloed shadow dappling the ground."

Throughout his poems, Roberson persists in trying to see for himself, to sort through and assess all the available data, no matter where it leads him. The results can be dire, melancholy, harsh, erotic, tender, and sometimes comic. While he brings his study of science, and of observing and collecting information, sharply to bear in his work, it doesn't mean that he is a literalist. A visionary power heightens all of his experiences, as in the poem "Flight Record":

> Some cities look like embers of a fire
> when you fly in. Against the faint points
> of the glowing ash, what might have been
> the scale of flames you don't want to think about.

The leaps the poet makes in this stanza are scientifically objective as well as prophetic and apocalyptic. Every line in the stanza builds from an initial, not particularly far-fetched poetic insight that cities, seen from the air at night, resemble the embers of a dying fire. And yet the perception comes across as heightened and hallucinatory, a warning "you don't want to think about." Paradoxical though it may be, it seems to me that in undoing Blake, Roberson became his truest heir.

Roberson's materialist vision of being "of the earth," of being a thing among things, marks a significant break with a time-honored poetic tradition that centers on the "I," as well as with the postmodern belief in the death of the self (or author), which privileges the social milieu over all else. While much of the poet's work is rooted in personal experience—from camping in the Andes to walking the streets of Chicago—his aim is not to achieve a coherent subjectivity in which a transparent "I" discursively relays a moment or event in which a personal and cultural experience become interchangeable.

In the place of revelation and transcendence, he offers this view of time:

> But we are on this company line, we are on
> *our* payroll of   *our* clock.
> We make lots of money known as
> times to spend.

We are responsible for how we "spend" our time. The lines are choreographed to register the hesitations of thought and the twists, turns, and eruptions of insight and realization. Here again, the poet questions where the inalienable right to pursue happiness has led us. The poetic self in Roberson's recent poems is as much a third person "he" on the way to becoming an "it," as it is an "I." For what the poet recognizes is that all of us live in infinite time, which is merciless, inhuman, and democratic in its unavoidable transformation of all that it contains. Getting off a plane, he writes:

> I accept the change
> from thin air, empty handed for all I've seen,
> from air to the walk away again in all my flesh,
> accept what I have to leave
> of flight for feet.

In addition to accepting the consequences of infinite time ("the grave / there is no step out of, the compost earth," the poet recognizes two other cycles of time, the historical and the individual, and how they and our various conceptualizations of them affect each other in myriad ways. Amid the realization that he is constantly moving closer to becoming part of the "compost earth," Roberson writes poems that move in unexpected directions, shift gears suddenly, and detail the perceptions, memories, thoughts, associations, and questions he has about nature, of which he is an infinitesimal part who is able to have the following experience:

> And once, coming in late down the Hudson
> into Newark, I could look up Forty Second
> the whole way across Manhattan like peeking
> through a crack into more light than light
> across the universe, by the convergences
> a worm hole off to the side on night's horizon

Each perception can suddenly and unexpectedly lead to a physical awareness of infinity, that which contains us all and cannot be fully experienced. Can we, in our boundedness, respect and honor the unbounded?

Ed Roberson's poems detail the gamut, from the intimate and social to views of deep time and glimpses of infinity, and braid together all of these perceptual experiences. Within a single poem, he can embrace the "cicadas' sound" and "cataclysmic novas" ("Planetarium") without losing his bearings. I cannot think of another poet who covers as much physical space, articulates as many different kinds of landscapes, and details as many conceptions of time, often in a single poem. He can shift between the exterior physical world and the interior domain of the imagination as fluidly as rain running down an office tower window. Among his many sources, I can point to the poet's firsthand, in-depth experience of the world's one-sided exploitation of nature; to his learning about how little humans see of the world they move through ("As if we are always asleep, / the jaguar's tracks are there in the morning,"); to commonplaces of urban life; to his understanding of colonialism's promotion of the use of nature; to his articulation of domestic space and relationships; to detailing his progress towards mortality. Roberson recognizes the deep roots of slavery, "un-Whiting-Out" that the destructive development of nature and colonialism, particularly in its manifestation, expansion, and growth of the slave trade, springs from the belief, often religious in origin, that there is an elected "we" that exists outside of nature and is superior to it.

Both fertile and poisoned, this is the ground from which Roberson's poetry emerges and from which it grows. The poems in *To See the Earth before the End of the World* are grouped under five headings: "Topoi," "The World, Then," "Chromatic Sequences": "Playground and Parks Department Music," and "Of the Earth." They zero in on places and events the poet has experienced, where earth and world overlap and collide.

Throughout the book, the poet ponders time passing in terms of deep time, historical time, and the individual's consciousness of mortality, and considers how they are all connected. The poems are motivated by his belief that "[c]losely observed realities" are the most reliable measure by which one sees oneself "in the brief moment / that we are / of the earth." Such motivation can lead to an unexpected perception of the differences between races, which the poet (or his alter ego) expresses in the poem "1948: Art and Third Grade":

> Earliest of those purely observed what
> I felt only myself see   by the third grade
> was meat in the butcher shop   pig's feet
> the skins looked like my seat partner's hand
>
> and I felt   this sadness for her   she was ugly and
> she wasn't supposed to be being white
> it was my secret that I could see it
> as meat   and supposed to be s'pose to be really looked at

Roberson stops at the perception. His refusal to build on it or develop a generalization is one of the hallmarks of his poetry. He doesn't try to get outside of the perception and possess it, as if it is something that could be used to market a larger view of history. He recognizes that his early materialist understanding of the social world protected him ("it was my secret that I could see it / as meat").

One subject Roberson returns to is the transition from flying in a plane to walking ("accept what I have to leave / of flight for feet"). At the same time, he can be precise in his awareness of being lost and circumscribed ("We can't see over the curve, / so horizons / front for the whole beyond, / lessening limit"). Perceptions collide and blur into another ("the glass facets kaleidoscope a rose / window back / of themselves full of the flash petals of grace,"), reminding us that daily life is a matter of constantly focusing, refocusing, sorting, and making choices.

As Roberson moves from word to word, and from line to line, he is always open to turns of perception and thought, replete with interruptions, shifts, hesitations, stutterings, and unstoppable bursts, all of which he scores on the page. He doesn't deliver his findings so much as enable his thinking and seeing to become ours. A speck adrift in the wake of the cataclysm that gave birth to this universe, he details the signposts he encounters in the labyrinth we call reality. Scientific objectivity and visionary exhilaration are indivisible. Roberson's poems challenge readers to reorient their relationship to nature, to reinvent themselves and the way they see reality and each other. Rooted in ethics and philosophy as well as a love for scientific data and precise observation, Roberson's poetic innovations are of the deepest kind.

V.

The Great Kenward

Michael Silverblatt—host of the nationally syndicated radio program *Bookworm* and reader of everything interesting—concludes the first paragraph of his essay, "Make the World Safe for Kenward Elmslie," which serves as the introduction to the reprint of Elmslie's *The Orchid Stories* (Cave Song, 2016), with this observation: "He's the most extravagant, and extravagantly overlooked poet, in America." You might think Silverblatt is stretching things just a bit, but he isn't. Not really. As he goes on to say: "Elmslie is the nearly invisible fifth member of the quintet that includes Frank O'Hara, John Ashbery, James Schuyler, and Kenneth Koch."

Elmslie published his poems in *Poetry* magazine in 1960, and his first book, *Pavilions,* came out in 1961. Between then and now makes more than fifty years of work. And yet, in some ways, his writing cannot quite be contained by such definitions as "poetry" and "fiction." One example that comes to mind is Elmslie's collaborative volume *Sung Sex* (Kulchur Foundation, 1989), for which Joe Brainard—his longtime companion—did sixty-five drawings, one for each poem. In addition to collaborating with artists (Donna Dennis, Ken Tisa, and Trevor Winkfield), he has also written many songs and librettos, including one for an opera adapted from Anton Chekhov's play *The Seagull* (1974), with music by Thomas Pasatieri.

In *The Orchid Stories,* the unnamed narrator has this to say about the improbably named Dr. Schmidlapp:

> I disliked Dr. Schmidlapp right off, as for one thing he tended to personalize nature. He was wont to refer to seeds as "expert hitchhikers," to say that sloths "tie on the old feedbag," and to

liken the genes to a pack of cards, which is shuffled and arranged in many different ways, dealing each of us a "Grand Slam" or a "Full House."

Elmslie elegantly balances Schmidlapp's personalizations between sense and nonsense. It's easy to imagine a young poet somewhere in America using a similar association in a poem and thinking it quite brilliant. To Elmslie, the phrases are just words in a sentence, nothing more. Once he has written them, he moves on without ever calling attention to what he's just done. Seeds, sloths, and genes—Schmidlapp's list works only because of the way he characterizes them. Elmslie never comments on this because it would call attention to him as an author, and he has no interest in doing that. Such modesty is increasingly rare in an age of braggarts, experts, and self-promoters. What we should not lose sight of is that Elmslie's modesty has produced some of the most exquisite sentences one is likely to read. Moreover, by not claiming to tackle a Big Subject, he actually gets at quite a lot of stuff, such as the isolation and pain of growing up gay in America in the 1940s and '50s. He can start off light and smoothly spiral down to something else, all in the blink of an eye:

> She was laughing, laughing away. Inside her mouth, I noticed gold fillings. Her neck had creases. She wore face powder. Her mouth curved downwards, even when laughing, and two hard lines led from her mouth down to her chin. The first chin. Then came the second one that wobbled when she laughed. She had an old lady body odor, like sweet gas. Gray wisps were stuck to her neck, which bulged. Her wig was tilted. She was wheezing.

Elmslies goes from "laughing" to "wheezing." When he writes "The first chin," you laugh, knowing that he has just warned you that everything is about to go horribly wrong. There is a warmth and tenderness in this writing that you don't ever get in Ronald Firbank or Raymond Roussel, both of whom he learned from, along with Henry Green, Giorgio de Chirico's *Hebdomeros,* songwriters such as Cole Porter, and the innuendo filled dialogues of movies from the 1930s and '40s. I have the feeling Elmslie knows some of Carole Lombard's ditzy monologues as well as he knows the opening sentences of Franz Kafka's "The Hunter Gracchus."

From lists to letters, to travel brochures, to public announcements, to regional vernacular, to terms of endearment you might use on your pet kangaroo, to concrete poems and shaped verse—every kind of writing makes an appearance in *The Orchid Stories*. What elevates Elmslie's preposterous aggregations into another realm is their oracular significance:

> If only one had been born Swiss, the daughter of a well-to-do grocer. One could expand the fine foods department, correspond with grocers all over the world, searching out an out-of-the-ordinary olive, a cheese from a high altitude in the Andes, dried footstuff from a remote oasis in the Gobi-hein?

Originally published in 1973—long before America discovered food and the word "foodie" became a way of identifying yourself—Elmslie predicted the lengths to which we would go to prove our refinement and sophistication when it comes to our taste buds. Now everybody is eager to announce that they have eaten or drunk something known only to a few adepts ("each cinnamon and lemon and cardamon pellet was tiny"). Here again, Elmslie makes nothing of this insight and goes on—conscientious and wild. No word ever feels extraneous, which is remarkable given the ornate heights he can effortlessly attain.

Time and again, Elmslie builds something absurd out of ordinary, never allowing it to crash to the ground:

> One finishes one's coffee, one's lip is bleeding from a metal sliver imbedded in the sugar cube which refuses to dissolve however hard one hacks it with one's spoon, and the spoon handle bends if much pressure is exerted, until it is curved, like an old-fashioned baby spoon.

It's great that Song Cave has brought *The Orchid Stories* back into print. Elmslie is the perfect writer to begin reading in an age that worships profligacy and the collecting of luxury items and art trophies. As in the sentence about coffee that I just cited, he can morph from a realist opening shot ("One finishes one's coffee") to a cartoon image at the end ("like an old-fashioned baby spoon") while passing through a moment of extreme, self-destructive violence ("one hacks it with one's spoon …).

Elmslie's writing combines scientific detachment with erotic intensity, mixing this cocktail with dream-like absurdity, deadpan humor, and movie camera detail:

> Also—right hand makes whirling motions in hollow of Barry's stomach button, like corkscrew driving in.

This is Elmslie's genius—I don't know what else to call it. He weaves together the most diverse bits of information and never once seems arbitrary. It all makes a certain kind of awful sense, at once hilarious and horrible. In gorgeous sentence after gorgeous sentence, he reminds us that Lautreamont's chance meeting of a sewing machine and an umbrella on a dissecting table now seems as fated as Abraham Lincoln and Mary Todd going to Ford's Theater on Good Friday, April 14, 1865.

There are fourteen stand-alone tales (or disconnected chapters) in *The Orchid Stories,* in which certain characters—often in sets of three—appear. The first set we meet is Mattie and Edith and Bubbers. They live on "a fine old Kentucky estate known as Locust," which they call "Low Cost." Elmslie inhabits sound at a level few other writers do—it makes sense that he is also a librettist. He brings together the high-toned, the vernacular, the metaphorical, and the whimsical. He can be as detached and exact as a pathologist in a morgue ("Decapitated head floating in harsh crimson light, pulsating.") Or he can be as outrageous as he is precise ("I'd based my style of living quarters on a nineteenth-century Yankee hospital room which I modeled on a photograph—part of a foto-essay about Walt Whitman and his war experiences as a male nurse.") Or he can tune us into sounds—the constant buzz and chatter we swim in—as he does in his narratives from Locust (Low Cost) as well as a family's private language for body parts ("that's what Mummers called the blotches on my behind: 'acid underwear transom wallops.'"). This last sentence comes from "Streetcar," which is one of the best stories I have ever read about the weirdness and pathetic self-involvement of adolescence ("My counting mania included my own skinny body.).

What comes through in every story—and in every sentence—of *The Orchid Stories* is the incongruity of life and how, in some strangely comical and weirdly nightmarish way, it all makes sense ("banana fritters at the bus terminal café"). Silverblatt's introduction isn't just another extended blurb. One of the most careful and thoughtful readers I know—he is the host of *Bookworm,* a nationally syndicated radio program that features interviews with authors—Silverblatt rightfully characterizes *The Orchid Stories* as "an ongoing fantasia of representation." There is much else he tells and uncovers, including a surprising link to the great Irish writer Aidan Higgins. *The Orchid Stories* is a book about language in words you won't want to turn away from.

Language Is Not Colorless:
The Amazing Writing of Sawako Nakayasu

Since the beginning of this century a number of poets of Asian descent writing in English have published books that have helped redefine the field of study known as Asian American poetry, while challenging the various received definitions of what constitutes avant-garde or innovative writing.

Predictably, the gatekeepers of the avant-garde have overlooked these poets, partly because they believe that identity and language are separate domains. Based on the assumption that one should aspire to be a post-identity writer, this oversight is further proof of how invested certain authorities are in maintaining a problematic narrative populated almost solely by white writers.

Those who argue for post-identity writing are advancing that English is colorless and even neutral, which may be true if words remain unused. But use and context are another matter. Moreover, the old binary opposition between voice (or what Robert Grenier disparaged as SPEECH) and text (existing printed material, which, at the very least, implies some kind of approval and stability) is no longer viable. It might have been true in the 1970s, when the L-A-N-G-U-A-G-E poets, who were calling attention to the materiality of language, were rising into prominence, but globalism and immigration (or migration) has changed the situation. By introducing varieties of pidgin, slippage, sonic confusion, mispronunciations, misspellings, malapropisms, graffiti, and unknowing false signs into English, globalism has upended the rules defining areas of fixed vocabulary, grammar and spelling. We are living in a cauldron of relentless collisions.

This is what the poet and translator Don Mee Choi said in an interview that appeared on the *Lantern Review* blog (December 5, 2012):

> My English was strange for a long time. I'm sure it still is. When my younger brother was growing up in Hong Kong, he spoke Korean, English, Cantonese, and Japanese all mixed up together. He and his Japanese friends communicated perfectly in this mixed-up language. They were too young to censor themselves. The same thing was going on in my head except that I was older and knew how to censor myself. I only freely talked funny with my sister and a Chinese friend who also knew how to talk funny. At school, I wore my uniform and memorized and recited things perfectly that I didn't understand at all. I always failed because that funny voice inside me always butchered my English. So translating and writing is like this for me. I wear my school uniform and try to memorize and recite poems perfectly, but I always end up butchering them. My primary technique for translation and my own poetry is failure.

In addition to Don Mee Choi, the poets and writers of Asian descent who have altered the literary landscape include: Sesshu Foster, Sawako Nakayasu, Hoa Nguyen, Cathy Park Hong, Brandon Shimoda, and Monica Youn are just a few of the writers that come to mind. Many of them write across genres. Beyond being of Asian descent and writing in English, what they share is an engagement with the materiality of language. I see their engagement with language as signaling a paradigm shift away from the lyric 'I'-centered poetry of the generation that emerged in the 1970s and '80s. Such a shift suggests that an anthology of these and other writers should be put together, focusing on their openness to experimentation, while establishing a distance between them and the writers collected in *Aiiieeeee!: An Anthology of Asian American Writers* (1974), which was edited by Frank Chin, Jeffrey Chan and Lawson Fusao Inada, and *The Open Boat: Poems from Asian America* (1993), edited by Garret Hongo, which included some of my poems.

Among the poets I have mentioned, all of who deserve further attention, I want—in this essay—to single out one, Sawako Nakayasu, whose books of poetry and translations constitute an impressive body of work. In the last month, I have gotten her two most recent books: *The Ants* (Les Figues, 2014), a series of prose poems, and *The Collected Poems of Chika Sagawa* (Canarium Books, 2015), which she translated from the Japanese. Ugly Duckling Presse is about to release her translation of *Costume en Face: A Primer of Darkness for Young Boys and Girls* by Tatsumi Hijikata. An innovative Japanese choreographer, Hijikata (1928–1986) founded the extreme dance performance art called Butoh.

While I have not read all the books and translations that Nakayasu has published, I have read enough to know that I will be reading be the rest. In addition to these two books, I would recommend you read *Hurry Home Honey* (Burning Deck, 2009) and *Texture Notes* (Letter Machine Editions, 2010), as well as her translation, *For the Fighting Spirit of the Walnut* by Takashi Hiraide (New Directions, 2008). In these five books you get a sense of the breadth of her investigation into the possibilities of different forms and language itself, whether writing in English or translating from the Japanese.

This is what Nakayasu has said about poetry:

> I work mostly in poetry because it claims to be neither fiction nor non-fiction, because it acknowledges the gap between what really was or is, and what is said about it. Is the woman really in a box? It depends on who you ask, how they see it, or what constitutes a box. I like to claim that all of my poems are "true."

This is what she has said about translating:

> One of the difficulties in translating poetry is balancing multiple demands at once—for example, to make it simultaneously faithful and beautiful. Yet it got me to thinking about faithfulness and its opposite, perhaps also in terms of defining what it means to be 'true.' (What good is a faithful partner if he or she is not interesting in the first place?) At some point I started experimenting with unfaithful or less faithful, roguish translations. I wanted to find different ways of being "true" to the work I was translating.

In these two statements I sense a feeling of inexplicable distance. It is apparent to me that Nakasayu recognizes that she lives both inside and outside two languages (English and Japanese) and is never completely grounded in either one. As she states, "it depends on who you ask" or, as I hear it, it depends on which Nakasayu you ask. I don't mean the one who is conversant in English and the one who is conversant in Japanese. I am not being reductive, and it is not that simple. Nakasayu uses words to construct a space, often an intimate one between the writer and reader, the lover and the beloved, friends. This space is distinguished by its instability, and the slippages that arise.

Nakayasu's poetics probably share something with this section from the 111 prose poems that make up *For the Fighting Spirit of the Walnut*:

> Entering the room, a pulse is taken right when the heart is crushed upon a color-printed newspaper. And so it is today, too, a line of poetry goes without shooting you, and is nothing more than a soundless watery segment floating up for the first time, finally, enfolded in the gathering dusk of a long detour.

You cannot reduce this to a theme or a story, nor can you decipher it, and yet the language is hardly difficult. There are no obscure words, but persistent questions do arise: whose pulse is being taken when the heart is crushed? Here, heart hardly seems a metaphor. Or is it? In this poetry about poetry the body is central, which locates both Nakayasu and Hiraide's work in a very different province than the one explored by Stéphane Mallarmé.

According to Nakayasu:

> Sagawa Chika is Japan's first female Modernist poet, whose work resonated deeply with, and helped shape, the most dynamic shifts and developments in the poetry of that era. She was a singular and remarkably inventive poet who had developed a poetics influenced by French literary movements as they were imported to Japan, English and American Modernist writers whose work she translated, and contrasts between her nature-filled upbringing and

cosmopolitan Tokyo. Despite her death in 1936 at the young age of 24, it is impossible to overstate the importance of her remarkable oeuvre, which was created in less than six years of poetic production during one of the greatest social and cultural shifts of her nation's history.

While reading both the "Introduction" to *The Collected Poems of Chika Sagawa* and the translations, it occurred to me that Nakayasu is changing what Americans know of both the history of Modernism in Japan and contemporary Japanese writers. Sagawa absorbed Dada, Surrealism and Futurism, both the literature and the visual art. Her writing shows the influence of Cubism, the "collapsing of foreground and background." Her translations include James Joyce's *Chamber Music* and poems by Charles Reznikoff.

As Nakayasu astutely points out in her "Introduction":

> [...] Sagawa' poetics allow us to read her poems not as fixed, stable objects, but something more architecturally complex, inviting us to read (or see) the poem from various angles.

Here is the poem "In White":

> Flickering above the grass like a flame
> An amethyst button sparkles
> And you descend slowly
> The turtle dove lends its ear to a lost voice,
> A mesh of sunbeams cuts through the treetops.
> Green terrace and dried flower petals.
> I remember to wind my clock.

In translating Hiraide, Nakayasu chose a writer who works in various genres and unclassifiable forms, and cannot be conveniently labeled a novelist or a poet. Hiraide's novel, *The Guest Cat,* which was translated by Eric Selland, was a surprise bestseller. In the "Preface" to *For the Fighting Spirit of the Walnut,* Nakayasu writes:

> [...] *For the Fighting Spirit Of The Walnut* [...] once again commanded great attention, as it marked a crucial, albeit early, turn

in Hiriade's career, in which he begins his lifelong explorations of prose as the Idea of poetry, extended syntax, and a poetics of the grammatical line.

Of course, this is also true of Nakayasu. It is not hard to figure out why Nakayasu translated poems and prose by Sagawa and Hiraide into English. In Hiraide, one also reads (sees) him collapsing foreground and background:

> The sound of bursting flesh of fruit scatters between your ears. The forefront of this spray beckons to those outside of sorrow.

The writings of Sagawa and Hiraide are crucial to Nakayasu's own work, meaning that she has developed her poetics without necessarily locating herself within the Western tradition of avant-garde literature. This doesn't mean that she hasn't learned from European and American writers, but that she complicates any essentialist reading of lineage.

The Ants is the third book of Nakasayu's poetry that I have read. *Hurry Home Honey* is a book of love poems unlike any other. Caryl Pagel has characterized *Texture Notes* as "a daybook, a pillow book, a journal, and a map." Each book is distinguished by its grammar and syntax. *The Ants* is made of more than seventy prose pieces, only a few of which are longer than a page. In prose poems such as "Ants in a Japanese Can," "Chinese Patriot Ants," and "Korean Ants Too Erudite for their Own Good," Nakasayu writes about ethnic food ("soup dumplings"), the movement of language from one culture to another ("one of the 13,500 of the traditional, non-simplified Chinese characters"), game shows ("*Jeopardy*"), and a "Japanese-Greek chorus."

Nakasayu's *The Ants* is a rich, dense mélange of material derived from a breathtaking range of sources, including local customs, mistranslations and science fiction. You get the feeling that she has read everybody, from Gertrude Stein to Andre Breton to Rosmarie Waldrop, and made them her own. A feeling of dislocation, often inflected by a wise humor, spreads throughout the book, starting with the first sentence of the first piece, "We the Heathens":

We go to have Chinese for dinner and my friend who is visiting from another planet is horrified (and perhaps a little excited also), until I explain to her that we are having Chinese food, not Chinese people.

Ants appear in nearly every one of the prose pieces. They are the Other, the self, performance artists, immigrants and so much more. It is difficult to imagine Nakasayu writing in a way that separates language from identity, which is to say her work is neither colorless nor "avant-garde." She is a masterful writer and translator whose work I consider indispensable.

Introduction to *New Generation: Poems from China Today*

> *The chair of poetry must remain empty, for poetry does not collaborate with society, but with life.*
> —Frank O'Hara

Wang Ping, in an interview[1] with the poet and translator, Arthur Sze, made a number of useful observations about the current state of contemporary Chinese poets and poetry. The poets who emerged in the wake of both the Tiananmen Square Massacre, which occurred on June 4, 1989, and the rise of the dissident poets associated with the Misty School, many of whom are currently living in the West, tend to be less idealistic, less lofty in their language. The reasons for the younger generation's desire for what might be called "plain speech" are due less to a generational shift than to a change in both political and social circumstances. Rather than publishing and editing in the relative openness that existed in the years preceding Tiananmen Square, the current generation of experimental poets is writing in a climate of extreme repression. Consequently, while experimental poets of the earlier generation often had print runs of 15,000, this generation has both fewer outlets and less likelihood of reaching an audience of any size. In the years before Tiananmen Square, Gu Cheng and Bei Dao could not only make a living from writing poetry, but they also began gaining a reputation abroad. In contrast, the poets Wang Ping has chosen to include in *New*

---

1. Arthur Sze, "Writing in a Zigzag Way: An Interview with Wang Ping" *Manoa* (Volume 10, Number 1, University of Hawaii Press, Honolulu, 1998), Editor: Frank Stewart, Feature Editor: Arthur Sze, pp 59-64.

John Yau

Generation: Poems from China Today (Brooklyn: Hanging Loose Press, 1999) survive in an authoritarian society with little hope of being read by either those who share their mother tongue or by foreigners.

It is one thing to be a poet in a country that doesn't care about poetry, quite another thing to write poetry in a country where censorship makes it dangerous for both writer and reader. In America, poets can feel sorry for themselves, while in China self-pity would be an extravagance. And yet, what is self-pity but a desire— or perhaps more accurately a *cri de coeur*—for dignity. For whether one is a worker in an assembly plant or a person sitting in a room and writing, one wants to be afforded a certain amount dignity for what one does. But perhaps dignity is not always something conferred upon the individual by an external source. Certainly, Frank O'Hara's argument with the confessional poet Robert Lowell was about dignity. O'Hara thought Lowell was undignified to write about himself as he did, to repeatedly confess to feelings of impotence and isolation. He felt the older poet's poems of self-pity were manipulative, and that what Lowell really wanted, but never admitted, was power.

How do you resist both the tug toward self-pity and the desire for power? And, at the same time, how do you get beyond all the temptations to accommodate yourself to an untenable situation? For one thing, the poet has to rethink what it means to be a poet. Given the long and central position poetry has held in Chinese culture, this is the daunting task the current generation is addressing both in their poetics and their poetry. Among other things, it means understanding one's relationship to both the past and present, to rich literary tradition and an oppressive political system.

Among their literary forebears, the contemporary Chinese poet has to address Lu Chi, who might be considered one of the founders of Chinese poetry. In his "Introduction" to his translation of *The Art of Writing: Lu Chi's Wen Fu*,[2] Sam Hamill writes:

---

2. Sam Hamill, *The Art of Writing: Lu Chi's Wen Fu* (Minneapolis: Milkweed Editions), p. 11

In the history of Chinese letters, Lu Chu holds a position similar to that of Aristotle in the West, but with one paramount distinction: virtually every Chinese poet since the fourth century has gone to school on the Wen Fu, and most memorized it. He is revered by traditionalist and experimentalist alike.

Composed around AD 200, *The Art of Writing* is the first *ars poetica* written in China. After the "Preface," Lu Chi begins:

> The poet stands at the center of the universe,
> >   contemplating the enigma,
>
> Drawing sustenance
> >   from masterpieces of the past.
>
> Studying the four seasons as they pass,
> >   we sigh:
>
> Seeing the inner-connectedness of things,
> >   we learn the innumerable ways of the world.

Eighteen centuries later, in "The Brown Notebook: Rejecting Metaphor (Excerpts)," excerpts of which have been admirably translated by Wang Ping and Ron Padgett, Yu Jian writes:

> *We have forgotten language. Metaphor becomes a means*
> >   *of transportation. It disguises itself as poetry.*
>
> Language games become life games. Metaphor equals
> >   mask.
>
> *Poetry today rejects metaphor.*
>
> Real poetry rejects readers. It rejects the reading habit,
> >   not reading itself.
>
> Poetry is not a noun, but a verb.

> Poetry is its own reason for being. Poetry begins from language and ends in language.
>
> Rejection and depth. Reject 'instinct' 'inspiration,' or 'passion.'

Writing "poetry begins from language and ends in language," it seems very likely that Yu Jian—perhaps inspired by the writings of Ludwig Wittgenstein—is being critical of *The Art of Writing: Lu Chi's Wen Fu*, and any poetic assertion regarding the poet's relationship to the universe.

Here, it is useful to recall a trajectory that begins in the 20th century with Ezra Pound. Deriving his poetics from his study of Chinese ideograms, it was Pound who asserted that sincerity was "man standing by his word." While Pound is anti-metaphorical, he does advocate the use of clear, non-poetic images in poetry, a possibility he was only able to fully formulate after he studied Chinese ideograms. After him, William Carlos Williams would go one step further and propose No ideas, but in things." In order to go beyond the Modernist tradition of Pound and Williams with which he first identified, Robert Creeley would argue no ideas but in words. In 1960, Creeley wrote: "I mean then words—as opposed to content. I care what the poem says, only as a poem—I am no longer interested in the exterior attitude to which the poem may well point as signboard."[3]

Like Creeley, Yu Jian also wants to rid language of rhetoric, poetic devices, all the mechanisms meant to trigger a predictable response on the reader's part ("Real poetry rejects readers. It rejects the reading habit, not reading itself."[4]). Whereas Jack Spicer claims, "No one

---

3. Robert Creeley, "A Note on the Local," *A Quick Graph: Collected Notes & Essays* (San Francisco: Four Seasons Foundation, 1970) pp. 32–33.

4. Gao Minglu, *Edited by, Inside Out: New Chinese Art* (San Francisco: San Francisco Museum of Modern Art, and New York: Asia Society galleries, 1998) Ex. Cat. In "From Elite to Small Man: The Many Faces of a Transitional Avante-Garde in Mainland China," Gao Minglu writes: "Wenda Gu, Wu Shan Zhuan, and Xu Bing were among the artists who created series of works or installations using Chinese characters." p. 159.

Common to all three artists is the desire to either disrupt or subvert language's capacity for reference. Wenda Gu restructures Chinese ideograms by reversing

listens to poetry," Yu Jian believes "Real poetry rejects readers." He isn't preoccupied with the lack of an audience; he doesn't derive his dignity from knowing how many readers he does or doesn't have. Despite the very different circumstances in which *The Brown Notebook: Rejecting Metaphor (Excerpts)* was written, Yu Jian's desire to rid language of its capacity of illusion is familiar to us in the West. The particular of the circumstances in which this desire is expressed are made all the more clear when we read "Individual" by Liang Xiaoming:

> You and I raise our mugs
> And drink our tea
> We smile at each other
> And nod elegantly
> We're fastidious
> We talk about business,
> Study our fingers
> And express our opinions.
> Finally
> We walk our separate ways
>
> At the gate we shake hands
> And look into each other's eyes
> When we descend the stairs
> I wave at you
> If you're ahead of me
> And say "come again"
> Or if I'm the first
> You wave at me
> And say "walk slowly."
>
> Then we flee
> In different directions,

---

various components as well as writing them upside down. Wu Shan Zhuan juxtaposes "randomly selected phrases" and Xu Bing "hand-carved more than two thousand wooden type elements," which he then printed. None of the characters in his project *Book from the Sky* (1987–1991) can be pronounced.

> And if it's raining
> We have our raincoats
>
> (Translated by Wang Ping and Gary Lenhart)

Think of all the poems Du Fu wrote lamenting the immense distance between, or lack of communication from, his friend Li Bai, and the lack of nostalgia, not to mention the highly circumspect state ("study our fingers"), the reader encounters in "Individual" becomes all the more poignant. Think of Pound's translation of Du Fu[5] in Cathay, and one becomes more conscious of the origin of certain states of lamentation and self-pity that appear in many contemporary American poems. Aware as he so clearly is of Chinese literary tradition, Liang Xiaoming also knows there is no turning back, no recourse to the past, which, if anything, has been embalmed by the present political situation.

The two nameless individuals might "smile" at each other, but there is a current of joylessness, and of the inability to celebrate this brief moment of meeting, that suffuses throughout the poem. And yet, what is remarkable about the poem, what makes it stand in stark contrast to both Classical Chinese poems and to much contemporary American lyrics, is the poet's utter absence of self-pity, his rigorous refusal to lament his present circumstances, which we might remember is post-Tiananmen Square. At the center of his refusal is an unstated understanding of language, that it is something that is used either publicly or surreptitiously. One should, however, never confuse the two.

In the poem, "This Not the Last," Mo Fei writes:

---

5. See Hamill, p. 28. See also Gary Snyder, *Axe Handles: Poems* (New York: Counterpoint, Reprint Edition, 2005). In the title poem, Snyder refers to both Lu Chi and Ezra Pound. He believes there are models near at hand. While one branch of the American Modernist tradition originates with Pound and his formulation of Chinese poetry and language, contemporary Chinese poets are responding to that very tradition from a very different vantage point. Snyder sees himself as continuing a tradition, while Yu Jian and Mo Fei feel compelled to find an alternative to, as well as disrupt, their long literary tradition. In this regard, they share something with avant-garde visual artists such as Wenda Gu and Xu Bing.

I'm not the last
person to be punished by language.
The new wooden house
Gets knocked down by a tree.

The prisoner
Sets traps around himself.
If he escapes alive,
He'll take his crimes with him.

He has no other shortcut.
A knife blade separates life and death.
Light is cut open
And bent by the lonely sky.

The world is painful as fate.
Words are shackles.
Once he's learned how to confess
No one can ever defend him.

(Translated by Wang Ping and Lewis Warsh)

Surely, when Mo Fei writes "A new wooden house / gets knocked down by a tree," he is aware of Lu Chi's well-known statement—"When cutting an axe handle with an axe, / surely the model is at hand." Mo Fei, however, is no utopian; he recognizes that the models he has been given are false. Quietly, and without avant-garde fanfare, he has reversed Lu Chi's statement, because he knows that any agreement with it would amount to nothing more than sentimental affirmation, empty words. Living in China, amidst its disregard for nature and its push towards economic domination, Mo Fei has experienced first hand what utopian thinking can bring to bear in the individual's life ("The world is painful….").

In contemporary China, language and the use of language does not exist apart from the individual's body. All concepts are likely to be empty unless one's body is part of the equation. One has to stand by one's words; there is no other choice. This is what living in China after Tiananmen Square has made clear. Otherwise one lives in a web of lies and hypocrisy. This is the difference between the conditions under which Yu Jian wrote *The Brown Notebook: Rejecting Metaphor (Excerpts)* and those in which Pound claimed that the ideal state the poet should strive for is *sincerity*. Sincerity in Pound's time did not necessarily get you condemned to jail or, as on the morning of July 4, 1989, killed.

I would also make the distinction beween Yu Jian's *ars poetica* and those made by the various poets connected with the Language movement. For the Language poets, the majority of whom have also rejected "metaphor,' "instinct," "inspiration," and "passion," the primary concern is with the social body. The difference is that "Chinese culture is a 'metaphor,'" while America is based on exchange. One of the guiding principles behind the Language poets's emphasis on the materiality of words is their belief that the social body, and all the places where an exchange occurs, is what the poet should challenge. By declaring that both author and narrative have died, and all the so-called stories have been told, they are questioning the nature of meaning, which is a form of exchange.

In contrast to the Language poets, Yu Jian and his fellow poets cannot construct either a poetics or a poetry that exists apart from the individual body. This has nothing to do with either individualism or exchange. Rather, in China the individual body and the social body are synonymous in a way that they have never been in America: Yu Jian and his fellow poets live in a society where exchanges must be sanctioned, and sanctioned exchanges might be, at best, metaphors or illusions. In order to circumvent restrictions and censorship, they must write in what Wang Ping calls the "zigzag way."[6]

"The world," Mo Fei tells the reader, "painful as fate. / Words are

---

6. [...] I guess Chinese poets have had a history of writing in a zigzag way, you know, alluding to the politics and what is going on; we're quite good at that." Arthur Sze, "Writing in a Zigzag Way: An Interview with Wang Ping" *Manoa* (Volume 10, Number 1, University of Hawaii Press, Honolulu, 1998), Editor: Frank Stewart, Feature Editor: Arthur Sze, p. 61.

shackles. / Once he's learned how to confess / no one can defend him." What does Mo Fei mean by the phrase, "learned how to confess." Mo Fei knows he isn't the first or "last person to be punished by language." It may be an old story that he is telling us in plain words, but it isn't one we have listened to very well. Perhaps it is time that we do listen, and try and hear what these poets are saying. In her selection of poems and poets, Wang Ping, along with her co-translators, many of whom have already distinguished themselves as both poets and translators, bring us the news. What we might learn from reading this news is that poets writing in one of the world's oldest languages have much to tell us about the kind of zigzag measures one must use to stay alive. Foremost among those measures is recognizing all the uses that language, and those who use it, can be put to. As Robert Creeley put it: "At some point reached by us, sooner or later, there is no longer much else but ourselves, in the place given us."[7] Wang Ping's anthology *New Generation: Poems from China Today* brings us poems from that place, which is equally part of this world.

---

7. Creeley, p. 34.

The Need for Opaque Identities

On March 25, 1941, Wifredo Lam (1902–1982) sailed from Marseille, France, to Cuba, where he was born. He was the child of a mixed marriage: his mother was Ana Serafina Castilla, whose legacy was Spanish and African, and his father was Enrique Yam-Lam, who was Cantonese.

He was returning to a country that he had left nearly 20 years earlier, in 1923, when he sailed to Spain to further his knowledge of European art. In Spain, where he ended up staying for fifteen years, he was for a time a student of Salvador Dali's former instructor, Fernando Alvarez de Sotomayor. As has often been pointed out, it was while Lam was living in Spain that he met Pablo Picasso, who encouraged his interest in African art. In 1938, at the beginning of the Spanish Civil War, Lam went to Paris, where he met many poets and artists in the short time he was there, as well as had an exhibition at Galèrie Pierre Loeb. In his mid-thirties, he had become a promising, minor figure in the Paris art world—a status that he would change after he returned to Cuba.

During his journey home, he and his fellow passengers and friends, such as André Breton, were detained in Martinique because the Vichy government regarded them as traitors. It was during this period of detention that he and Breton met the Martinican poet Aimé Cesaire, who had written *Cahier d'un retour au pays natal* (*Notebook of a Return to the Native Land*) in 1938.

In this book Cesaire used the term "Négritude," a poetic and theoretical affirmation of the importance of African culture as it had manifested itself in the Caribbean, brought there by slaves. In 1943, Lam provided the illustrations for the Cuban edition, which was translated by Lydia Cabrera. The publication of this signal poem—which was the first and only time that Lam, Cesaire, and Cabrera collaborated—introduced the concept of Négritude to Cuba and its Spanish-speaking population.

Cesaire was not without his critics. The most important one was Édouard Glissant, a Martinican who was 15 years Cesaire's junior. In the late 1940s, Glissant began formulating an alternative to Cesaire's "Négritude." The term he came up with was "Créolisation." Cesaire had argued for a Pan-African identity for all people of African descent living in the diaspora, while Glissant believed in a non-hierarchical and local situation in which the children of mixed marriages could construct their own identity. Whereas Cesaire believe in a static sense of identity, which could be traced back to Africa, Glissant believed in a fluid one. Glissant, who rejected Cesaire's essentialist view of identity, believed there was no single black, diasporic experience, and that each set of circumstances helped generate different results.

Having written about Lam for the first time in 1988, I was naturally interested in the new exhibition, *Lydia Cabrera and Édouard Glissant: Trembling Thinking,* at the Americas Society, curated by Hans Ulrich Obrist, Gabriela Rangel, and Asad Raza. Along with early editions of books by Cabrera and Glissant, magazines containing their articles, drawings by Cabrera, and a wonderful film interview with Glissant, the exhibition contains works done in different mediums by Etel Adnan, Kader Attia, Tania Bruguera, Manthia Diawara, Mestre Didi, Melvin Edwards, Simone Fattal, Sylvie Glissant, Koo Jeong A, Wifredo Lam, Marc Latamie, Roberto Matta, Julie Mehretu, Philippe Parreno, Amelia Peláez, Asad Raza, Anri Sala, Antonio Seguí, Diamond Stingily, Elena Tejada-Herrera, Jack Whitten, and Pedro Zylbersztajn. Many of the works—but not all—directly address or deal with Glissant and Cabrera and their considerations of identity as plural in nature.

This is the kind of group exhibition that rarely happens in New York—a gathering of artists from different countries, cultures, generations, and aesthetic approaches focused on the issues surrounding the construction of identity. And while one could quibble about aspects of the show, including the dearth of context provided by the wall text, there was a lot of material to see and think about. If one purpose of a group exhibition is to inspire viewers to learn more about the different artists and writers they have encountered, then this show has more than succeeded.

In the catalog essay, "Trembling Thinking, or Ethnography of the Unknowable" written jointly, the exhibition's curators state:

> For Cabrera and Glissant, thinking beyond narrow understandings of identity was a practice of necessity–one from which we can learn. But in order to do so, we must listen to both carefully, as we live in a time of defenses erected against "others."

At a time when the President of the United States can proudly announce that he is a "Nationalist" and the recently elected President of Brazil said that he would rather his son die than be gay, the self-determination of one's identity has become a matter of life and death, whether it is as blunt and final as a death sentence or the lifelong agony of living a closeted life.

Later, in the same essay, the authors point out that Cabrera asserted "there is no way to understand Cuba without studying its Black culture." We know that Cesaire's concept of "Négritude" inspired Lam, but much less seems to have been said about how Cabrera might have helped shape the way he accessed his memory and imagination. Lam's curiosity regarding his origins took him beyond African art. His interest was not confined to form, as content and function were equally important to him. Participating in Santeria religious rituals as a child, he recognized the gods as powerful spirits. After returning to Cuba, he realized that he did not want to keep making European art. Rather, he wanted to make Cuban art that was not for tourists. Doesn't Lam's ambition align itself with Glissant's formulation of the local? Don't Lam's figures exist in a jungle that is not to be found in Africa, but in the Cuban sugarcane fields of the artist's imagination?

Alongside Cabrera's focus on culture, we should remember that Glissant believed "there was always something unknowable, something opaque, inside each person, which, rather than being what divides us, is what links us." As more and more societies demand conformity and enforce an oppressive view of transparency, Glissant's "opacity" presents an alternative.

Cabrera and Glissant did not have time to be cynical or ironic. For them, resistance was vital and could be enacted on many different levels and in many different ways, including their own writing, which challenges distinctions. Glissant was a poet, a philosopher, and novelist. Cabrera was a poet, artist, feminist, and prolific scholar of Afro-Cuban religions. If you are at all interested in any of these issues and the intellectual history of the Caribbean, especially in Cuba and Martinique, you should go see *Lydia Cabrera and Édouard Glissant: Trembling Thinking*.

The exhibition contains *Flamariouss* (2006), a book collaboration between the Korean artist Koo Jeong A and Glissant; *Hommage à Édouard Glissant* (2014), an accordion book of colored brushstrokes by Etal Adnan; a set of 12 small works done in acrylic and sumi ink on rice paper by Jack Whitten for his painting *Atopolis: For Édouard Glissant* (2014). It seems to me that Glissant's friendship with artists, and what inspired them to ponder, should be the focus of a comprehensive exhibition. I know, for example, that Irving Petlin met Glissant in Paris. I am sure there are many other artists who were directly inspired by Glissant.

In Kader Attia's video, *Héroes heridos* (2018), a series of interviews with refugees and emigre activists living in Spain, one of the interviewees uses the term, "feminization of poverty" to describe the pressure on refugee women to work as prostitutes. As Glissant points out in the film interview, which greets the viewer in the front gallery, capitalism has survived the longest of all systems because it could adapt to world chaos. However, he also believes that all systematized approaches to daily life are ultimately doomed to fail.

While Lam's relationship to Cesaire is well known, at least in poetry circles in the US, his relationship to Cabrera is less so. And yet, they lived near each other in Cuba during World War II, and he did at least one portrait of her, *Retrato de Lydia Cabrera* (*Portrait of Lydia Cabrera*) (1940s). Might not her studies of Black culture in Cuba aided Lam in his drive to introduce aspects of his youth into his art?

I think it is worth considering that Lam painted Cabrera's portrait while his work was undergoing change, and he had begun to recover aspects of his childhood, which included the memory of his godmother, Antonica Wilson, practicing Santeria, a pantheistic Afro-Cuban religious cult that was a syncretic combination of Yoruba belief and Catholicism. I see this as an example of Glissant's "créolisation." In fact, I think we could replace the formal term "hybrid," which I and others have used to describe Lam's art, with the culturally inflected term "créolisation."

Cabrera published over one hundred books during her lifetime, few of which are available in English. *Afro-Cuban Tales* (University of Nebraska Press, 2004), translated by Alberto Hernandez-Chiroldes and Lauren Yoder is well worth buying. Cabrera was a brilliant, complex figure whose work should be better known to an international audience.

I like that the curators focused on two individuals rather than one. Cabrera and Glissant agreed on many things but they also went their own way. One was from Cuba and wrote in Spanish, while the other was from Martinique and wrote in French. This diversity, which is central to the exhibition, is reflected in the array of material the curators presented.

There are names that will likely to be new to the visitor, including Amelia Peláez, who traveled to France with Cabrera in 1927 to study painting. Her *Mujer con pez* (*Woman with Fish*) (1948) is a knockout. Another highlight is Tania Bruegera's figurative sculpture, *Displacement* (1998/2005), which is made from Cuban earth, glue, wood, nails, and textiles. A video projected onto the wall documents the sculpture as a costume being worn at a public street performance in Cuba. The vitality is unmistakable and communal, which is different than a performance held in a museum.

In this modestly sized exhibition, the curators introduce us to the multi-layered, complex cultures, traditions, and legacies that are part of the history of the Caribbean, amalgams that underscore the significance of interracial and cultural marriages and the possibilities they beget.

VI.

Trevor Winkfield's Undomesticated Imagination

Trevor Winkfield has a small but intensely devoted following, and much has been written about this English painter who moved to New York City from London in 1969.

As the editor of an important mimeograph magazine, *Juillard*, in the late 1960s, he became associated with poets and writers such as John Ashbery, James Schuyler, Harry Matthews, Ron Padgett, Larry Fagin, Charles North, Kenward Elmslie, and others connected to the New York School.

In addition to collaborating with many of these writers, as well as providing inimitable designs for their books, he is the author of two marvelous collections, *Georges Braque & Others: The Selected Writings of Trevor Winkfield, 1990–2009* (2014) and *The Scissors' Courtyard: Selected Writings, 1967–75* (1994), and the translator of a cornerstone text, *How I Wrote Certain of My Books* by Raymond Roussel, with an introduction by John Ashbery, which was first published in 1977. Among the artists he has written or spoken eloquently about, I would list Jasper Johns, Maurice Denis, Burgoyne Diller, Charles Filiger, Gerald Murphy, Giorgio de Chirico in 1918, and Patrick Henry Bruce.

This is how Ashbery describes Winkfield's paintings: "At times it as though Bosch and Beatrix Potter had collaborated on a Book of Hours […]." Later, in the same review, he cites Jean Cocteau's description of Roussel's writing as fitting Winkfield's work "perfectly": "a suspended work of elegance, fantasy and fear." Whatever territory Winkfield has brought us to, it is not like anywhere else, as Ashbery's conjoining of Bosch's macabre fantastical domain with Potter's world of benign bunnies surely suggests.

While I was on my way to see his current exhibition, *Trevor Winkfield—Saints, Dancers and Acrobats,* at Tibor de Nagy Gallery, I began to wonder—as someone who has followed his work since the late 1970s, and who has read many of the things written on his work, as well as much of his own writing—if I could add anything to what has already been said.

Winkfield begins with a collage, which is a hybrid of geometric forms and representational motifs rendered in solid colors. Whether the resulting image is a bird or an unidentifiable thingamajig, it is composed of outlined abstract shapes, which may be patterned or evenly colored. Over the years the artist has accumulated a vocabulary that ranges from heraldry to cartoony biomorphism, from crisp patterns to sly nods to artists he admires, such as Rene Magritte, Piet Mondrian and Kazimir Malevich. Along the way, he seems to have become an expert in vexillology, the study of flags.

The painting is a copy of the collage, presumably with a few minor tweaks and adjustments. What we see is an airless world of monochromatic forms, geometric structures, and outlined shapes, often joined together to assemble a graphic totem joining abstract and representational forms. Winkfield's outlined shapes share something with the painter Nicholas Krushenick, who was inspired by Japanese woodcuts.

Like M. C. Escher and Mondrian, Winkfield is interested in the division of the picture plane. For his current exhibition, he constructed the layered space in his paintings by arranging different-sized, monochromatic rectangles atop of each other. In *The Floating Crocodile and Her Keeper* (2013), two rectangles are placed side-by-side, each holding its own image—an abstract totem or candy-colored *personnage*—as if they were the panels of a diptych. The black, green, violet, and yellow bands bordering the rectangles frame the totems as well as underscore their separateness. Other paintings, such *The Painter in Her Studio* (2014), come across as if there were a painting by Peter Halley or Burgoyne Diller emerging from behind Winkfield's large, dominant rectangles. The spaces between the planes are as eye-catching as the forms occupying them. At the times, the cropped shapes along the edges vie with the abstract totem for attention.

Winkfield's world is oddly atomized: it is made of parts joined to other parts to make unlikely gatherings. The combinations are inexplicable, a seamless combination of the sinister and innocent. He has taken the collages of Max Ernst to a new place. I am also reminded of the private symbolism of David Smith's totems and the imaginary worlds of Odilon Redon. It is as if he is an assemblagist who had neither the objects nor the space to make his work, and had to paint everything on a small table.

In Winkfield's matchless paintings, the *personnages* may be things animated by one's imagination. Didn't we used to spend long hours talking to a stuffed animal or doll? Weren't these objects friends who could keep our secrets? In *The Sundial* (2017), Winkfield depicts a sundial rising from stylized foliage. Seen in perspective, it is crowned by a brown semicircle from which stylized flames shoot upward, a visual pun on the words "sun" and "dial." It is a sundial and a dream of a sundial. In the upper left-hand corner, Winkfield has placed three triangles within an inset white rectangle, suggesting the pyramids or a geometry lesson. So much happens in a Winkfield painting that is not instantly apparent. For all of their strong, solid colors and bold forms, these are not quick paintings. We cannot domesticate the otherness of Winkfield's images, what I have been calling his totems and *personnages*.

There was a moment in modernism when it became expedient to make something simple and exuberantly friendly, perhaps with a trace of irony. One sees it in the silly balloon dogs of Jeff Koons and in the gloppy images of Garfield and Star Wars troopers in Katherine Bernhardt's oversized paintings. This has nothing to do with elitism vs. accessibility, though many observers have couched it in those weighted terms. The latter celebrates the triumph of capitalism by offering trophies for both indoor and outdoor settings, the bigger the better.

Modest in scale, exact in execution, mysterious and aloof in outcome, Winkfield's invented forms tell us that all is not lost, that capitalism does not yet own our imagination—that the excessiveness of the mind's eye does not require the profligacy of high-end production or large expanses of real estate. Despite all the voices clamoring otherwise, it is still possible to exist in this world and not join those who rejoice in the triumph of popular culture.

An Arcadian Moment in New York's Lower East Side, circa 1969

For anyone interested in poetry; underknown art and artists; the artists and poets of the New York School after the death of Franz Kline and Frank O'Hara (in 1962 and '66, respectively); collaboration; collage; a do-it-yourself spirit; the Lower East Side (particularly from the late 1960s until the late '80s, decades before it was gentrified); and the persistence of bohemian life, despite all the efforts to stamp it out, the exhibition *A Painter and His Poets: The Art of George Schneeman*, thoughtfully curated by Bill Berkson and Ron Padgett at Poets House, is a must-see. One reason is to see the painting, *Untitled (Nude Group)* (1969), in which thirteen people, many of them poets, sat nude in George and Katie Schneeman's sun-filled apartment at 29 St. Mark's Place. As far as I know, it is the first time this painting has been exhibited in New York.

Although I wasn't familiar with Schneeman's work at the time, he was one of the reasons that I left Cambridge, Massachusetts, in 1974 and moved to New York. Cambridge and Boston were places for the well brought up and polite, while, in my mind, New York was the artistic epitome of the unruly and impolite. I would pass Robert Lowell in Harvard Yard and we would nod to each other, though we never actually spoke. I saw the Jules Olitski retrospective at the Museum of Fine Arts, Boston, in 1973 and realized that this was as good as it was going to get, and that wasn't enough for me. There was so much more to see and learn firsthand.

Fast-forward forty years. Each time I leave my apartment, I look up and see a collaborative lithograph by Schneeman and Ted Berrigan hanging above my front door. Under the "ten things" Berrigan claims to do every day, I read: "play poker, drink beer, smoke pot, jack off and curse." He also cites O'Hara's *Lunch Poems* and Charles Reznikoff's first novel, *By The Waters of Manhattan*. Schneeman, for his part, has drawn bowling pins, a ship, and flowerpots. This was the shared culture among the writers and artists that I met when I moved to New York—not the corporate norm that so many critics and magazines find it necessary to comment on, photograph members of, and broadcast. It is this meeting of artist and poet, of the mundane, joyful and crude, that I pass under, entering the world (I would like to think) with some trace of their spirit in my head.

Schneeman was essentially a self-taught artist who studied the Sienese masters, such as Sassetta, Giovanni di Paolo and the Lorenzetti brothers, while living in rural Tuscany from 1958 to '66. Isolated from everything that was going on in contemporary art, he took his cues from early Renaissance painting while Pop Art, Minimalism, Color Field painting and Painterly Realism were gaining attention in New York and elsewhere. He learned the difficult technique of fresco and, starting in the early 1970s, began making what he called portable ones. He also worked in egg tempera, which, historically speaking, preceded oil painting. Although Schneeman had five exhibitions at Holly Solomon between 1976 and '81, only one of which sold well, most of his career took place off the grid. From 1981 to '96, he had solo exhibitions in his studio on the Lower East Side.

In 1966, after, as he says, eking out a living in the Italian countryside, Schneeman and his wife Katie and their three children moved to New York, ostensibly so that the children could grow up American. The decision to move to New York was most likely influenced by his friendship with the fiction writer Steve Katz and the poets Ron Padgett and Peter Schjeldahl, whom he and Katie had met and befriended while living in Italy. It is while living in New York that Schneeman becomes a modern artist. This is how he puts it: "In the late 1960s and early 1970s I was influenced to some degree by Pop Art and Minimalism, which in some ways are remarkably similar to early Italian painting."

Schneeman never lost his passion for fresco, a bright, all-over light, or white and muted colors. In fact, it was while looking at Schneeman's fresco portraits of poets, which are lined up in the vitrines at Poet's House, that I was reminded of another overlooked New York School artist, the Italian-born Giorgio Cavallon, whose work was championed by Frank O'Hara and John Ashbery. Schneeman and Cavallon shared a similar palette of white and muted colors, influenced I believe by the harsh Mediterranean sun. This is how Bill Berkson puts it in the brochure accompanying the Poets House exhibition:

> The culture George made for himself pervaded his own art, including his collaborations with poets and his portraits of them, which, like his paintings generally, are full of the same "gentility and asceticism" he wrote of discovering in the Lorenzetti brothers, Sassetta, and other early Sienese masters—qualities matched, and often overridden, in his other work, especially in his collaborations with poets, by a counterthrust of roughness and profanity.

It also occurred to me that if you consult the work of Clement Greenberg, Harold Rosenberg, Dore Ashton and Irving Sandler— just to pick four well-known writers working from the '50s through the '70s—you will only get a partial history of the New York School of artists (forget about the poets) because they seldom if ever paid attention to those who were not part of the marketplace or didn't show in a commercial gallery. As Corinne Robins pointed out in 1997, the seemingly inclusive chronicler Irving Sandler failed to mention any artist of color in his book, *The New York School* (1978).

On June 17, 1969, which was Ron Padgett's 27th birthday, thirteen people who were more or less the same age took off their clothes and sat demurely on the couch and floor of Schneeman's apartment, their knees drawn up. If their poses tell us anything, it is that they are rather shy around each other. The young men's hair is almost as long as the women's. The paint is thinly applied giving everyone a slightly washed-out look. The muteness of the colors and the thinness of the paint recall Schneeman's love of fresco painting. There is a pale cerulean blue sky filling the window in the background on the upper left side. Some of the figures have been cropped, underscoring a collective energy that pushes beyond the painting's borders.

Even now, more than forty years after Schneeman completed the painting in what I believe was one session, there is something bohemian, daring, innocent, sweet, utopian and, paradoxically, antisocial about *Untitled (Nude Group)*. On an early summer day, in the midst of the Vietnam War, race riots and assassinations, a group of people got together and declared: we are white, naked and vulnerable. Alex Katz and Fairfield Porter, two figurative artists associated with the same group of artists and poets, never made anything remotely similar to Schneeman's gathering of thin, naked young men and women. I see this painting as a kind of unspoken manifesto of a painter and thirteen of his friends, a challenge to not compromise, not become corporate. It is the mutual innocence of the scene that grabs me, the fact that thirteen people would participate in Schneeman's dream to paint an urban Arcadian scene full of young, beautiful nudes. It brushes aside cynicism without raising a finger.

George Schneeman, Quietly Radical

I happily own a large lithograph that George Schneeman and Ted Berrigan collaborated on. This prized possession hangs above the front door of my apartment, and I pass under it whenever I go out. In the lithograph, Berrigan cites Frank O'Hara's *Lunch Poems* and Charles Reznikoff's first novel *By the Waters of Manhattan,* while Schneeman has drawn a ship and bowling pins. These are some of the ten things that Berrigan says he does every day: "play poker, drink beer, smoke pot, jack off and curse." It is a celebration of a world in which art and daily life are inseparable, which is one of the reasons I moved from Cambridge, Massachusetts, to Manhattan in the mid-'70s.

In 2014, I reviewed the retrospective exhibition *A Painter and His Poets: The Art of George Schneeman,* which was thoughtfully curated by Bill Berkson and Ron Padgett at Poets House. That exhibition included the amazing painting *Untitled (Nude Group)* (1969), in which thirteen people, many of them poets, sat nude in George and Katie Schneeman's sun-filled apartment at 29 St. Mark's Place, while blood was being shed all around them, in race riots, assassinations, and the Vietnam War. This exhibition *George Schneeman: Going Ape* at Pavel Zoubok, offers another side of this self-effacing, under-appreciated artist: ceramics and small egg temperas on panels in which he made copies of his collages.

Schneeman, who started painting while he was in the army and stationed in Italy, was self-taught. After getting out of the service, he and his wife Katie stayed in Italy until 1966, when they moved to New York so that their children could grow up in America. They settled in the East Village because Padgett and Peter Schjeldahl, whom Schneeman had befriended in Italy, convinced him that this was where he wanted to be. The rest is history.

By all accounts Schneeman did hundreds and hundred of collaborations with poets, including Padgett, Berkson, Berrigan, and Schjeldahl, as well as Larry Fagin, Dick Gallup, Alice Notley, Allen Ginsberg, and Anne Waldman, many of whom were part of the second wave of the New York School of Poets. It is not surprising that Schneeman never became a commercial success. Collaborations with poets are hardly what collectors pine for. According to the poet and critic Carter Ratcliff: "Never very intent on a career as a gallery artist, Schneeman chose instead to be a friend of the poets." But in a real and deep sense, Schneeman was an integral part of a historical moment that took place on the Lower East Side between the 1960s and '80s, before gentrification. He contributed designs for flyers, posters, and calendars to the Poetry Project at St. Mark's Church, where generations of poets have done readings. Even if you did not know him, his presence was felt in the thriving literary scene that centered in the Poetry Project.

There is a lot in this small exhibition to recommend. The collages Schneeman did with Berkson are diaristic accounts of whatever they were watching on television (baseball or perhaps a movie) or talking about: the title of the great noir film *Out of the Past* (1947), starring Robert Mitchum, Kirk Douglas, and Jane Greer, directed by Jacques Tourneur, is written on one collage. The film actress Ann Dvorak, who retired in 1951, is another name that is likely unknown to many, but it has also found its way onto another work. There is a richness of pop culture associations mixed with crude phrases in the mixed-media work *Ten ways to watch it*, which also includes a seated male nude and the memorable phrase, "Have a heart like a steel banana." The writing and images (drawn, painted, collaged) are slight and yet powerful: they have a gritty urban feel to them.

The selection of ceramics, which Schneeman taught himself to slip cast, includes three in brown and black dating from 1980–81. These are incised with portraits, two of which are identified as *Rene (Ricard)* and *Susan Rothenberg*, while the third is untitled. On another ceramic, *Untitled (Stocking Vase)* (1980), which is primarily white with an orange stripe at the top and near the bottom, the artist has depicted a pair of stockings draped over a coat hanger—a meeting of domesticity and the erotic.

There is a portrait in acrylic and collage called *Untitled (The Locket)* (1967), in which Schneeman depicted his wife Katie the year after they moved to New York and were living in a small apartment on East 7th Street near Tompkins Square Park. According to Katie, he bought the locket in a junk shop across the street for her as a Christmas present. It cost 35 cents. Thinly painted in muted ocher and surrounded by white, reflecting Schneeman's love of fresco, making the locket the composition's focus. In the upper left corner Schneeman has affixed a framed holiday greeting from the Casablanca Bar in year 1946, which includes a real thermometer. This too likely came from the junk shop and probably cost less than 35 cents. This is Schneeman's aesthetic: use whatever is lying around the house. In a country devoted to materialism, Schneeman's gesture strikes me as radical and rebellious without announcing that fact.

Done between 2000 and 2006, the paintings after collages were done in egg tempera on panel. They constitute a distinct body of work within Schneeman's oeuvre and should be better known. They are made up of fragments: an image of a woman's hands gripping her insteps, her feet shod in red high heels. She seems to be standing on a white platform. To her left, and in a completely different scale, is a pilgrim carrying a blunderbuss. Between them is an object that looks like a large compass or sundial mounted on a pedestal. In this and other paintings, there is a clear invitation to supply a narrative. Their juxtapositions never feel arbitrary, and they cannot be quickly unpacked. This where they get their staying power, and yet there is something mysterious and even sweet about them. Perhaps a show solely devoted to these works is what should happen next.

Why I Am a Member of the Ron Padgett Fan Club

One mind-bending sensation a reader is likely to glean from Ron Padgett's *Collected Poems* (Minneapolis: Coffee House Press, 2013) is that the poems wrote themselves, and that he just happened to be in the room when they showed up. There is even a substantial section in *Collected Poems* that Padgett titled: POEMS I GUESS I WROTE (2001). Who wrote these poems, if he didn't? Was it the Angel of Poetry, Saskatchewan Sam, or benevolent pixies, or did they each just appear, spontaneously generated, at one time or another? Only Padgett could have achieved the appearance of such effortlessness.

Padgett's writing strikes me as essentially without an identifiable style. Of course, this is absolutely false. He does have a style; it is just that it is neither literary nor a form of branding. His writing isn't traditionalist, surrealist, avant-gardist, minimalist, metaphysical, pataphysical, philosophical, scientific, conceptual, extravagant, obscure, metaphorical, or riddled with puns. While he has a huge bag of tricks, particularly in the early books, *In Advance of the Broken Arm* (1964) and *Great Balls of Fire* (1969), he seems never to rely on a particular device—collage, for example—to generate work over a long period. He does not try to be profound, which is not to say his poems are modest—as that can become, and often is, a pose. They are not about a favorite pet, though animals do run and even somersault in at least one poem. The writing doesn't seem to be driven by any cause or trauma. They are not political or claiming to be agents of social change. Finally, the poetry is not autobiographical in any overt, attention-getting way (The "look what happened to me school" that continues to be prevalent).

Despite all the many things that Padgett's poems are not—and I have only touched the tip of the iceberg—there are a few things about the poems, prose poems, lists and gatherings that you can count on. They are apt to be occasional, funny, and about something quotidian or underfoot—such as reading a French-English dictionary, drinking chocolate milk or having a fantasy about seeing his father sitting on the front porch as it rains. But for all the humor and air of innocence that dances through the poems—as nimble and elegant as Fred Astaire and Ginger Rogers—other feelings, at once dark and even unfathomable, are hinted at, without Padgett stepping in and spelling them out.

It seems to me that Padgett recognizes that certain events exist in the domain of the unspeakable, and they don't necessarily have to be devastating and traumatic to become something not written about. To write about them is to cheapen them as well as turn them into a commodity. It is to go into the comfort and encouragement business.

In the prose poem, "The Poet's Breakfast," which was included in *You Never Know* (2002), Padgett begins:

> What does a writer do? A writer sits and goes through hell. I'm not exactly going through hell, but then, I'm not driven by the belief that the world is waiting for my next bit of hard-earned genius.

He goes on: "I seem to feel that since I can do nothing to save souls, it is my job to slow the material world's inevitable slide into rack and ruin." And, as the poem proceeds—jumping (as one's thoughts do) from the pleasures of "raking and piling the grass" to "Juan Gris's 1914 painting, *Breakfast*," which "became part of [him] in 1962, when [he] first saw it"—one gets a sense of Padgett's genius, which is to track the places, feelings, memories and events conjured up as well as manifested, however fleetingly, by the meandering mind. In this he shares an affinity with certain aspects of Abstract Expressionism, and with those artists whose works are a record of the painting coming into being. It is writing that is both necessary and without pretense.

Padgett recalls seeing Gris's 1914 painting *Breakfast* with his lifelong friend, the precocious Joe Brainard (1942–1994). They met in high school, while growing up in Tulsa, Oklahoma. Padgett and his friend and neighbor, Dick Gallup, were seventeen when they started a literary journal, *The White Dove Review* (1959–60), which published young and well-known poets such as Allen Ginsberg and Jack Kerouac. Padgett asked Brainard, whose work he admired but who he didn't know at the time, to be the art editor. After the three of them, along with the older poet and friend, Ted Berrigan, who was stationed in Tulsa at the time, moved to New York, and began to be known in the city's downtown literary and art circles, John Ashbery affectionately dubbed them the "*soi-disant* Tulsa School of Poetry."

At the time that Padgett wrote "The Poet's Breakfast," Brainard was HIV positive and would die of AIDS-induced pneumonia a few years later, at the age of 52. The enjoyment of the details of everyday life—this is what Padgett and Brainard shared in both their life and work, and it is something that is found throughout *Collected Poems*.

Padgett's memory of seeing the Gris painting leads to him to a memory: "I should add that I was looking at it with Joe Brainard, who knew how truly beautiful it was, and I was seeing it through his eyes...." And then after finishing this thought, Padgett immediately follows with: "And now, as Joe and I drive to town, I'm struck by how bizarre it is that in a few years he will be gone and how brave he is to keep enjoying the details of everyday life. I am forty-nine years old and surrounded by death. Does writing help? Probably not."

There are neither Job-like howls, nor self-pity in these poems. Instead, there is the recognition that whatever else life is, it is also 'bizarre."

Padgett's devotion to the pleasures of the everyday, no matter how seemingly incidental, occasional and small, transform his poems into unlikely celebrations. He is one of the most self-effacing poets writing today; his work is quiet, gentle and funny, but that should not lull the reader into thinking he has modest ambitions, because he doesn't. He is a poet who refuses to show off, refuses to let us know how much he has read, refuses to act like a prophet or speak to us as if we needed to hear what he has to say, to learn the lesson that he has to teach us. He has none of those elevated views of the self that are all too often associated with poets, or that poets adopt in order to convince themselves of their importance.

I remember when I first became a loyal reader of Ron Padgett. I had bought a secondhand copy of *Great Balls of Fire* shortly after I moved to New York in 1975. This is where I first read "The Complete Works," a fitting title for one of Padgett's longest poems, which is basically a list of descriptive, declarative sentences in which a single letter has been removed, added or substituted:

> Tin is a soft, lustrous metal which becomes brittle when heard.
> Edgar divided the dainties among the fiends.
> Dick wept farther and further into the dense wood.

In this and in the one titled "Y . . r D . . K," Padgett underscored the materiality of words; they were things made up of smaller things: letters. Adding or removing a letter changed the thing's identity, such as "friends" becoming "fiends." I was hooked and since then have bought every book whose cover claims that Ron Padgett is the author.

My appreciation of Padgett continued to grow throughout the 1970s, with the publication of *Toujours L'Amour* (1976), *Tulsa Kid* (1979) and *Triangles in the Afternoon* (1979) in rapid succession. And then, just as I began thinking that there would be a new book by Padgett every couple of years, it took him more than a decade to publish his next book of poetry, *The Big Something* (1990), followed five years later by *New & Selected Poems* (1995), which I thought left too much out. This is one reason why *Collected Poems* is so satisfying; it gives the full range of what has done.

Padgett never seems to get embarrassed by the odd and silly places his mind takes him. Toward the end of his prose poem, "The Woodpecker Today," which begins with a very clear and precise description—"The wings of the redheaded woodpecker flashed white as he landed on the deck rail, well fed and magisterial ..."—the poet recalls "an article that explained why woodpeckers don't get headaches." And then he follows the implication of this memory to its logical but impossible ending: "As these thoughts ran through my head, for a moment I saw a small helmet materialize on the woodpecker's head—a silver Detroit Lion's helmet. I hope he comes back. I would like to get the entire uniform on him." On the opposite page is the prose poem, "The Ape Man," which begins" "Why is it that I seem to want to write so often about writing? I am not theoretician of language." Later, he states: "Perhaps it can't be put into words, because words can't be used to describe themselves, just as an eye can't see itself."

Padget's refusal to theorize goes against the grain of much that is being written today, poems as manifestoes and declarations of what can and can't be done. He seems to have no interest in being right, which is refreshing. He recognizes that stating what your poems are up to doesn't make it true. Instead, he writes a poem titled "Charley Chan Wins Again," another favorite, which begins:

> Now honorable leg broken.
> The fog drifts over the docks.
> It is a terrible movie
> I can't watch, but I do.

It is that assent—his embrace of a guilty pleasure—that is so central to Padgett's poetry, and what distinguishes his body of work from others. He recognizes his foibles. He doesn't seem afraid to write something trivial or ordinary, because domestic life can be a full and wondrous adventure.

VII.

Ian Hamilton Finlay's Philosophical Gardening

Ian Hamilton Finlay, Marcel Broodthaers and Cy Twombly: I see them sitting in a neoclassical gazebo overlooking a shimmering lake, talking passionately about poetry, different kinds of script (from handwriting to calligraphic lettering to typefaces), gardens, and the distinction between cultivated flowers and wildflowers. Their literal writing—from Finlay's concrete poems to the pairing of words and images in Broodthaers's graphic works to Twombly's transcriptions of poems by various poets—is what initially enthralled me, but this early enchantment has blossomed into much more.

Like many poets of my generation, I first learned about Finlay when I came across his concrete poems in the indispensable gathering *An Anthology of Concrete Poetry,* edited by Emmet Williams, and published by the legendary Something Else Press, under the guidance of Dick Higgins, in 1967. Recalling that early encounter—I was in my first year of college—I wonder if it was Finlay's playful variations on the same letters and words that interested me in the possibility of language being something to both to read and look at? Or did the roots of my fascination start much earlier, when I was a child happily watching my mother using a brush and ink to practice her calligraphy on Sunday afternoons?

In 2016, Broodthaers had a retrospective at the Museum of Modern Art in New York; Twombly had one at the same museum in 1994–95, 15 years after his 1979 retrospective at the Whitney Museum of American Art, which opened the eyes of a lot of people. For a variety of reasons, however, Finlay's work remains little known in

America. As such, anyone with even a passing interest in the meeting of poetry and art, language and object, should go to the exhibition *Ian Hamilton Finlay: "The Garden Became My Study,"* at David Nolan and leisurely explore both floors of the galleries—while technically not part of the exhibition, there is a selection of concrete poems in the open office area on the second floor that I urge visitors to see, as it hints at the creative scope of this far ranging, inimitable artist.

Finlay's work can be tender, sweet, caustic, satirical, unsettling and downright gnarly. Not derived from a dictionary or thesaurus, his use of language comes from his deep reading in divergent subjects, from the French Revolution to classical literature, and a punster's sensitivity to homophones and other links. By this, I mean that instead of appropriating readymade definitions, as a number of conceptual artists have done, he lived inside language—from sound to orthography to calligraphic and pictorial possibilities. For Finlay, like the poet Arthur Rimbaud, who wrote the sonnet "Voyelles," language already existed as matter.

In 1966, when Finlay was in his early 40s, he moved, with his wife, Sue, and children, to a small farm on the moors of Pentland Hills, near Edinburgh and little more than hour by car from Glasgow. There, on seven acres of land, he spent the rest of his life concretizing words and passages he read (and reread) into sculptures and art works, which were then integrated into different gardens and areas that he carefully cultivated. Not surprisingly, he became a gardener who seldom left his garden, which he called Little Sparta because he was at war with the rest of society.

In order to make these works—in materials such as wood, clay, bronze, and concrete—he collaborated with craftspeople of all kinds, as well as poets and printmakers. For Finlay, the garden was not simply a place of beauty, but rather a liminal space bordered by nature and culture, where visitors are invited to meditate on the different ways time passes, from the cycle of seasons to the recording of history. His garden became a philosophical inquiry into and reflection on our relationship to the natural world. He was influenced by his readings, which began with the Presocratics, often considered

Western civilization's first philosophers and scientists, and included such writers and thinkers as Virgil, Jean-Jacques Rousseau, and E. M. Forster.

Almost all the works in this exhibition address the themes of the garden and the imbalanced relationship between nature and culture. The one exception is a rectangular stone plaque, *Only Connect* (1998), made with John Andrew. The piece, measuring 7⅞ by 11½ by 1⅞ inches, is engraved with the phrase "Only connect," which comes from the novel *Howards End* (1910) by the English writer, E. M. Forster. It is useful to cite it, as it gives further insight into Finlay's thinking:

> Only connect! That was the whole of her sermon. Only connect the prose and the passion, and both will be exalted, and human love will be seen at its height. Live in fragments no longer. Only connect, and the beast and the monk, robbed of the isolation that is life to either, will die.

Finlay recognized that humanity had become estranged from the natural world, and that we see the latter as something to subjugate and profit from. We live fragmented lives, completely out of tune with nature, the seasons, and the various cycles of time. His approach to art was to make connections, to bring things into proximity so that we would consider the links, which we might find challenging, illuminating, enchanting or disturbing, as when he connects Mondrian's plus/minus sign to the swastika, which he did in a print not included in this exhibition. And yet his provocations are not only to be unsettling. He wanted us to see further, and to hear Forster's imperative to connect, to try and attain a more holistic relationship to nature.

In *Osiris, Osiers* (1983), made with David Ballantyne, we see two similarly sized brown ceramic plaques mounted on the wall. The word "Osiris" has been incised in one plaque; the word "Osiers" in the other. The obvious link is the shuffling of two letters ("r" and "i" becomes "e" and "r") to spell two words, which leads us to ask: what has Finlay connected?

In Egyptian mythology, Osiris is the god of the underworld who grants the dead everlasting life. He is associated with the coming of spring and the yearly flooding of the Nile, which, in ancient times, made the land around it fertile. Osiers are willows that grow in wet habitats; their flexible shoots and twigs are used for basketry and furniture. By linking the two—one is the product of man and the other something found in nature—Finlay asks us to recognize the way we deal with nature and natural resources. Are we committed or not to the renewal of a resource?

In the installation *Homage to Seurat* (1995), made with Gary Hincks and Candida Ballantyne, a blue wheelbarrow, a blue watering can, and a partly blue hoe, all of which are speckled with mostly red and yellow dots, has been placed in the middle of the room, in front of a wall painting. The painting is defined by a band of brown dots. Inside, we see a few lines and a lot of numbers, suggesting we are to "connect" the dots, so to speak. Even as this joke surfaces in your consciousness, you realize that the dots you must connect are those on the gardening implements to the white space demarcated by numbers and a few gracefully billowing vertical and lines, offset by one horizontal. As you begin thinking about this, you might notice that the dotted frame is brown (earth) and the garden implements are blue (water and sky). It quickly becomes apparent that the numbers and lines allude to one of Seurat's maritime scenes and that we are to connect gardening with the ocean, which we also harvest. However, do we replenish what we harvest?

By compelling the viewer to make the connection and go on to discover what links his pairings, often between language and things, Finlay invites us to contemplate our relationship to the earth and how we use it. As much as I have learned about and seen his work, including a memorable afternoon spent at Little Sparta, I am still astonished at all the different ways he plays with words, typography, and lettering. In *EVENING* (1967), the first three letters (EVE) are typographic equivalents of engraved letters, while the middle letter (N) of this seven-letter word is solidly colored in the lower half, but not in the upper half. Finally, the last three letters (ING) are solid blue. It seems that the sun is setting on the left and night approaches from the right. Visually, Finlay's representation of the word reminds us that "evening" is the period between day and night, and that we are on the "eve" of night.

It is amazing how much can be teased out of Finlay's work. This is true even of what seem at first to be the simplest ones. The density of Finlay's thought, in tandem with his incredibly supple, visual imagination, led him to produce a powerful and provocative body of work that remains too little known in America.

When Capri Was the Place to Be

Jamie James, who worked as a freelance writer in New York City for two decades and now lives in Lombok, Indonesia, writes about expatriates—people who leave one culture or place for another. As it says on his page at the Guggenheim Foundation website (he was awarded a non-fiction writing fellowship in 2014), he is interested in "expatriate artists who adopted the culture of their newfound home as their own."

In *The Glamour of Strangers: Artists and the Last Age of the Exotic* (Farrar, Straus and Giroux, 2016)—which is a dazzling threading together of biography, travelogue, literary and art criticism, and judicious sympathy—James writes about expatriate artists or what he calls the "artist-exote," among them Walter Spies (1895–1942), a Russian-born German artist and composer who moved to Bali in 1927, and whose highly detailed, dream-like landscapes have captivated many viewers, myself included. Other figures included in the book—which focuses on six creative personalities—are the writer Isabelle Eberhardt, the poet and novelist Victor Segalen, and the filmmaker Maya Deren, each mesmerizing in his or her own way.

In his most recent book, *Pagan Light: Dreams of Freedom and Beauty in Capri* (Farrar, Straus and Giroux, 2019), James turns his attention to the different people who relocated to the small, rocky island of Capri, which lies 22 miles off the coast of Naples, "peaking up from the sea like a perfect meringue, just out of reach, but it has always been a world apart."

Starting with Augustus Caesar, who bought Capri in 29 BCE, and Emperor Tiberius who moved there from Rome in 26 CE. James gives a full, intriguing, detailed history of the island's colorful visitors and expat residents, including a wild panoply of 19th- and 20th-century figures: Civil War veterans interested in the landscape's geological formations—especially the Blue Grotto—along with writers, artists, rogues, madmen and madwomen, and thieves.

In his conjectural biographical sketch of Tiberius, which is based on his reading of Suetonius and Tacitus, both of whom wrote about this often maligned emperor, James offers his analysis of what the writers are likely to have made up and what might be factual. He even delves into their motivations for developing a particular slant on the emperor. This is just one of the many insights in this always interesting book.

The list of the island's latter-day visitors is impressive and diverse: Marquis de Sade, Pablo Neruda, Romaine Brooks, Maxim Gorky, Joseph Conrad, Mark Twain, Graham Greene, and D. H. Lawrence. A brief sojourn there by Oscar Wilde and his lover Alfred Douglas was said to have inspired others seeking sexual freedom to live on Capri, whose two harbors are hardly welcoming. But James is not interested only in the lives of the famous, but also in lesser-known and forgotten figures.

"Capri surely provides the setting for more works of fiction than any other island of its size" is how James opens one early chapter. One of those books—"the finest of the Capri novels "—is *South Wind* (1917) by Norman Douglas (1868–1952), whose literary star has long since fallen. In addition to his nuanced analysis of the strengths and weaknesses of *South Wind,* James goes into detail about Douglas's life, including the people he knew and which writers have been influenced by his work. James possesses the rare gift to be able to do this: he is both bookish and a world traveler. As a researcher, he will follow a thread whether it is found in a little-read book of poems or in a conversation he has with a longtime resident of Capri.

He traces the family history of the French writer Jacques d'Adelswärd-Fersen (1880–1923), whose home, Villa Fersen, is one of the island's main tourist attractions. A persona non grata in Paris, Fersen moved to Capri after a scandal involving French schoolboys got him locked up, as well as ruined his marriage plans. James unravels the truth from fiction in *The Exile of Capri*. Roger Peyrefitte's fictionalized biography of Fersen and his lifelong companion, Nino Cesarini. In the book, "Jacques, seventeen, is traveling with Robert de Tournel, a poet his elder by some fifteen years, the earliest manifestation of what would come to be known as the gay lifestyle, though not as his lover."

James digs up all sorts of details from Fersen's life, dating back to his time in Paris, as well as anecdotes about his biographer, Peyrefitte (1907–2000), who boasted that the Catholic Church, which he repeatedly attacked, called him "The Pope of Homosexuality." James can pivot from a description of the landscape to a subtlety gradated literary analysis, to a piece of unfounded gossip, to a trial record reported in a French newspaper, all in the service of presenting a fuller picture of his subject. If he feels it is necessary, he will digress for pages at a time to reveal a trail he has followed. I never felt disinclined to follow him, nor did I think that he was wandering off the subject. This is what is remarkable about *Pagan Light*.

In another chapter, James briefly details how Futurism's founder, Filippo Tommaso Marinetti, invited Fersen, who "was losing himself in the amorous reveries of classical antiquity," to write for his magazine, just as he had contributed to Fersen's important journal, *Akademos*. It was "a flirtation of convenience on both sides" because the gay Fersen, who loved the past, was the opposite of the heterosexual Marinetti, who wrote in his Futurist Manifesto: "We will glorify war—the world's only hygiene—militarism, patriotism, the destructive gesture of freedom-bringers." This kind of incongruous detail is just one of the animating features of a book replete with biographical information, hearsay, literary critique, history, and much else.

James has an encyclopedic knowledge of his subjects at his fingertips: he seems to have read the most obscure and hard-to-find books and articles on his subjects and, more importantly, is able to present what he has dug up in precise, gorgeous prose. He is comfortable reading Latin texts, French fin-de-siècle poetry, and trashy pulp, and discussing the strengths and weaknesses of each. Unless otherwise stated, all the translations in the book are credited to James, a feat in and of itself.

One of the most fascinating figures James writes about is the artist Romaine Brooks. Thorough in his research, James seems to have read the different versions of her unpublished memoir, which details her childhood. James calls her early life "a hellish vortex of suffering that surpassed the travails of Dickens's most pathetic orphans."

If readers think that James is being extravagant in this description, they need to read on as he relates her "marriage of inconvenience" to John Brooks, a well-known freeloader in the circle of the writers Somerset Maugham and E. F. Benson, who also lived on Capri, and her affairs with various women and men, including "the most influential poet of his era," Gabrielle D'Annunzio. While he is at it, James lists the three reasons why D'Annunzio is no longer much thought about in terms of his writing.

This, of course, is what James does throughout *Pagan Light*. So many interesting people went to Capri in search of some kind of freedom. For years, the island was a haven for people who did not fit into what we now call a heteronormative society. Many were artists, writers, and composers—members of a bohemian world that seems to no longer exist, at least on Capri, which "was," as one of islanders says, "an international laboratory for the avant-garde, a place where ideas were born, a new artistic vision, and given to the world." Like so many other places of refuge that—due to their remoteness and geography—were once apart from the world, Capri, he tells us, is now a brand.

How Frederic Tuten Became a Writer

Between 1946 and 1947, shortly after his father, Rex, left the family, 11-year-old Frederic Tuten "developed rheumatic fever and was moved to my mother's big bed, where I convalesced for almost year." Meanwhile his mother "slept in the living room on my old cot behind a moldy old screen." During his long recovery he began reading the books his mother borrowed from the local library: Robert Louis Stevenson's *Treasure Island* and *Kidnapped* and Mark Twain's *Huckleberry Finn* and *Tom Sawyer* were among his favorites. He was left with a heart murmur, but eventually he returned to school. "[S]eated in the last row by the huge window that faced the street, I was the tallest in the class [and] had no friends."

This briefly summarizes one of the first chapters of Tuten's *My Young Life* (New York: Simon & Schuster, 2019). Though less than 300 pages long, it has nearly 70 chapters. Each of the short chapters precisely details a specific moment of realization, however wayward and, at times, harrowing, that the author experienced on his bumpy, digressive path to becoming a writer. The result is a beautifully composed, accumulative portrait of Tuten at different stages of his young life.

Starting out in the Bronx as a naïve, vulnerable, abandoned, angry, self-involved romantic, he drops out of high school and dreams of moving to Paris and being a celebrated artist. We also see him as a lustful teenager going to porn movies in Times Square, a high school student taking drawing classes at the Art Student's league, a young adult flunking out of the City College of New York, a drinker and a hero worshipper, an unhappy graduate student at Syracuse, and a habitué of Greenwich Village before moving to the East Village when it was dangerous, eventually becoming the consummate writer that he is today. Yet the memoir stops around 1964, long before he publishes his first novel in 1972.

What's remarkable about the chapter cited above, and all the others in *My Young Life* is Tuten's ability to transport you back in time. A perfect mimic with an impeccable sense of the vernacular, he can pick up the rhythms of speech from those around him:

> My father, from Savannah, Georgia, loved Royal Crown cola, pork sausages, pickled pig knuckles, pork chops, and hominy grits. Where did she find such stuff in our Jewish neighborhood, where we had moved a year after I was born, my mother telling me later that she wanted me to be raised among people who prized education rather than among the southern Italians not too far away on Arthur Avenue, where I could become a truck driver, a Mafia lowlife.

These two sentences show what a terrific writer Tuten is. The first is a tight list held together as much by sound as by meaning. Shifting immediately from his father's terse masculinity to his mother's hesitations, the second sentence is a meandering declaration made by Tuten's mother, who has moved from an Italian neighborhood to a Jewish one in the hopes of bettering her son's chances in the world. But, as the author elects to never point out, it is much easier to buy pork sausages and pork chops in an Italian neighborhood than a Jewish one.

By letting the reader put the pieces together, the author remains in the character of the young boy living in the Bronx to comment on what he has just written. This is the marvel of his writing: he seems to effortlessly become one of his earlier selves—whether barely formed or ill informed, whenever it is called for. If this book were movie, every scene would be a crystalline shot taken from mid-distance. The camera would never get too intimate, so as to linger on every blemish, real or otherwise, nor would it back up far enough that one could see everything within a larger context.

At the end of a chapter in which he returns to school, Tuten adds an extensive footnote about seeing Rex for the first time, after

41 years, after he learns from his uncle that his father is dying in a hospital in Jersey City. In the hands of a less exacting writer, the use of a footnote to explain what has happened since the brief period the chapter focuses on could have easily become a gimmick. But Tuten moves seamlessly from one time to another, something he has done in his fiction. For instance, in his novel, *Van Gogh's Bad Café: A Love Story* (2005), Ursula, a beautiful 19-year-old morphine addict and photographer, steps from Van Gogh's café to Manhattan at the end of the 20th century. And in what many have rightfully called a literary icon of American Pop Art, *The Adventures of Mao on the Long March* (1972), Tuten merged parodies of writers he admired (Ernest Hemingway and John Dos Passos) with his own wild inventions and found text, creating what John Updike loftily characterized as "a collage of his soul's contents [...]."

Along the way to becoming a writer, Tuten meets a panoply of characters, including the ex-con John Resko who became a celebrated painter and author. Another person we meet is Leonard Ehrlich, who published his only novel, *God's Angry Man* (1932), a character study of the abolitionist John Brown, long before Tuten took a fiction writing class with him at the City College of New York in 1955. In both of these cases, and many others, Tuten remembers his relationship with someone the world no longer remembers. Every one of these people warrants a footnote, which the author provides, often implicating himself in losing touch. In other footnotes, Tuten steps back from his early self and gives the reader a wide-angle shot:

> There was little to show for my six years of writing because I worked in a totally undisciplined, desultory fashion, in fits and starts, in moods exultant and despairing.

Tuten does many remarkable things in *My Young Life*. He moves from one neighborhood to another—the Bronx, Mexico City, East Village, West Village—never once getting nostalgic about a place that no longer exists. We learn in a few sentences that his mother thought he should get steady employment in the post office rather than go to college. It turns out the postman was the father of the writer Ed

John Yau

McBain, who wrote *Blackboard Jungle* (1954) under the pen name Evan Hunter and was the author of the 87th Precinct crime series. Rather than dwell on this missed connection or point out the irony, he moves to the next chapter of his life taking this reader right along with him. For Tuten, there were not two roads diverging in the yellow wood. There was only the one he took: the one that he looks back upon and writes about lovingly and brilliantly.

Wallace Berman's Magical World

In 2007, New York University's Grey Art Gallery held the exhibition *Semina Culture: Wallace Berman & His Circle,* which I reviewed for *The Brooklyn Rail.* Half a century earlier, in 1957, Berman had his one and only exhibition at the legendary Ferus Gallery in Los Angeles. Two weeks after the show opened, the LAPD Vice Squad shut it down because Berman included a copy of his magazine, *Semina* (1955–1962), in one of his sculptures. The magazine was deemed "lewd" and Berman was fined the considerable sum of $150. While he continued publishing *Semina* and writing in the magazine under the pseudonym Pantale Xantos, he never exhibited his work publicly again. In 1976, less than 20 years later, a drunk driver killed him on his 50th birthday near his home in Topanga Canyon.

By all accounts, Berman was a force of nature. He loved art, jazz, and poetry. He designed the original logo for Dial Records and his drawing appeared on their compilation, *Be-Bop Jazz* (1947)—the first pressing of Charlie Parker. He disdained commercial success and the straight world, and seems to have never had a job. His circle included poets, artists, dancers, small-time criminals, and Hollywood figures, such as John Altoon, Toni Basil, Joan Brown, Cameron, Bruce Conner, Jay DeFeo, Llyn Foulkes, Loree Foxx, George Herms, Jack Hirschman, Dennis Hopper, Jess, Philip Lamantia, Michael McClure, Dean Stockwell, and Russ Tamblyn, who played the role of the knife-wielding Riff in the musical film *West Side Story* (1961).

If you have any interest in the wild array of people who defined the West Coast beat/bohemian world, and the various ways it overlapped other worlds, including Hollywood and rock 'n' roll, then you must read *Tosh: Growing Up in Wallace Berman's World* by Tosh Berman (City Lights Books, 2019). The preface by the actress and poet Amber Tamblyn is a poignant reminiscence of growing up in a social milieu in which "Berman was a mentor to an entire world in which my father and other artists like him lived." Although she never met Berman, she talks about the large influence he cast on many lives, including her own.

Tosh Berman, who was born in 1954, was an only child who grew up in a family where he met just about everybody his father knew or even briefly hung out with. And the list of those who made an impression upon him is remarkable by any measure. Being a child and young adult in this world, Berman could have easily romanticized it—as so many people have—but he does not. This is one reason why the book is important.

The other reason is that he was both a firsthand witness and a participant in so many different situations and social exchanges, which he writes about with a welcome and unexpected critical clarity. The book consists of 50 short chapters, one for each year of his father's life. Each episodic chapter focuses on a memory Berman has of a place, historical event, or person. One chapter is titled "707 Scott Street," the address of the Bermans' home in San Francisco. The poet John Wieners was a neighbor and the actress Leslie Caron babysat Tosh. Another chapter is titled "JFK"; assassinations and death were also part of the world the author grew up in.

What makes this book doubly special is that Berman refuses to perpetuate certain myths about this bohemian/beat culture. Early on, he writes that his father "was very much an American male of that era." This meant, "He required a woman who would support his one-way route to art-life and not put restrictions on his time and his need for attention." He writes of his mother, Shirley Berman, "If I'd been her, I wouldn't have married him, which might seem to be an odd thing for the offspring of that relationship to say. But the women of that era had a bad deal in terms of gender equality." Wallace's charisma does not blind Tosh to the former's faults and even, in retrospect, disappointments.

There are so many memorable chapters, moments, and observations in this jam-packed book, all written in a relaxed conversational voice, I had a hard time picking out one to be representative of all the others, which is a good thing. Yet some incidents stand out more than others—for instance, that Mick Jagger "rubbed the top of my head and said, 'Cute tyke.'" More importantly, we find out that Brian Jones, the founder and original leader of the Rolling Stones, became a friend of the family.

There is a chapter on Toni Basil, who introduced Jones to the Bermans, and "who made introductions and secured us invitations to the other world that co-existed alongside Wallace's social set." Basil, who came from " a very particular background," had "one foot planted in the rock 'n' roll and movie business and the other planted in the bohemian/beat scene." She worked with Elvis Presley, John Lennon, David Bowie, and with Bruce Conner on his groundbreaking film *Breakaway* (1966), and later introduced him to members of the band Devo. I knew from Conner that Basil was an important figure in the Berman circle, as he spoke glowingly about her a number of times during our friendship, but, until I read Chapter 21, I knew little else about this fascinating individual.

Until I read this book I did not know that Andy Warhol and Tosh Berman crossed paths. Warhol shot some of the scenes of his first full-length film, *Tarzan and Jane Regained ... Sort of* (1964) at the Berman house, "and I totally recall my role as Boy, the son of Taylor Mead's Tarzan." I won't spoil it by telling more, but the whole chapter is interesting to read on many levels—not just for its anecdotal history.

The book is a mixture of memory and astute commentary. Some of the memories clearly came from the author's mother, Shirley. Photographs are scattered throughout, nearly all of them taken by Wallace Berman. At some point you might wonder if there was anyone in the world of art, rock 'n' roll and Hollywood that the author did not meet. Jasper Johns, Jim Morrison, Neil Young, and Judy Chicago make appearances. By this time, you should be tantalized enough to buy this book.

VIII.

"Purity" and the "Avant-Garde"

I am sick of the term "avant-garde," a European invention that has been presided over and refined by white critics since the French banker, mathematician, and social reformer Olinde Rodrigues first used the term in 1825. Contemporary discussions about the artistic avant-garde seldom address race because the term has come to be a force for maintaining pedigree, establishing lineage and bloodlines—bloodlines largely presided over by supervisors and administrators: those individuals who control access to the descriptor "avant-garde," and determine the reception of poetic works through publication, reviewing, and public readings.

Most recently, the ideal of avant-garde poetry has become tangled up with another term: post-identity writing. According to the Conceptual poet Kenneth Goldsmith: "Uncreative writing is a postidentity literature." In 2008, he summarized Marjorie Perloff's keynote address for the Tuscon, Arizona Conceptual Poetry Conference, writing that she "questioned the values of a poetics based on identity in a time when neither phone numbers nor email addresses tell us where caller and recipient are actually located, nor does an email address provide vital statistics about its possessor; when an AOL or Yahoo address, for example, reveals neither nationality, ethnicity, race, religion, age—and often not even gender." If such marks of identity are now passé, then why did the 2010 Arizona legislature find them so dangerous as to require prohibition? Law HB 2281 bans public school courses that, among other things, "advocate ethnic solidarity," including, for example, Mexican American Literature.

Recent debate around this topic shows that it is not, in fact, obvious or dead. If anything, I agree with Daniel Borzutzky's recent

Harriet post responding to Cathy Hong Park's essay, "Delusions of Whiteness in the Avant-garde," in which he characterizes the avant-garde's dismissal of "identity poetics" as "central to the United-Statesian avant-poetry's subjectivity-masking, first-person denying, retro-1970s-we're-not-so-into-narrative-and-emotions-because-they-are-subjectively-fabricated-phenomena-whose-conservativism-needs-to-be-combatted-with-revolutionary-anti-subjectivity-or anti-creative-'texts.'" As the white cultural gatekeepers frame it, experimental writers of color either don't exist in the "colorless" (read "white") world of the "avant-garde," or they are late arrivers, like hyenas feeding off the carcasses left behind by white writers.

The choice for writers of color seems to be to write within prescribed notions of acceptable experimentation (a choice that exists not so far from the nostalgic wish to return to a racially unmarked domain known as "Great Literature"), or be invisible. The second option is frequently the only option available to non-black writers of color. As Dorothy J. Wang points out in her "Preface" to *Thinking Its Presence: Form, Race, and Subjectivity in Contemporary Asian American Poetry:* "Langston Hughes might be included [in a Modernist poetry survey] as the token black—or what amounts to the same thing, the exceptional exception—but surely no other Harlem Renaissance poet (not to mention an Asian American poet such as Jose Garcia Villa)." Being "the exceptional exception" is like being dubbed a member of "the model minority." Who wants the honor?

In my essay, "Please Wait by the Coatroom," first published in *Arts Magazine* (December 1988), I wrote of visual artist Wifredo Lam's masterpiece *The Jungle* that it "hangs in the hallway leading to the coatroom of the Museum of Modern Art. Its location is telling. The artist has been allowed into the museum's lobby, but, like a delivery boy, has been made to wait in an inconspicuous passageway near the front door." My essay was a close reading of the museum's characterization of Lam as a follower of Pablo Picasso, rather than as a Chinese and Afro-Cuban artist of originality.

In order to support this colorless (or postidentity) viewpoint, William Rubin, the director of the department of Painting and

Sculpture at MoMA from 1973 to 1988, contextualizes Lam's use of ethnic sources as solely a consequence of his connection to Surrealism; he writes in the exhibition catalogue *Dada, Surrealism and Their Heritage* (1968) that "Wifredo Lam was the first Surrealist to make primitive and ethnic sources central to his art." This elision suggests that Lam's race and cultural background have nothing to do with his aesthetic choices, a formal viewpoint which neatly aligns itself with Perloff's and Goldsmith's touting of a postidentity world. While the term "postidentity" might strike some in the literary world as provocative, it is not new, having been borrowed from the art world and the narrative that links the progress of art with formal innovation and historical determinism, in which the goal is art about art—a questionable paradigm at best.

Rather than considering what I had to say about Rubin's misguided assumptions, the Museum of Modern Art removed the painting and put it in storage, literally and metaphorically removing all evidence of its existence. They seemed to have had no interest in engaging in a conversation. More recently Al Filreis, in recalling a critical review I wrote of Eliot Weinberger's anthology *American Poetry since 1950: Innovators and Outsiders* (1993), wrote on his widely read blog: "Yau doesn't have a political bone in his body and nothing really explains his attack (unless, as Weinberger hints, Yau had just lost his sanity)." Seemingly, being an Asian American poet and critic who had written critically about MoMA's presentation of Wifredo Lam in 1988 had nothing to do with why I was critical that an anthology of thirty-five "outsider" poets included only two black writers, Langston Hughes and Amiri Baraka, and not a single Asian. Filreis saw nothing problematic about emphasizing the centrality of anti-Semitic Ezra Pound as the forerunner of avant-garde poetry, as the single tree from which all of us are descendants. Instead of questioning Weinberger's assertion, Filreis chose to reinforce the view that "nothing really explains [my] attack" and that perhaps I had lost my "sanity." Aside from the misinformed view that I did not have a "political bone [in my] body,' which reveals that he had not read what I had written about Lam and others, Filreis suggests that any questioning of Pound is an act of insanity.

All these white individuals in positions of artistic power share the same strategy of personal attack: Say anything that thoroughly discredits the messenger while ignoring the message. At the same time, other than in cases of the "exceptional exception," separate the writer's or artist's identity from the work. These authorities seem not to have considered the possibility that their assumptions were racist from the start, and that racial identity isn't something you put on and take off, like a shirt or shoes. To claim that someone "doesn't have a political bone in his body" is to assert that you know that individual inside out, that you in fact both own that person's body and can personally speak for it—must speak for it, actually, particularly if he has "just lost his sanity" and cannot talk for himself. Should Weinberger and Filreis make such claims about me or anyone else? Or are these assertions of a postidentity world part of the ongoing narrative of white privilege that is synonymous with accepted views of the "avant-garde?"

Marilyn Chin: Poet, Translator, Provocateur

A few weeks ago, on Centre Street—just north of Canal, the longtime boundary between Chinatown and the rest of Manhattan—I was on a panel, *Re-imagining Asian American (and American) Poetry,* at the Museum of Chinese in America (MoCA). Dorothy Wang, author of the recently published book *Thinking Its Presence: Form, Race, and Subjectivity in Contemporary Asian American Poetry* (Stanford University Press, 2013), hosted the panel. In addition to me, the panel included the poets Marilyn Chin and Paolo Javier. Each of us was supposed to read for twenty minutes, and then we would begin discussing Dorothy's book.

Never one to ease the audience into her work or otherwise make it simple for them, Marilyn began her reading with the poem, "So You Fucked John Donne" from her book *Rhapsody in Plain Yellow* (2002):

> So, you fucked John Donne.
> Wasn't very nice of you.
> He was betrothed to God, you know,
> A diet of worms for you!
>
> So, you fucked John Keats.
> He's got the sickness, you know.
> You took *precautions,* you say.
> So, you fucked him anyway.
>
> John Donne, John Keats,
> John Guevara, John Wong,
> John Kennedy, Johnny John-John,

The beautiful, the wreckless, the strong.

Poor thang, you had no self-worth then,
You fucked them all for a song.

The poem is part sonnet, part schoolyard vernacular. It is written (or should I say spoken?) in a confrontational, accusatory voice that mixes a sly misreading ("A diet of worms for you!") with high-toned formal restraint and different aspects (or should I say cultures) of American slang. The striking thing about Chin's poem is the smoothness with which she both embeds and disperses her irreverence within the constraints of rhyme, repetition and meter.

As in many of her poems, Chin is interested in folding together different languages and intonations. This is perhaps true of many poets, but Chin's roots and experiences are planted in two very different languages and cultures: she was born in Hong Kong in 1955 and grew up in Portland, Oregon. In "Identity Poem (#99)," also from *Rhapsody in Plain Yellow,* she writes: "Are you the only Chinese restaurant in Roseburg, Oregon?" Difference and dislocation are conditions she is always conscious of.

Chin, who published her first book of poems, *Dwarf Bamboo* (1987) nearly thirty years ago, had her fourth book of poetry, *Hard Love Province* (2014), come out recently. She has also published a novel, *Revenge of the Mooncake Vixen: A Manifesto in 41 Tales* (2009). With these books, as she does in her most widely anthologized and perhaps best-known poem, "How I Got That Name: An Essay on Assimilation," the poet combines different discursive forms to create a hybrid or what Édouard Glissant would call "a creolisation." The roots of irreverence seem to have begun in the poet's childhood, as well as a sense of the absurd. Here is the first section of "How I Got That Name: An Essay on Assimilation":

I am Marilyn Mei Ling Chin
Oh, how I love the resoluteness
of that first person singular
followed by that stalwart indicative

of "be," without the uncertain i-n-g
of "becoming." Of course,
the name had been changed
somewhere between Angel Island and the sea,
when my father the paperson
in the late 1950s
obsessed with a bombshell blond
transliterated "Mei Ling" to "Marilyn."
And nobody dared question
his initial impulse—for we all know
lust drove men to greatness,
not goodness, not decency.
And there I was, a wayward pink baby,
named after some tragic white woman
swollen with gin and Nembutal.
My mother couldn't pronounce the "r."
She dubbed me "Numba one female offshoot"
for brevity: henceforth, she will live and die
in sublime ignorance, flanked
by loving children and the "kitchen deity."
While my father dithers,
a tomcat in Hong Kong trash—
a gambler, a petty thug,
who bought a chain of chopsuey joints
in Piss River, Oregon,
with bootlegged Gucci cash.
Nobody dared question his integrity given
his nice, devout daughters
and his bright, industrious sons
as if filial piety were the standard
by which all earthly men are measured.

Think of the sense of betrayal, absurdity, anger and embarrassment that follows being given a new (or transliterated) name by your father that your own mother can't pronounce. However, to read this work purely as a product of the poet's ethnicity is to do both poet and poem a disservice. Didn't Andrew Warhola change his name to Andy Warhol? He wanted to assimilate and often made up stories about where he was born. Chin recognizes that she can't do the former and won't do the latter. Isn't assimilation and its impossibility a crucial issue in America today?

In addition to being a poet, novelist and anthologist, Chin was one of the translators of *The Selected Poems of Ai Qing* (1982). An important modernist poet and proponent of free verse, Ai Qing was sent to a labor camp in 1958 because he openly criticized the communist government for its treatment of the proto-feminist writer, Ding Ling. He is the father of the Ai Weiwei, the internationally known artist who befriended Allen Ginsberg and knew Bei Dao, Gu Cheng and other American and Chinese poets and artists when he had an apartment/crash pad on Manhattan's Lower East Side between 1983 and 1993. For these poets and artists, language–its use and misuse–is central. When the *New York Times* publishes an article, "Does Poetry Matter," it once again bypasses the real question: Does language matter?

In Chin's most recent book, *Hard Love Province* (2014), simultaneity is one of the operative modes. This is the first section of the poem, "Nocturnes":

> Beautiful moon the murderer begins to sing
> The thief takes off his mask to smell the heliotrope
> A dirty girl's face against a clear night pane
> Dreams of a strawberry pie at Marie Callender's
> A junkie steals asters from a rich man's grave
> And spreads them on the modest mound of his mother
> A lone girl walks with moonlit haste in the shadows of
> the maquiladoras

As elsewhere in the book, Chin's use of spaces and phrasing slows down time, almost cinematically, as if everything is being seen and/or remembered in slow-motion.

For her the contradiction is that the world goes on despite her grieving. In "Formosan Elegy," she writes:

> I sit near your body bag and sing you a last song

In "Cougar Sinonymous," one stanza reads:

> I climb the Acropolis swim in the Aegean
> Flirt with Kouros but don't give him my name
> Drink tea at high noon eat octopus at dusk
> A woman at forty is proud of her lust

The shift from the autobiographical "I" in the first line to the more inclusive category of "A woman at forty" in the last line typifies Chin's project: she regards herself as a spokesperson, unashamed of her physical desire. She is, as the poem's title states, a "Cougar." One key to Chin's work is her volatile simultaneity of reverence and irreverence, anger and tenderness, all understood through the lens of longing without a stitch of self-pity.

Chin, whose awareness of race and the collisions between them, doesn't shy away from difficult subjects and, to her credit, doesn't try to reach overarching conclusions or offer a sentimental salve. This is the first section of her prose poem, "Study Hall, Deterritorialized"

> The brown boy hits me, but says he is sorry. The brown girl, his sister, says it's because he likes me. I say, *yuk! He likes me. Well, I hate him.* The black girl pinches me and says, *Scaredy-cat, tattletale, little pussy, I dare you to hit back.* The white girl grabs my Hello Kitty purse and spills my milk money. I karate-chop her arm. The white boys says, *My father says that your father's egg rolls are made of fried rat penises.* I answer, *Yep my father says that the reason why his eggrolls are made of fried rat penises is because Americans are weirdos and like to eat fried rat penises.* The black girl laughs deep from her gut and high-fives me. Just as I am redrawing the map, my little fresh-off-the-boat cousin from Malaysia starts weeping into her pink shawl like a baby, *wa wa wa.* The white girl muffles her ears, *Can't you shut her up.*

Chin stays in character, never stepping away from the poem to become a detached observer who puts a particular spin on the events. She neither allegorizes the situation nor turns it into a symptom of something larger. Chin never says more than she can say. She doesn't use the "I" as way to garner sympathy. For all their narrative drift, her poems are not anecdotes, little stories meant to call attention to the speaker's suffering or privileged status. As she writes in her poem, "Two Inch Fables:"

> This late capitalist immigrant bitch
> Will ransom your pretty ass home

At the same time, later in the poem, she can ask:

> What can you do with so many poems
> Sprouting dead hairs in an empty coffin

The toughness in Chin's poems is something we have yet to reckon with. She embraces and writes about the conundrum of being a daughter of two cultures, a woman growing older, a woman grieving for her lovers, both of whom have died, a woman remembering her childhood. All of these subjects have been written about before. And yet, Chin brings something fresh and daring to her work. She is unrivaled in her audacity.

In contrast to W. H. Auden, who wrote, "For poetry makes nothing happen," Chin, in her poem, "From a Notebook of an Ex-Revolutionary," counters with:

> Jon Yi was born in the caves of Yenan,
> Did the Long March on his mother's breast.
> He grew up and became a Red Guard,
> Placed a dunce cap on the very same mother,
> Marched her to Xinjiang, to die of hard labor.
> Twenty years later in Sonoma, California
> He confessed to his loving wife—I am a weakling.
> A spineless scoundrel, a turtle's spawn.
> A lackey, a whelp-dog. He squealed and squealed,
> *History made me do it! History made me do it!*

Foreign Sounds or Sounds Foreign

Brandon Som's first book of poems, *The Tribute Horse,* won the 2012 Nightboat Poetry Prize. According to the copyright page, it was published in 2014, so I don't feel too badly about being so slow to read it

Som knows that language and sound contribute to identity, especially if immigration is part of one's current family history. Wasn't this also true of Louis Zukofsky, who grew up on New York's Lower East Side speaking Yiddish and didn't begin to learn English until he started school? Doesn't Som's musical and linguistic terseness, his use of found text, and homophonic translations suggest that he has learned from the Objectivists? Isn't his "debt of sound" also true of Zukosky and others who grew up in a household where English wasn't the primary spoken language? Or is the avant-garde tradition not open to Asian American writers?

In a recent interview with *Interlochen Review* editors Nim Holden, Ray Kearns and Sarah Arnett, Som said:

> I'm both Chinese-American and Mexican-American, or Chicano. I grew up in these households where Chinese was primarily spoken or Spanish was primarily spoken, and I wasn't fluent in these languages at all, so I grew up really hearing the music of these languages more so than understanding their meaning. That was really important to me and I think it probably led to me becoming a poet because I spent a lot of time developing a kind of interiority, a kind of inner life, a kind of meditative life. I think it's also led to me foregrounding and prioritizing music within my own poetry. I'm really interested in what your question suggests, this kind of multi-lingual experience on the page. I think that's the experience

that so many of us have, and I really see the poem as a space for recording all of these languages and their music.

In citing that his "interiority" developed partly in response to growing up in a household where he "wasn't fluent" in the language spoken by his parents, Som speaks about an immigrant experience. His opening prose "Elegy" gets right to the heart of this book: "My grandfather, aboard at twelve, practiced a paper name." He was an illegal immigrant, who found a way to bypass the Chinese Exclusion act of 1882, the only law in American history that denied citizenship or entry into the United States based upon a specific nationality. The term "paper son or daughter" refers to Chinese people who purchased fraudulent documents stating that they were blood relatives to Chinese Americans who had citizenships in the United States. Such faked documents likely required you change your name as well as memorize a fake family history.

In the series, "Coaching Papers," which is named after the crib sheets Som's grandfather memorized on the ship carrying him to America, the poet returns to this world of sounds in 12 poems comprised of four two-line stanzas. Som uses clusters of close sounds to string words together:

> A ship's bow's shapes writes an *A*
> To mark the indefinite way. A name
> Is a persona, per son, per song.
> Sonar searches the sea by singing

Som uses sound, rather than narrative, to access a little-known history of the illegal immigration of Chinese into America. The voice of the poem is multiple and changing. When Som uses "I," he becomes his grandfather. In another poem in the series, he writes:

> At sea, a boy recites a name.
> The sea records it in waves.

The boy is Som's grandfather but also all the other Chinese youths who came to America as a paper son or paper daughter.

There are tight and open lyric sequences as well as prose poems in *The Tribute Horse.* The reader will encounter Spanish, Latin, and Pinyin, the official Romanization of Standard Chinese. There is a sequence, "Seascapes," that brings together "the horizon" and "our own inarticulate selves." In "The Nest Collectors," Som connects finding a "twig nest" with the Chinese delicacy of soup made from the "blood-spittle" of "swift nests." This isn't just another poem about exotic or native food, because Som includes different histories for each of his subjects. The music of the lines shifts throughout the poem.

In "Oulipo," comprised of 18 four-line stanzas, the poets writes a homophonic translation of a Li Po verse he saw carved into the wall on Angel Island, which is in the San Francisco Bay. The island housed a U.S. Bureau of Immigration inspection and detention facility, where Chinese immigrants might spend years before being granted entry to the United States. Many of these immigrants carved poetry into the walls of their barracks. Som's poem carries some of the sounds of Li Po's poem into English: it is an act of historical recovery, but it is more than that. Sounds are promiscuous: they will mingle with any other sound and with silence.

> Trundled nights of a nun
> Fissures between rival tongs
> You sell wontons here
> Detuned doo-wop songs

In the collision of different sounds and cultures—which Som has no doubt experienced his whole life—he recognizes that there is no pure moment to return to, no essential identity to define, and that such ideals are sentimental illusions. He seems to have taken Zukofsky's formal radicalism (or poetry guided by sound, which also infuses the work of Gerard Manley Hopkins and Harryette Mullen) and steeped it in the particulars of his life and the larger history of immigration. The lines sing and hold their own within any stanza or overall poem. The results are ravishing.

The Meme After the Fall of The Tower of Babel

Before focusing on Susan Wheeler's latest book of poems, *Meme* (2012), I want to cite an exchange from her interview with Robert Polito that appeared in *Bomb* 92 (Summer 2005):

> **Robert Polito:** I think of your earlier poems in *Bag o' Diamonds and Smokes* as composed of all these swirling vernaculars: the languages of pop culture, or of various professions, or even of modernist poets like Frost, and of course Pound. You've written so smartly about Bob Dylan's possession of the forms and variety of American speech, and that's how I've come to think of you. A collector perhaps, or a magpie. Your pleasure in our random, fleeting, and lost slang is palpable. How did you come to this absorption in vernaculars?
>
> **Susan Wheeler:** God knows, as my mother would have said. I'm beginning to get an inkling, as I've been writing a series of poems that use her idiomatic expressions—she grew up in Topeka, and had a strong portion of Pennsylvania Dutch as well, but who knows where she got phrases like "busier than a cranberry bog merchant." Other things, of course: a soft spot for "colorful speech," attempts to "read" idioms in order to fit into a group or out of one, an awe of good talkers, especially those who use highly idiomatic speech, Catullus—(laughter) What does Armand Schwerner say? "Extension of the dramatic monologue into plurilogue."

One of the arguments advanced by Language poets is that the text has replaced the lyric poem along with the idea of voice or what has been called speech. Many have traced this shift to the moment when Robert Grenier declared "I HATE SPEECH" in an essay entitled "On Speech" that appeared in the first issue of the magazine *This* (Winter, 1971), which he started with Barrett Watten. Fifteen years later, in 1986, Ron Silliman—in his "Introduction: Language, Realism Poetry" to *In The American Tree* (1986), the anthology he edited—stated that Grenier's announcement was both "a breach—and a new moment in poetry."

Essentially, Grenier's statement divides the practice of poetry into two distinct groups—those who believe in the text, found material, the possibilities of collage and the polyvalent, and those who believe in the lyric "I," sustained narrative and the poet's recognizable voice or "speech." If we use Kenneth Goldsmith's refining of Grenier's statement, you could say that the practice of poetry can currently be divided into the "uncreative" and the "creative."

Whatever terms are used to describe the dialectic, Susan Wheeler belongs to neither group. In fact, her use of "idiomatic expressions" and what Polito calls "swirling vernaculars" and "lost slang" advances a third possibility, which is that one can be "a collector ... or a magpie" who, among other things, calls up the voices that one has heard at different points in one's life. This view of poetry runs counter to the postmodernist belief in the death of the author. For in addition to intimations of the cessation of interiority and memories, the death of the author implies the birth of the text and of the internet as the storehouse of memory. Within this understanding of poetry, there is only surface and collage. In Wheeler's poetry, however, which she began publishing in 1998, her understanding of hearing (of listening to) and being sensitive to "the forms and variety of American speech" defines an area of poetry that the dichotomy of text and speech ignores.

I would go further and state that, in her "absorption in vernaculars," Wheeler shares something with other woman poets, including Matthea Harvey, Harryette Mullen, Laura Mullen, Cathy Park Hong and Evie Shockley. These poets recognize that what William Carlos Williams called American speech is actually made up of a multitude of slangs and vernaculars, which are encoded transactions and commentaries existing on the margins of both commonplace speech (as used in the mass media) and text (as used in the academy). By deploying, recovering and inventing different slangs and vernaculars, Wheeler and the others I cited recognize that America is made up of a mass of different languages and that none of them are central. There is no demotic but there are many languages, each with its own slang.

The *New Yorker* writer Malcolm Gladwell gives us a succinct and useful definition of "meme": "A meme is an idea that behaves like a virus—that moves through a population, taking hold in each person it infects." Wheeler's *Meme* is divided into three sections: "The Maud Poems"; "The Devil–or–The Introjects"; "The Split." In her interview with Polito, Wheeler cites her mother's idiomatic expressions as a source for the first section: "When I finish the mom poems, 'The Maud Project,' I only want randomness." "The Devil–or–The Introjects" is the shortest section, made up of eight untitled prose pieces ranging from one to five sentences in length. "Introjection" is when one replicates the behavior and attributes of others; it involves identification and internalization. In this section there is a recurring "she," although it is not clear whether "she" is an external figure, an internal force or a combination of both. As the title of the third section, "The Split," suggests, it is about the end of a relationship.

Despite the autobiographical current running through these poems, they are remarkably and, to my mind, powerfully free of anecdotes, overt narratives, and stories—all the things that are central to confessional poetry as they sequester it. Wheeler's poems don't culminate in revelations or epiphanies. Rather, I get the sense that the "Maud Poems" are carefully considered aural montages of a particularly powerful and recognizable voice, of distinctive phrases and orders of syllables that implanted themselves in Wheeler.

In order to write these poems, the poet seems to have taken dictation à la Jack Spicer.

She's a Pill

> Oh, dangling long sleeves in the Mercurochrome.
> Parking her punch on her knees.

> I'm not a joiner.

> In the night, a visitation, small as a thumb,
> enters the sealed house and ascends.

> Mother wouldn't have stood for that long. Drippy-dropping around
> on heels. Leaving the blue cheese out.

The deeper source of "The Maud Poems" is matriarchal speech as a form of instruction, which was used by a distinct, rather isolated social group ("Pennsylvania Dutch") at a certain moment in history to perpetuate longstanding ideas about correct behavior. While that specific group may have diminished, others have replaced it. There are as many as two hundred languages spoken in New York City alone. Each has its own idioms. While the division of poetry into text and speech was useful in the 1970s, it seems out of touch with the current state of the world. Wheeler's citation of Armand Schwerner— "Extension of the dramatic monologue into plurilogue"—feels more attuned to the different idioms and encodings one encounters on a daily basis. I would also advance that Wheeler and the other poets I cited recognize that idioms and slangs are evidence of the various processes of entropy and change each language undergoes at any one moment in time—that what interests them is the further changes that can be made to language; such developments are in fact central to their poetry practice.

Wheeler's "Maud" evokes intimate family moments without ever devolving into anecdotes centrally occupied by a highly sensitive "I." She doesn't focus on dramatic moments, but on the everyday rituals when, as Georges Perec might say, nothing happens. The poet is acutely sensitive to the odd colorfulness of whoever is speaking, the sense of rightness that informs everything she says. More importantly,

Wheeler neither defines herself as a victim nor privileges her feelings over others. There is a precision of observation that becomes weird, if thought about: "No, cocktail onions are just picked small." By slowing down this speaker's answer until it becomes words on a page, Wheeler underscores the imperious assumptions the speaker has made about the relationship between her leisure and the unseen labor. In these observations, the reader senses the poet's growing consciousness of the network of capital that binds and separates us.

All the poems in "The Split" are untitled. There are lists, compressed haiku—like fragments, limericks and bits from made-up vaudeville songs. On opposite pages, we read these two verses:

> I picked up a gal in a bar.
> She said she'd ignore my cigar.
> But when I was done
> Relieving my gun
> She said I was not up to par.

> He stumbled outside to his car
> He couldn't have gotten too far
> For when I replied
> *Your trigger's what died*
> He lit his exploding cigar.

It's as if there are two choruses in a Greek play informing the audience as to what exactly is going on. Lowbrow humor and rhyme are used to shape feelings of rage, rejection, disappointment and impotence. This isn't an "anecdote," as Wheeler writes elsewhere, but "an event" in the form of facing ditties.

While one of the recurring themes in "The Split" is the end of a relationship, the scope of the subject extends in widening directions, from dead pets to God. One list poem begins every line with "Bye":

> Bye, kid in first grade on your paddle cart
> Bye, Lorrain, Outward Bound in the snow
> Bye, Motorcycle David

John Yau

Near the middle of the poem:

> Bye Dad, bye Mom.
> Bye, Duncan's dancing bear shining, shining.
> Bye, great dogs I have known. Cats. Raccoon I hit.

And at the end:

> Bye to the husband who was the best wife.
> Bye to those I fear dead.
> I know you all in his absence tonight.
> I know you all in his absence tonight.

From limerick to elegy and prayer, and from prose to nursery rhyme, Wheeler uses different forms and ways of juxtaposing words, phrases and stanzas. Humor and sadness, celebration and dirges are inseparable. Her poems are infectious.

IX.

Nicholas Moore, Touched by Poetic Genius

Twenty-five years ago, Anthony Rudolf said it best in his "Preface" to the second edition of Nicholas Moore's *Spleen* (Menard Press, 1990): "The neglect of Nicholas Moore, a complex, many-sided, mysterious and disturbing poet is, well, a complex, many-sided, mysterious and disturbing phenomenon." By then, Moore (1918–1986) had been dead four years, and, in addition to *Spleen,* the only book of his that one could readily find was *Longing of the Acrobats: Selected Poems* (Carcanet, 1990), a gathering of around 85 pages, which the English poet and editor, Peter Riley, had put together from published and unpublished work. For the devoted handful who wanted to find more poetry by Moore, the subscription-funded *Lacrimae Rerum* (subtitled *Last Poems, 1985*) (Open Township and Poetical Histories, 1988), which was done in a regular edition of 375 copies, was the only other book to be had. According to Riley, who transcribed the poems and saw them into print. "These poems were all written between January 1985 and Nicholas Moore's death in January 1986."

Given this paucity, which has continued unabated for a quarter of a century, the publication of Nicholas Moore's *Selected Poems* (Nottingham: Shoestring Press, 2014), a volume of more than 200 pages spanning 1936 to '86, edited by John Lucas and Matthew Welton, with an introduction by Mark Ford, is certainly cause for celebration. At the very least, this substantial volume reintroduces us to the work of a poet who hasn't been read or thought about, except by staunch fans, since 1950. With examples from every period of Moore's life—from the earliest lyrics written when he was eighteen to the last poem, written shortly before he went into Orpington Hospital in January 1986, where he died—*Selected Poems* is the first welcome step toward revealing the breadth of this poet's accomplishment over fifty years, the different paths that he alone took.

One reason that Moore is almost unknown is that the *Recollections of the Gala* (subtitled *Selected Poems, 1943–48*) (1950) was last time he published with a commercial press. As Ford tell us in his "Introduction," the other reason is that:

> [...] from 1950 to the mid-sixties he composed a mere handful of poems, and published only one book, a meticulous guide to the culture and crossbreeding of the iris.

Without going into what happened to cause this silence and withdrawal, let's backtrack a decade. Between 1941 and 1950, Moore published seven books and two chapbooks—two anonymously and one under a pseudonym. Again Ford is illuminating: "Between 1945 and 1948 he had no fewer than 32 poems published in *Poetry (Chicago)* alone, and in 1947 he was awarded their Harriet Monroe Prize." Most likely, it was during this time that John Ashbery first came across, and admired, Moore's poetry.

One reason I would urge you to buy *Selected Poems* is because it contains the entire *Spleen*, a sequence of 31 poems that Moore wrote in less than two months in 1968, after many years of hardly writing at all. The poems were written in response to a poetry translation competition, which was hosted by *The Sunday Times*, with George Steiner serving as the judge. The poem chosen for the contestants to translate was "Spleen (III)" by Charles Baudelaire, a sonnet-like, eighteen-line rhymed poem that begins:

> Je suis comme le roi d'un pays pluvieux,
> Riche, mais impuissant, jeune et pourtant trés-vieux
> (I am like the king of a rainy country,
> rich but helpless, decrepit though still a young man)

Although Moore claimed that he wrote the poems because of "a disagreement [that he had] with Dr Steiner's thesis in his introduction, namely that it was a good thing that so many modern poets were interested in translation," it is clear from the poems that the competition unlocked something in his imagination. It enabled him to bring his health ("diabetic bones" and "gangrene") and the iris into the poems, that is to say, he was able to transform his bleak circumstances into poetry.

Moore's translations include two poems dedicated to "Nicholas Moore" which were written respectively by the anagrammatic "Conilho Moraes " and "Rosine MaCoolh." The dedication to the translation titled "The Prince of Wails" reads: "for Pee-Wee Russell—a prince in his own right—and that wailing clarinet." The supposed author of this poem is yet another anagram, "Alonso Moriche," with a return address that begins, "c/o Private Eyeballs." Other jazz musicians Moore mentions in the sequence include Yusef Lateef and Claude Hopkins, who died in 1984, having never achieved the recognition of other bandleaders such as Duke Ellington or Count Basie.

In his "Foreword" to the second edition of *Spleen* (The Menard Press, 1990), the poet Roy Fisher gets right to the core of Moore's translations:

> There is no specific tone or direction to the 'black fun': it inhabits the classic bleak world of the satirist, where the rudderless impulses for good struggle among scoundrels and impostors, and there's also an element of the wacky, knuckle-crackling, self-generated glee of the isolate who's not sure whether there's really anyone out there to share his jokes.

I believe that Moore's *Spleen* is one of the great, weird, neglected books of poetry written since the end of World War II, and that it belongs in a category all its own, like Frank Kuenstler's *LENS* (New York: Film Culture, 1964), another inimitable, gleeful work by an isolate. In *Spleen,* Moore writes thirty-one translations of Baudelaire's poem in order to prove that translation is impossible, while in Kuenstler's *LENS,* which took twelve years to write, the poet sets words against themselves by inserting a homophone into a two-word phrase or multisyllabic word ("purr.Version" and "fact.Simile" are good examples), which he strings together in dense, paragraph-like blocks.

John Yau

This is how Mark Ford, in his introduction to *Selected Poems*, describes Steiner's response to Moore's poems:

> Moore was not one of the winners announced some two months later, but in his roundup Steiner drew attention to a bizarre series of entries that he assumed came from the same poet, although sent under a range of strange pseudonyms (W.H. Laudanum, H.R. Fixon-Boumphrey, Jago McFaithfull Fabb, Rosine MaCoolh, Alonso Moriche, Lhoso Cinaremo) and with various spoof or absurdist return addresses (The Hamerican Impassy, P.O. Hoax I aaaaaaaaa): day after day, Steiner wrote, these versions had arrived in 'fantastically mottoed' envelopes, typed in green or brown; their author, he speculated, was possibly American, certainly steeped in Wallace Stevens and 40s jazz, and although "*hors classe*," the dizzying range of approaches adopted ("parody, pastiche, straight, dialect, free verse, heroic couplets, quatrains, alcaics") revealed more than an occasional "touch of poetic genius."

Moore was born in 1918 in Cambridge, England, the oldest child of the philosopher G. E. Moore and Dorothy Ely. Moore's father was one of three philosophers teaching at Trinity College, Cambridge, the other two being Bertrand Russell and Ludwig Wittgenstein. Together, they are considered central figures to what is known as "analytical philosophy" and, as the elder Moore titled one of his papers, "The Refutation of Idealism" (1903).

Moore's poetry is essentially lyrical and autobiographical. Between 1936 and 1948, many of his poems are love poems to his wife Priscilla. Others are dedicated to jazz musicians and to Wallace Stevens, whose work he was one of the first in England to write about. After 1948, a number of the poems are about the emptiness and anger that he felt after Priscilla left him for another man, taking their five-year-old daughter, Julia, with her.

According to Ford, "[Moore's] attempts to branch out in the years after the breakdown of his marriage to Priscilla were stymied by a seemingly endless series of disasters." And yet, Moore's work differs significantly from what is known in America as "confessional poetry," because, as dramatic as the poems can become ("I ran after you I ran after you" is the first line of "Running to Paradise"), Moore comes across as given neither to shame nor to histrionic self-dramatization.

Even in an erotic poem titled, "When I First Held Your Naked Body," he approaches everything with a slight detachment that, in this instance, becomes an unlikely combination of interlocking perceptions, ranging from the courtly to the wistful, and imparting tact to tenderness. Here is the first stanza:

> When I first held your naked body
> It seems to me it was shiny like a seal's.
> Cool and fresh, and eager, and you moved,
> Lightly, exotically, in a world you loved.

Moore could go from using unadorned, matter-of-fact, almost conversational language, which he broke down and reassembled in musical phrasings, lines and stanzas, to declarative, decorative language full of assonance, inspired by his love of Wallace Stevens.

These are the opening lines of "Pepe-le-Moko au Montrachet-le-Jardin" one of his translations of "Spleen," which he dedicated to "Mrs. Alfred Uruguay," the title of a poem by Stevens:

> Beau Roi of Serpentines in thunderous mish-mash!
> Golden glissadings, O empty effendi of air,
> The tutor's fulgurations, fine flickerings of frenzy, leave
> You like a Dodo in the abattoirs;

In addition to the poems I have cited, *Selected Poems* contains three examples of his 'pomenvylopes,' which are poems and commentary Moore typed onto envelopes and sent to friends and acquaintances. In one of the "pomenvylopes" reproduced in *Selected Poems*, he writes, among other things:

> We also listen to The Supremes and we sure
> do think Mary Wilson characteristic
> soul bon-femme of the Noo World."
> Mike and Boris Pasternak

Who knows how many of these exist? According to Rudolf, "Over the years Nicholas Moore sent me 100 'pomenvylopes,' which sometimes contained letters, sometimes were the letter. These cherished envelopes are covered with poems, jokes, quotes, etc." Peter Riley also received a large number of "pomenvylopes." In these works, Moore shares something with another inveterate correspondent and isolate, the mail artist and collagist, Ray Johnson.

This is the first stanza of Moore's late poem, "A House of Words":

> The words themselves have taken on
> Their own personalities, like bricks or slates,
> Or the quiet roofs of the villages,
> Thatched.

So far Moore's *Selected Poems* is the best record of the remarkable journey undertaken by this poet in words, and, during the last twenty years of his life, about words, growing old, and much else.

Why I Am a Member of the Christopher Middleton Fan Club

This is my list of the essential books of Christopher Middleton, the ones I believe you should read if you want to learn what he has been up to for the past 60 years: *Collected Poems* (Carcanet, 2008); *Faint Harps and Silver Voices: Selected Translations* (Carcanet, 2000): *Jackdaw Jiving: Selected Essays on Poetry and Translation* (Carcanet, 1998); *Crypto-Topographia: Stories of Secret Places* (Enitharmon, 2002); *In The Mirror of the Eighth King* (Green Integer, 1999); *Palavers, and A Nocturnal Journal* (Shearsman Books, 2004); *If From The Distance: Two Essays*, with an introduction by Alan Wall (Menard Press, 2007). These seven books contain examples of all the genres and forms Middleton has written over the course of his career: poems, concrete poems, translations, prose (which cannot be categorized), essays, and journals. Ideally, there should be a selected prose that brings together all the different kinds of writing he has done; an up-to-date, comprehensive collection of his essays; a selection of his collages (*The Troubled Sleep of America*—40 collages with texts—was exhibited at the Laguna Gloria Museum, Austin, Texas, in 1982); and a selection of his journals (none of which he wrote for publication, but which he now seems to be willing to publish). As it is, my list of published works adds up to around 1,500 pages, a formidable achievement by anyone's standard.

I have not included on my list Middleton's collections of translations of Robert Walser, Friedrich Nietzsche, Christa Wolf, Elias Canetti, Georg Trakl, Friedrich Hölderlin, Lars Gustafsson, and Andalusian poems "from Spanish versions of the original Arabic" (with Leticia

Garza-Falcon). Middleton is a prolific translator, who began translating Robert Walser's compressed fictions in the 1950s, long before this Swiss writer was on anyone's radar in America or England. However, if you are still reluctant to plunge in or don't know where to begin—I would suggest the *Collected Poems* is a good place to start—you could begin with what I consider the best introduction to his oeuvre: "Christopher Middleton: Portraits," edited by W. Martin (*Chicago Review* 51: 1/2, Spring 2005). The issue contains illuminating essays, reminiscences, testimonies, an interview, bibliography, and examples of his writing. In his "Introduction," W. Martin believes "a *Collected Letters* would be delightful to read at the very least." One standout essay among many is Gabriel Levin's "Middleton in Asia Minor":

> The stratification of languages and cultures—Hittite, Greek, Byzantine, Ottoman, Turkish—is, I believe, what has lured Middleton repeatedly since the early '80s to this vast stretch of land which once comprised the northern arm of the Levant. It has been for the poet a quest in awe of revelation. (*Chicago Review*, p. 119)

Despite all this, Christopher Middleton is a poet—an innovative lyric poet, in fact, and matchless prose writer—who has continued to be overlooked, at least to the extent that, except for the *Chicago Review* (kudos to them), mainstream book reviews, middlebrow periodicals, and adventurous little magazines have consistently failed to address his work, particularly in America, where he has lived for over 40 years. On the rare occasions when they have addressed his work, reviewers tend to regard him as an anomaly, and make convoluted qualifications regarding his singular achievement, all of which ends up marginalizing him. Here is what Alfred Corn wrote in the *New York Times Book Review*: Middleton's "effort is to escape the artifice of received literary ideas, and he has at least succeeded in doing that; his poems don't sound like anyone in particular, not even his models. The gains bring with it definite losses." In arguing that it is better to sound like someone else than to not "sound like anyone in particular," Corn seems to be emphasizing that Middleton has neither an instantly recognizable "I" in his poems nor has he tried to develop a signature style. Here I part company with Corn and agree with Robert Kelly: "Style is death." Middleton's defining sin seems to be that his poems and prose don't sound like anyone else's, and they can't be characterized by their style, which is not to say that he is without, as Corn implies, preoccupations or themes.

This is the rather deplorable situation that I would like to help redress, however inadequately knowledgeable I must admit to being when it comes to discussing the many subtleties of this poet's achievement. I am not alone in this feeling. In his review of *Intimate Chronicles* (1996), the far-more-intellectual August Kleinzahler laid the problem bare: "His analysis, for example, of Mallarmé's 'Le Tombeau de Charles Baudelaire' would frighten off wiser men than I from having a go at Middleton's own poetry" (From an essay originally published in *The Threepenny Review* [Winter 1998] and reprinted in the *Chicago Review*). This is where many people reading and reviewing Middleton's work go wrong; they confuse his vast erudition for narrow eccentricity. They think he's trying to pick up where Ronald Firbank or another strange limner has left off, and that is not the case at all.

Clearly, Middleton has gained a small though loyal public, which is the case with many poets whose work I care about, but, for reasons I find perplexing, he has never crossed the line into the realm of wider recognition—Rae Armantrout, Susan Howe, Louise Glück, Paul Muldoon, Charles Simic, Mark Strand, and his friends Keith and Rosmarie Waldrop are practically famous compared to him. Outside his books, you are not likely to come across his name; he isn't mentioned on literary blogs; year after year, he isn't listed among the nominees for prizes; and he isn't a past winner of an award or fellowship we immediately recognize; he isn't talked about as a teacher of creative writing—all those questionable measures we use to determine a poet's importance. As far as I know, he has never received a Guggenheim Fellowship or, perhaps better yet, if he has received one, he has chosen not to list it among his achievements.

Aside from these mainstream markers, you don't hear him being mentioned as an example of some tendency, good or bad. Certainly, no ready profile, however misinformed and generalizing it might be, comes to mind when we think of him, which isn't the case with his peers: John Ashbery, Robert Bly, Robert Creeley, and W.S. Merwin. In fact, I can think of many slightly celebrated poets whose work I don't ever want to read again—even if I am stuck in a dentist's waiting room, sitting next to the latest issues of the *New Yorker*—being embraced far more often, and tendentiously, in literary and semi-literary periodicals. And it is certainly easy enough to think of figures whose very names are mentioned in a hushed voice befitting a martyred saint—a status that Middleton has clearly shunned. What I am lamenting, however, is his absence from every list that I can think of, except neglected poets.

The bare bones of Middleton's biography are as follows (my primary sources include *Palavers, and A Nocturnal Journal*, (Shearsman Books, 2004) and "A Retrospective Sketch" which was included in the *Chicago Review*). He was born in Truro, Cornwall, England in 1926. His father was an organist who started teaching music at the University of Cambridge in 1930. His mother read D. H. Lawrence. Growing up in Cambridge, "a city bristling with old bookshops," he was by 15 "a nestling antiquarian." He spent three and half years in the R.A.F. (1944–1948), studied German and French at Merton College, Oxford (1948–1952), where his classmates and friends included Rodney Needham and Guy Davenport. He "was never a student of 'Eng. Lit.'."

He taught English at the University of Zürich (1952–1955). While teaching German literature in King's College, London (1955–1965), he became interested in the Levantine, the worldwide symbolism of Paradise Mountains, Dada, and Expressionism. During this decade, he "helped to make the new German writing of the '50s and '60s accessible to British and American readers. [He] wrote reviews, gave radio talks. This work opened up the task of translating...." He first came to Austin, Texas to teach for one year in 1961–62. In 1966, at the age of 39, he returned to the University of Texas and taught German Literature and Comparative Literature until he retired in 1998. He thinks of where he lives in Texas as a "poor man's Mediterranean."

He has literally hundreds of pieces of music in his head, no doubt because of the influence of his father. According to W. Martin, "It was through [Middleton] that I learned to read Hölderlin, the French and Russian symbolists, Plato of the Symposium and Phaedrus, and above all to appreciate the poetic power even of discursive language."

I want to call attention to a few salient features that stick out from this brief biographical sketch. Middleton doesn't have a homepage on the Web, and his Wikipedia entry is remarkable for how little it tells us. He is a widely learned poet and translator, not a constricted theorist and academician. He belongs to the generation that, in America, includes the poets I previously mentioned, as well as points to two English poets who spent much of their adult lives here, and who were widely admired during their lifetime, Thom Gunn (1929–2004) and Denise Levertov (1923–1997). Born exactly between these two public figures, Middleton is all but invisible compared to them. Is this because he was neither part of any group, nor been associated with any movement? Since coming to America in 1966, he was never part of an English department and seems to never have taught creative writing. This goes a long way to explaining why he remains an obscure figure compared to many of his peers. He never put himself at the center of a constantly changing group of impressionable wannabe poets, and made no attempt to gain authority in this manner.

At the same time, I want to make it clear that Middleton is not a curmudgeon grousing about what went wrong with civilization, poetry, and human beings. He has never called attention to himself in that manner. In fact, for all his passion and rage, there isn't an ounce of Phillip Larkin-like grumpiness in him. He doesn't hate Picasso, Pound, and Parker, which one suspects many better known poets do, but have become savvy enough not to admit it. After all, how many celebrated poets have incorporated collage, alluded to history and other literatures, been particularly sensitive to the unstable relationship between sound and sense, and masterfully used shifting registers and dissonance in their work? How many prize-winning poets resist writing the smooth narrative poem with a beginning, middle, and end? Not a lot, but enough, I believe, for me to ask the following question. Why isn't Middleton's work more widely read or, barring that, more widely praised, however little impact that might have on sales and reputation? Why has this poet glided gracefully under the radar for his entire career?

Again, Kleinzahler's observations are helpful: "The poetry of Middleton is not easy to characterize, not least of all because no one Middleton poem truly resembles another, much less one book resembling another in style and subject matter." In other words, there is no carry-over, nothing that might, after you've read one of his poems, help you read the next. You always have to start all over again. If you look at a Jackson Pollock painting from 1948—a so-called drip painting done during the period after he made his first breakthrough to abstraction in 1947—whatever you glean from it (method, all-overness, accretion) will help you look at another done by Pollock a year or two later. This is less the case with Middleton. According to Kleinzahler,

> "[H]e is a philosophical poet, in his fascination with time and the phenomenological, by which I mean in the complex ways of perceiving and thinking about how we perceive. He is not anecdotal and certainly not confessional. Poetry, for Middleton, is very much involved in the act of retrieving in language the imaginative experience or moment, letting it find its own pulse and exfoliate on the page. It detests 'reportage' or 'brute discourse'; it wars against 'languishing idioms.' It is improvisatory."

This is what Alan Brownjohn wrote in the *New Statesman:* "His concern to produce an individual structure of perception for every place, thought, and experience he writes about results in a ceaseless and challenging originality."

Kleinzahler's observations hearkens back to Charles Baudelaire's definition of modernity as the conjoining of "the fleeting and the infinite," but after the death of God, with the promise of redemption the infinite once held now vanished into the cold vastness of the ever-expanding beyond, as I think Middleton recognizes. This doesn't mean the visionary isn't possible, just that received versions of it tend to resemble all those derivative, palatable, easy-to-get instances that so many poets parade before us. Middleton knows for all the seeming sameness of the world, it is never the same, and style helps deny that unending difference. Open and responsive from the beginning of his career, he was able to braid together distinct and different strands of perception, knowledge, and music, including the archaic and the modern, the mythic and familiar, and the unlikely and unexpected, without reducing either to an explanation of the other. He has never written poems that can be read as editorials on contemporary life; he never claims to be more sensitive than others. Which doesn't mean that he has removed himself from the world ("The poet of the abyss / Takes to walking the puppy," *Collected Poems,* p. 388) or from history or catastrophic events ("'Abstraction,' 'pure,' who can mean them now / And not in irony deplore their barbaric use? / Nothing out there pretends. In vague words fatality nests." (*Collected Poems,* p. 607) Rather, his poems don't culminate in a predictable poetic revelation, an "aha" moment that was telegraphed in the first line. He has never succumbed to that particularly American affliction of being cornball. The very first poem in his *Collected Poems* is a good example of what he does and doesn't do.

SEVEN HUNTERS

1
On skins we scaled the snow wall,
seven hunters; roped, leaning
into claws of wind; we climbed,
wisely, for no fixed point.
There was no point we knew.

Staggered upon it at noon.
Drifts half buried it. The coils
Horns eyes had to be hacked free.
We lashed, as the moon rose,
Its black flesh to sledges.

It was dead as a doornail,
thank God. Labouring
The way down, by lick
We found a hut, beer and bread.

2
Some came in cars, some barefoot,
Some by air, some sprang from ships,
Some tore in by local train,
Some capered out of bed
And biked there with babies.

Like flies they filled the hot square.
The cordon, flung around the heap
Of black tubes, when the eye blazed,
Could not see. The crowd did.
Then we heard the first shout.

Now in our houses the streets
And houses have gone.
Here, underground, we
Who were seven, are one.

"Seven Hunters" has two sections. Each section is made up of fourteen lines, divided into three stanzas—the two five line stanzas are followed by a four line stanza (a sonnet but not a sonnet). The lines consist of mostly one-syllable words interrupted by a two or even three syllable word ("The cordon, flung around the heap / Of black tubes, when the eye blazed,"). Musically, the poem is terse and insistent. "Seven Hunters" is an open-ended narrative in which the poet evokes two distinct worlds, but never brings them so close that the reader can reach out and grasp either one. Unable to extricate a story from this inseparable juxtaposition, the reader cannot arrive at some easy conclusion that the poem is about this or that. It is self-sufficient and in that regard has affinities with radical painting of that time. (In a recent email from Anthony Rudolph, I learned that

Alan Wall, whose "Introduction" to *If From a Distance: Two Essays* is well worth reading, believes "Seven Hunters" starts from William Wordsworth's poem, "We are Seven").

Except for the poems that had been privately printed in two earlier collections, "Seven Hunters" is the first poem in his first book, *Torse 3* (1962). By the late 1960s, with the publication of *Our Flowers & Nice Bones* (1969), Middleton no longer relies on juxtaposing two separate worlds, but is able to braid together distinct and unlikely strands of knowledge, memory, and perception into a fluid, changing whole, gaining for his work a greater fluency coupled with a subtler music ("You suddenly woke and saw / on the bedroom hearth an apple green / puddle of moonlight. It was the armadillo," (*Collected Poems*, p. 101)

Middleton's measured dispersions of vowels and consonants in "Seven Hunters" reveal a sensitivity to sound as a potent poetic force ("Some capered out of bed / and biked there with babies."). His use of enjambment is already linked to both a hesitation or delay in music and a time-based perception, and never seems contrived ("We lashed, as the moon rose, / its black flesh to sedges.") His essay, "Ideas about Voice in Poetry" (pp. 88–101, *Jackdaw Jiving*) is a must read if you want an idea of the role sound plays in his thinking about poetry. Citing Mandelstam, Middleton advances that the "poetic word can go against the whole grain of the Saussurian view of language as a system of conventional signs; 'The word is a psyche ..." (*Jackdaw Jiving*, p. 93). The poet must use words (both their sound and sense) to make the poem the place where the experience and possible transformation from one perceptual state to another occurs. Learning from his study of German and French literature, as well as from his encounters with Dada, Surrealist, and Expressionist writing, the poet will raise the music of his writing to far more complex and intricate possibilities.

In contrast to many of his peers, Middleton did not embrace a nationalistic sense of the English language or England after World War II. He did not retreat from the world, as many poets both here and in England did, and write local poetry. He did not strongly identify with a particular region, which is not to say that he disowned his past. Among poets emerging in the aftermath of World War II, he did something unprecedented and, to my mind, brave. He studied German and French, and met and translated German and French poets, among many others. His friends included some of the most radically innovative poets of the century, such as the multilingual Romanian-born German poet and honorary member of OULIPO, Oskar Pastior (1927–2006), and the Austrian poets Ernst Jandl (1925–2000) and Friederike Mayröcker (1924–). He became a cosmopolitan poet, which is perhaps why he has never been fully embraced in either England or America.

"Seven Hunters" neither typifies Middleton's poetry, nor exists as an isolated example. It is part of a possibility that he has explored throughout his career, the unpredictable meeting of the ordinary and the extraordinary, which can only be manifested in words, their particular music. Over time, this meeting has veered into the mythic, and, at other times, it is clearly rooted in specific instances, which includes something as unlikely as standing in the bathroom of the apartment of two good friends. The result is an ekphrastic poem on the tiles; "Berlin: Mommsenstrasse 7" ("Antiquish tiles in a house on Mommsen Street / Line three walls of a demure retreat: ... Blue bees seem to ride the backs of butterflies, / Rocks ring a pool. A warbler perches there ...") The poem locates poet and reader in a familiar act: ("While you pee / There's time to look around."), and the reader is immediately brought into what Middleton, elsewhere, calls the "secret places," in this case a bathroom. He believes that, as a poet, you can't bring yourself to the moment of perception. Instead, you must be open to what the world gives you. ("Almost anywhere there's a poem lying around / Waiting for someone to lift it up, dust it off," (*Collected Poems,* p. 623). Given the range of starting points and subjects in poems and prose, he has remained remarkably open to the world he inhabits, and is passing through, for more than 60 years of writing.

Middleton's poems seem to have their origins in at least five engendering possibilities. There are more, I am sure, but these are the ones that strike me as most prominent. They are rooted in the palpable world of direct experience, such as finding a dead "Tussock

Moth" or seeing "Navaho children … sprouted from sand." They can arrive unexpectedly as music, as in "Woden Dog" ("Wot doth woden dog / Por dog drageth plow"). They are encountered while reading ("Found Poem"), which is also the source of his many imagined dramatic monologues ("Mandelstam to Gumilev 1920"). There are his responses to a photograph or a painting. In fact, his ekphrastic poems are about many different kinds of works, including an oil sketch by Rubens, a kitsch print, a photograph of Chekov, the prints of Charles Meryon, a painting by Joan Miró, and a late painting by Balthus. Add to this list his poems on animals, which are every bit as good as any by D. H. Lawrence and, of course, Christopher Smart, but have a far greater range. He has written poems on cats (many times), armadillos (more than once), parrots, a coral snake, a wild horse, a magpie, and a puppy. In Middleton's universe, everything and anything can become a poem, if you are ready to receive it. He is as conversant with the dead as Jack Spicer, but never once calls attention to it.

By not using the poem to build up to a cathartic event that promises a moment of revelation for poet and reader, and refusing to use the space the poem occupies to tell the reader what it's about, Middleton knowingly risks obscurity. And yet I would argue that he has a higher regard for the reader than those poets who use the poem to announce what they are writing about and why it's important, as if we are children sitting in a ring, learning our lesson. Rather than straining after significance, I am convinced that he believes that it is everywhere, at all times, and that it is his responsibility to recognize it. In this sense, Middleton's poetry and prose shares something with the poetry of Gustaf Sobin (1935–2005). (This unlikely connection was inspired by Middleton's essay "Ideas about Voice in Poetry" [1983], in which he cites lines from a poem by the then-unknown Sobin on p. 97.) In fact, I think a comparison between Middleton's *Collected Poems* and Sobin's *Collected Poems* (Talisman House, 2010), which was edited by Esther Sobin, Andrew Joron, Andrew Zawacki, and Edward Foster, might prove useful.

Middleton certainly fits Theodore Enslin's lauding of Sobin as "an *amateur*, in the highest sense of the word: a lover of the thing itself." Born in different countries nearly a decade apart, and choosing as adults to emigrate to a country far from their own, both entered a diaspora in which they cut themselves off from their own language, and had to reinvent it in their writing. While both poets are highly responsive to what Middleton called the "collaboration between ear and eye ... reinforced by the other senses, if not subliminally regulated by those senses" ("Ideas about Voice in Poetry", p. 92), the difference is that his collaborations are as extensive as Sobin's are narrow. In part, it has to do with their attachment to place. As Zawacki and Joron point out in their introduction, "[f]rom the beginning of his apprenticeship to [René] Char until the end of his days," Sobin wrote in a "simple hut, with its small windows opening onto the wide fields of Provence." Within the narrow purview in which he chose to dwell, the poet focused all of his attention on articulating states of ecstasy and illumination, trafficking in what Joron and Zawacki call the meeting of "eternity and the ephemeral," a conjunction that knowingly invokes Baudelaire's definition of modernity.

Middleton chose to live in, as well as journey into, a wider field. In this regard he anticipates the artist who lives in the age of globalism and has no fixed studio. He has, to put it bluntly, a larger imaginative reach than almost any other contemporary poet that I can think of (John Ashbery and Robert Kelly, two poets I was lucky enough to study with, also have a similarly extensive imaginative reach). As Gabriel Levin puts it: "The diverse provenance of Middleton's own poetry is so great—we have, after all, poems from his native Cornwall and his adopted Texas, as well as from France, Germany, Mexico, Japan, Turkey—that speaking of one locus may be unjustly reductive ... (*Chicago Review*, p. 112). Levin goes on to say that "Middleton, not unlike Echo, is acutely aware of the interstices, the slippages and frictions, between sound and meaningful speech—poetry's 'this prolonged hesitation,' as Valery wrote, 'between sound and sense.' The poet's task is to recapture a voice that is there to be heard provided that he is licked by the flames of memory and desire" (p. 113).

About memory, I would point to "The Lime Tree" (*Collected Poems,* pp. 465–467), a poem about the relationship of son and mother, which is every bit as sensuously complex and disquieting as Robert Duncan's great poem, "My Mother Would Be a Falconress." Middleton's poem opens with these lines:

> Thank you for giving birth to me in the first place,
> Thank you for delivering me from the dark,
>
> You whose round arms I stroked with feeling
> Made presence atmosphere and contact known.
>
> And I wanted not that Englishness;
> I wanted deliverance from you so soon,

And about desire, memory, and the survival of the human trace in anonymous art—the poem strikes me as a self-portrait in which the "I" is noticeably absent—I will leave Middleton with the last word after one last observation. In the third and fourth lines of the poem it is clear how much more masterful he has become since "Seven Hunters" in his interlocking of vowels and consonants. A sinuous dance of sound and meaning reverberates throughout his poem "Figurine of a Chinese Drummer." Here the third and fourth lines of the poem—"Gouged, all of a glug, out of yellow muck, / Now he skips on a disk and beats his bongo" (from *Collected Poems,* p. 563).

Christopher Middleton's Prose

A few years ago, in an essay called "Why I Am a Member of the Christopher Middleton Fan Club," I stated the need for "a selected prose that brings together all the different kinds of writing he has done." *Loose Cannons: Selected Prose* (Albuquerque: University of New Mexico Press, 2014), which includes an insightful foreword by one of Middleton's most vocal and articulate champions, August Kleinzahler, is pretty close to the book I had in mind.

The thirty-three unclassifiable pieces, some no longer than three pages, were selected from prose written between *Flowers & Nice Bones* (1969) and *Depictions of Blaff* (2010), a span of forty-one years, a period during which the prose poem became an increasingly popular form in American poetry. Middleton's short pieces are not prose poems, however. As Kleinzahler states at the beginning of his "Foreword," "what Middleton "would refer to as 'short prose' are certainly [his] wildest, most accessible, and most entertaining work and count as some of his very finest writing." I suspect that one reason why they are not better known is because they are not short tales with a beginning, middle and end.

In other words, Middleton's short prose pieces are not prose poems as that term is conventionally understood, and they have little to do with the beloved Francophile tradition spawned by the posthumous publication of *Paris Spleen* (1869), Charles Baudelaire's book of fifty-one prose poems. Middleton's imaginative prose pieces are not motivated by disgust, nor do they seem to have an overriding theme, recognizable style or tic holding them together, as do the prose poems of Charles Simic and Russell Edson. They are not neat and tidy. They are in a league of their own, just as those fabulist concatenations found in the book *Tatlin!* (1974), by Guy Davenport, his friend and classmate at Merton College, Oxford (1948–52), are unclassifiable. As I see it, the imaginative prose of Davenport and Middleton constitute two of the more singular achievements in American letters.

Like Davenport, Middleton's erudition is unrivaled in its grasp and comprehension of many sources. A prolific, innovative translator, he started translating Robert Walser's fiction in the 1950s, in postwar, non-German-loving England, long before this unique writer was on anyone's radar. In 1957, Middleton published his eye-opening translation of Walser's *The Walk and Other Stories*. He has also translated the work of Friedrich Nietzsche, Christa Wolf, Elias Canetti, Georg Trakl, Friedrich Hölderlin, and Lars Gustafsson. Along with his interest in Dada, Surrealist, and Expressionist writing, all of which were largely rejected in England, Middleton was a devotee of the experimental work of his own time and became friends with some of the most radically innovative poets of the century, such as Keith and Rosmarie Waldrop; the multilingual Romanian-born German poet and honorary member of OULIPO, Oskar Pastior (1927–2006); and the Austrian poets Ernst Jandl (1925–2000) and Friedrike Mayröcker (1924–). The other difference that sets Middleton apart from his peers is that, in addition to not aligning himself with the French tradition, Middleton doesn't see himself as an heir to Ezra Pound, as did Davenport. Homer's Greece and Dante's Italy were not the center for Middleton. Rather, it was the Levant countries of Cyprus, Egypt, Iraq, Israel, Jordan, Lebanon, Palestine, Syria, and Turkey, and all that happened there, that held Middleton's attention.

One of the memorable moments I spent with Middleton was sitting with him in the mid-'90s in a café in Austin, Texas, where he has lived since 1966, listening to his enthusiasm, anticipation and excitement as he talked about his forthcoming trip to Yemen to learn more about Arabic. He was then in his early 70s and, as far as I could see, still an eager and curious student, someone who believes that learning never ends. Instead of claiming authority, he yearned to gain more knowledge.

Imagine prose that is neither anecdotal nor confessional, and you begin to get a sense of Middleton's unclassifiable writing. Add to this his resistance to arriving at predictable poetic revelations, moments that appear to be blessed by a sudden universal insight, and you get a sense of why his writing has never quite gained the attention it deserves. We want revelations, however cliché, because they promise us comfort. Middleton comes from another tradition, which counts Herodotus, Plutarch and Thucydides among its originators. He is not in the habit of providing solace to the reader.

Inspired by these ancient classical writers, Middleton is simultaneously contemporary and mysterious rather than nostalgic or soothing. In "The Birth of the Smile," within a span of less than two pages, Middleton goes from "the Sumerians" to "the smile inserted at the corners of Che Guevara's mouth by the thumbs of his murderers." Here, as elsewhere, Middleton is able to braid together different kinds of prose, ranging from history, myth and fable to a description gleaned from the mass media, without anything seeming forced or contrived. I cannot explain why it feels right that the author ends with Che Guevera's post-mortem smile, but it does. At the very least, he is reminding us that a smile and cruelty are linked often enough to be unsettling. The fact that he refuses to step back and moralize after reaching this insight is just one of the many powerful things he does.

In "The Turkish Rooftops," Middleton starts with the observation that "Turkish people like to sleep on rooftops," and then goes on to list the various things one might see on these rooftops ("Buckets, parts of cooking stoves, donkey saddles, lengths of rope, piping, sinks, scythes"), as well as to comment on "how, in Cézanne's paintings of Mont Saint-Victoire, the mountain changes its clothes, sky its diagonals that shine or rain down upon the roof of the mountain." What interests Middleton is the threshold between one order of objects and another. He is both scholarly and innocent and doesn't privilege one above the other. Each of the thirty-three pieces in *Loose Cannons* contains something marvelous. Each of his sentences is a seamless synthesis of perception, information and music.

Perhaps *Loose Cannons* will help change our perception of Middleton's considerable achievement. Instead of offering us easy

John Yau

reassurance, his prose (as does all his writing) seems motivated by what he states at the end of his "Prologue": "Beauty is exuberance." Here we might be reminded that the one lesson Middleton might have gotten from translating Walser or from reading Baudelaire is the latter's observation: "The Beautiful is always strange." The strangeness that Middleton leads the willing reader to is well worth beholding.

One More Thing I Want to Say about Christopher Middleton

For the fans of the poet Christopher Middleton (1926–2015), *Serpentine* (2018) is a welcome addition to his body of work, which includes *Loose Cannons: Selected Prose* (2014), *Collected Poems* (2008), and *Faint Harps and Silver Voices (Selected Translations).* Originally published by Oasis Books in 1985, *Serpentine* appeared in what Tony Frazer, the publisher of this edition by Shearsman, called "a slightly shoddy, if serviceable production." While a few of the pieces in *Serpentine* are also in *Loose Cannons: Selected Prose,* this reprinting fills a gap in Middleton's prose. A member of the generation of poets that includes John Ashbery (1927–2017) and Robert Creeley (1926–2005), like them, Middleton wrote in many styles, from the classifiable to the unclassifiable. *Serpentine* belongs to the latter.

The collection consists of 20 untitled pieces, 18 of which are in prose and titled in lower case on the Contents page, along with "a provisional postscript" and "publisher's note" by Tony Frazer. According to Frazer, the original edition "was reviewed only once, received scant distribution, and was never republished." This is a common fate for many poetry books, which, unlike the *Titanic,* sink without notice, all the words gone with nary a ripple. Frazer, who has been the editor and publisher of Shearsman Books since 1981, is to be commended for bringing *Serpentine* back into print.

This is what many people would call a book of experimental prose—an unfortunate description. According to a note on the back of this edition, Middleton is said to have "forbade such a definition from appearing anywhere in the first edition for fear of frightening off potential readers," which it seemed to do without any help. In his exercise, "How to Start a Drawing," Paul Klee famously said, "Drawing is taking a line for a walk." Something similar happens in Middleton's prose. It pivots to reveal a narrative that is discovered as it goes along, creating a state of shifting consciousness in which to register its realizations. In "wittenbergplatz" he writes:

> Something he said about the poem before getting into the 60 bus at Wittenbergplatz with five minutes to spare noticed the iron frame with place names across it like rungs of a ladder and could not see very well go closer they were the names of places like Auschwitz Bergen-Belsen Buchenwald Theresienstadt in alphabetical order and off the square on the corner he could see looking beyond the frame Sexpool a window and in the window a wax dummy woman wearing a black leather corselet chains a steel studded collar and on her head jauntily a military cap with several squat fir trees planted to commemorate the great undulant plains and forests [...]

At this point, Middleton starts another block of prose. Later, in "How to Start a Drawing," Klee suggests: "Let the Drawing Appear 'By Itself.'" This seems to most closely describe what Middleton does in Serpentine, which touches upon all kinds of subjects, from the hero eating a chicken he just cooked to "moving day in momnpopville after a trip to church." Each piece of writing takes the reader for a walk that is full of surprises, interesting detours, unsettling encounters, and much more. The prose can be crystalline, opaque, and sonorous. It is the prose of a cultivated man who seems to always be in touch with a reservoir of feelings, associations, and scholarship. And yet, in "wittenbergplatz," he is a person about to board a bus in Berlin. There is, in that sense, nothing special about him.

In thinking about *Serpentine,* Middleton's review of John Ashbery's *A WAVE* (1984), which appeared in *The New York Times* on June 17, 1984, came to mind. Middleton could be writing about himself in the opening paragraph:

> Reading John Ashbery's poems is a bit like playing hide-and-seek in a sprawling mansion designed by M. C. Escher. The mansion

is located in midcity and midcountry at the same time (or at least from its pinnacles one can see across open country). Just as abrupt shifts occur between levels in the buildings Escher drew, abrupt semantic shifts occur in Mr. Ashbery's poems. Non sequiturs spin off in various directions; phrasings of inspired concision telescope with prolix, prosier ones. Yet the reader has to concede, perhaps ruefully, that bewilderment on his part must be his own problem, for the poems have an air of sovereign intelligence. Whatever else may happen to shiver the linguistic timbers, the syntax and the voice are coherent, cool, levelheaded.

When people take a walk, some always like to know exactly where they are. Others don't mind being lost because what they encounter is the real substance of their wanderings. The prose in *Serpentine* has "an air of sovereign intelligence." Any reader who does not mind adventure, vertiginous moments, and getting temporarily lost should want to go on a stroll with Middleton in whatever landscape he explores.

Why I Am a Member of the Lee Harwood Fan Club

Mark Ford's blurb on the back of Lee Harwood's most recent book of poetry, *The Orchid Boat* (London, Enitharmon, 2014), inspired me to look up the original review from which it was quoted.

Written a decade ago in *The Guardian* (September 17, 2004), this is how Ford's astute assessment of Harwood's *Collected Poems* (Exeter UK: Shearsman, 2004) began:

> Lee Harwood, who is 65 this year, is still not known much outside the world of small press publications. His twenty or so volumes of poems and prose poems have been issued by tiny, often fugitive presses, such as Pig Press, Galloping Dog Press, Slow Dancer Press, Transgravity Press, and Other Branch Readings. But, like Jeremy Prynne, whose work drew fire earlier this year from the heavyweight academic professors John Carey and John Sutherland, Harwood has cult status among followers of the alternative British poetry scene.

Although a decade has passed since Ford's smart, sympathetic review, Harwood, a resident of Brighton since 1967, who has managed to fly under the radar in his own country for nearly his entire career, continues to remain all but invisible here. There are many reasons for this, none of which are particularly interesting.

And yet, it wasn't always so. Like others of my generation (I was born in 1950), who began reading poetry as teenagers in the wake of Donald Allen's groundbreaking anthology *The New American Poetry 1945–1960* (1960), I discovered some of what was going in the alternative English and American poetry scene through Fulcrum

Press, which published Basil Bunting's *Collected Poems* (1968), as well as Robert Duncan's *Derivations: Selected Poems, 1950–56* (1968). The press also published Harwood's *The White Room* (1968). Lewis Warsh and Ann Waldman had earlier published *The Man with Blue Eyes* (New York: Angel Hair Books, 1966), but I didn't own it until after I bought *The White Room*. This was my introduction to Harwood, and I have followed his work as best as I could ever since. His work hasn't always been easy to find, but it is now, which is why I want to go on record about this marvelous poet.

There are sixteen poems in *The Orchid Boat*, none longer than two pages. After finishing this book and thirsty for more, I decided to go back to Harwood's *Collected Poems*. Covering forty years (1964–2004), the *Collected Poems* is 522 pages long. I highly recommend it or, if one finds that too daunting, read his *Selected Poems* (Shearsman 2007), which is 140 pages long and includes poems written between 2004 and 2007. One may also find it useful, as I certainly have, to look up *Lee Harwood: Not the Full Story* (Shearsman, 2008), which contains six interviews by Kelvin Corcoran. My final recommendation is *Chanson Dada: Tristan Tzara, Selected Poems* (Black Widow, 2009), which contains all of Harwood's translations of the poet done over a period of twenty-five years.

One reason to read *Collected Poems* from beginning to end is because, as Ford stresses in his review, "Harwood's poetry is not only not 'difficult'—it is open, moving and exquisitely delicate in its attention to landscape, mood, and the pressures of time and history."

Ford makes another point in his review, which I think bears repeating:

> He makes use of avant-garde poetic techniques not to dramatize a radical skepticism about language or meaning, but in order to recover for poetry the kinds of "directness" or expressive energy postmodernism taught us to distrust.

This directness is what I think Harwood has to offer to readers and young writers who feel like they have reached an impasse.

In the "Foreword" to his *Collected Poems,* Harwood cites among his early influences Ezra Pound, John Ashbery, who he met in Paris in 1965, Tristan Tzara and Jorge Luis Borges. From these writers Harwood learned about collage and what could be done, as he says to Corcoran: "with fragments and suggestions." Later, he tells Corcoran that another influence is "Reverdy's idea of *The Daily Miracle*—of how amazing all the things around you are when you look at them and step back rather than take them for granted."

This is one of the keys to Harwood's poetry—his sharp-eyed, sympathetic attention to the unpredictable drift of the ordinary things, feelings and daydreams that fill our everyday lives because they are not to be taken "for granted." He is not driven to make a grand statement or be oracular.

This is the last stanza of his early "letterpoem" (ca. 1965):

> lunch-times I sit in the park
> watching the sun and damp grass.
> there's no big fiery blast to end this poem,
> no sudden revelation—"more's the pity"
> —and even this sounds too neat

While still in his mid-twenties, Harwood quietly and confidently refuses to join the high modernist tradition that includes T. S. Eliot. At the same time, he does not become part of another club; he is a man sitting alone in a park. I still find Harwood's confident acceptance of his unavoidable solitariness inspiring.

Another key to the poetry can be gleaned from this exchange between Corcoran and Harwood.

K.C.: "They are very physical poems, Lee. They are involved with the body, aren't they?

L.H.: Yes, there is the sexual side.

Later, in the same interview, Harwood states:

I just feel a strong sense of self can be a hindrance. That it detracts from the relationship between the writer and the reader and it imposes the author's personality, and that moves into the business of authority, which I detest. I don't think any writing should be an authority, rather than a questioning, otherwise it panders to the writer's vanity.

This is the conundrum that animates Harwood's best writing, from poems to prose. There is a strong sense of the sensual, sexual body—his love of men in his earlier work and later women—while at the same time a reluctance to impose any authority upon the relationship.

As Ford states in his review:

> His poetry never attempts to coerce us into a particular attitude to life, and indeed even avoids interpreting the experience it embodies. Instead, it creates a space in which perceptions, quotations, overheard snippets of conversation ("Being a working girl isn't all stars"), clippings from newspapers, outbursts of lyricism or unhappiness, inscriptions copied from gravestones can succeed each other without seeming either merely random or too programmatically shaped.

Later, Ford advances that Harwood's attention to the details of everyday life is comparable to the writing of James Schuyler, but Harwood's writing is plainer, less likely to contain an outrageous analogy. While there is some truth to Ford's observation, Harwood's mixture of the descriptive and objective is all his own. What comes across is the poet's sympathy and tenderness, a sense of "the daily miracle."

The other thing that struck me while reading the *Collected Poems* was his unabashed interest in narratives and storytelling, none of which resolved into anecdotes or what he called the "author's personality." The poems remain open and inviting—they evoke the private thoughts we often suppress, ignore, are ashamed of, or embarrassed by. Harwood isn't afraid of either courting sentiment or of arriving at the kind of emotional directness we associate with the work of Constantine Cavafy.

To his credit, Harwood took what he learned from Ashbery, particularly the collage poems found in the highly influential *The*

Tennis Court Oath (1962), and opened it onto his own territory, at once playful, tender and unexpected, as in the jump-cuts we enjoy in movies, from the high to the low.

What Harwood's poetry shows is that there is no correct way to go—you have to make it up as you go along until you finally reach something that is your own. Screw what the academics tell you about doing what they define as the correct thing. Without being either nostalgic or reactionary, Harwood rejected authority in his mid-twenties. His poise is something we can all learn from, as well as his awareness of the isolation it would bring. He recognized that separation was fundamental, an ingrained aspect of human solitariness, which he chose not to ignore.

At the end of his poem "Saint David's Daon the Leyn" (ca. 1988–1993), Harwood writes:

> A glint in the sharp spring air
> as a young girl wearing her best clothes
> walks along an empty country lane
> clasping a bunch of bright daffodils.

Harwood's poem conveys with extreme pictorial economy a perception that is tenderly sympathetic to the young girl's vulnerability, solitude, innocence and belief. We don't know what will happen to this young girl—it is a snapshot of her in time.

Is Harwood's lack of radical skepticism about language really a cardinal sin? Is straightforwardness a quality that we can no longer have? Is human solitariness an obsolete artifact, joined as we all are by the Internet?

Start with Harwood's newest book, *The Orchid Boat*. Here is the second stanza of "Departures," the book's opening poem, which was collaged from the poem, "The Sorrows of Departure" by the Chinese woman poet Li Ch'ing-Chao (c. 1084–1151):

She wrote:

> Gently I open
> my silk dress and float alone

> on the orchid boat. Who can
> take a letter beyond the clouds?

Is this what can longer be written in a poem because it is neither ironic nor hip? Is Harwood's compassion something to be dismissed or laughed at? Has poetry really come to that?

X.

Digging into Time and Memory with John Koethe

Why does someone end up being a poet? It is one thing to start out writing poems, because nearly everyone dabbles in it. But to keep at it until writing poetry becomes all you've really done is another matter. This is the mysterious impenetrable planet that John Koethe has orbited for many years.

During these yearly orbits, with the prospect of a future diminishing as he gets older, he often returns to this question: what does it mean to end up being a bunch of books on a shelf, especially a shelf that few people stand in front of, much less return to. This is just one of the subjects that Koethe patiently examines in *Walking Backwards: Poems 1966–2016* (New York: Farrar, Straus and Giroux, 2018).

As the title suggests, Koethe's subject is memory and time. Scattered throughout this collection are poems that originate with a Proustian moment, a brief, intense memory that keeps leading to other memories:

> I didn't start out to write a poem about my mother,
> But unchecked memories carry you away, like the shoes
> In *The Red Shoes*. I'm sure I loved her then:
> She was smart and funny and more down to earth
> Than my father, who, when he wasn't somewhere with the Navy,
> Affected these aesthetic airs and sang too loud in church.

These lines are from the poem "Red Shoes," which appeared in his book *ROTC Kills* (2012). The poem is around 70 lines long and begins:

> When I was eleven I'd accompany my mother
> To San Diego State College, where she was taking courses
> For some degree or other (she taught reading to kids).
> It was summer. Maybe she didn't want to leave me at home,
> Or maybe I wanted to come along—I don't remember.
> I was into microscopes and blood: I had a compound model
> With three lenses I bought at an optical store on the second floor
> Of a Chandleresque building with exposed ironwork,
> Like the building in *Double Indemnity.*

One of the marvels of "Red Shoes"—indeed of many of Koethe's poems—is how much ground he covers, how effortlessly he pivots from one thought (memory/perception) to another, how precisely he is able to register the drift of one's thinking in pursuit of something intangible.

> [.......] They're both dead now,
> And all I have to wrestle with are words, and yet these
> Syllables bring back the feeling of those summer afternoons,
> The red tile roofs, the blood and the ballet, as I sit here in the future
> I couldn't imagine then, waiting for one I can't imagine now.

A funny thing just happened. I stopped to check a review that I had written about Koethe in 2012 and realized that in that review I discussed this very poem, "Red Shoes," though not in the way I am now. My reading of "Red Shoes" has changed since I first read it. Isn't this why we return to certain poems, paintings, and films? Koethe's poems are not frozen descriptions of a revelatory moment—a field we stop by on a snowy night. They change, because we do. As he writes in his poem "The Great Gatsby": "I have read it dozens of times, starting in high school."

What Koethe does in "Red Shoes" is use the movie—which he first saw when he was eleven, and which, years later, he sees again in New York—to bring different parts of time together: his childhood, his parents getting older and dying, and the "future" he now inhabits, marked by what led up to this moment. What allows him to time travel and bring moments back is "syllables."

For all of his discursiveness, Koethe is a musical poet. He has written poems that rhyme and long meandering disquisitions on the nature of time passing.

His poem "The Secret Amplitude" consists of nine sections of three line stanzas in which rhyme is often used. In this poem, which appeared in *Falling Water* (1997), Koethe ponders "the experience of memory:"

> For over time, the personal details
> Came to mean less to me than the feeling
>
> Of simply having lived them, revealing
> Another way of being in the world,
> With all the inwardness it still sustains
>
> And the promise of happiness it brought.

This is the contradiction that animates Koethe's poems: the "promise of happiness" that courses through the work mixed with his awareness of a future "one can't imagine now." How do you live in time with no expectation of transcendence or sanctuary from its passing? In Koethe's case, you become a poet who spends years teaching in the philosophy department at the University of Wisconsin in Madison, while making trips to New York to see friends, who happen to be poets and artists, some of whom you met when you were still in college.

As he writes in his masterful poem "Ninety-Fifth Street:"

> For that's what poetry is—a way to live through time
> And sometimes, just for a while, to bring it back.

While the poem may be instrumental in making a private, erotic connection, as when he writes, "the blond light / Of a summer afternoon that made me think again of Sally's hair," it can do something very different in "Tulsa," which appeared in *The Swimmer* (2016).

"Tulsa" opens with an observation about the Civil War:

> It wasn't just the slaughter—though proportionally it
> Exceeded all our other wars combined—but what prefigured it
> And what it brought about.

From this recognition that the "slaughter" had a history that preceded it, Koethe instantly pivots to:

> There was the cotton gin
> That gave the South a one-commodity economy
> It needed slaves to run.

A few lines later we read:

> It's sickening to read the rationales, because they cut so close.

By now, it should be clear that Koethe keeps digging and revealing a subject; he is in pursuit of understanding something about time and history.

After stating that he has read the rationales, he goes on to cite some of them. This is from Mississippi's justification for slavery:

> None but the black race can bear exposure to the tropical sun
> These products have become necessities of the world,
> And a blow at slavery is a blow at commerce and civilization.

"Tulsa" is like a sequence of camera shots, beginning with an abstract and distanced one: 'It wasn't just the slaughter [...]" No matter what he is writing about, each of Koethe's lines is driven by his penchant for detail, which pulls us closer to the subject of the poem.

Fifty lines into the poem, after reading Koethe's detailing of the Civil War and the Reconstruction, particularly "the Compromise of 1877—the 'corrupt bargain ...'" when the "South" became "a separate nation after all," he changes the focus without notice: "In 1999 I flew to Tulsa for a literary festival." During this time there, his hosts tell him something of the history of Tulsa, including "the riots that occurred in 1921," which he gets down in exact and tormenting detail:

> There was a vibrant black community in a part of town called
> Greenwood
> (One of those thriving middle classes, I suppose), so prosperous
> with its
> Banks and businesses and homes that it was called "the Negro
> Wall Street."
> On Memorial Day there was an incident in an elevator in a
> downtown building
> That involved a young white woman and a young black man, who
> was jailed
> On suspicion of assault. A white crowd gathered, incited by an
> editorial
> In the *Tulsa Tribune* egging on a lynching. Skirmishes ensued,
> And then at last a huge white mob stormed into Greenwood,
> shooting
> Indiscriminately, burning stores and businesses and houses, while
> Biplanes
> From an airfield near town, left over from WWI, dropped
> firebombs
> And fired at people on the ground, until the Negro Wall Street lay
> in ruins.
> No one really knows how many died—hundreds probably, and
> thousands wounded.

Starting with one "slaughter," Koethe brings us to another that occurred more than fifty years after the Civil War ended. It is a slaughter that America has largely erased from its history.

Didn't the use of biplanes to drop firebombs on a civilian populace precede the aerial bombing at Guernica (April 26, 1937) by more than a decade? Didn't Americans bomb woman and children—noncombatants, as they say—long before the Germans did? Is this something mentioned in our history books?

Koethe, however, does not stop with this horrific event. He keeps digging after detailing it, and writing about how "the Tulsa Race Riots simply disappeared from history." He tells us the name of "the young black man" (Dick Rowland) who was used as a scapegoat, as well as the "real cause" of the riots: "the black community's continually accumulating wealth." And then, having reached this point, he steps back once again and writes: "In metaphysics and philosophy of language there's a view that holds/that if you want to know what something is, ignore what people say about it–/Look instead at where it came from." This desire to see where things came from, to understand the origin of our ongoing Civil War, for example, is just one of the many reasons why I think Koethe is a necessary and great poet.

Living in time, he writes poems that weave together different genres: poetry, essay, history, memoir, philosophical inquiry, and lecture. He can easily change tones and registers, swiftly move from abstract language to detailed representations of a painting, movie, popular song, or a story by John Cheever. He cites poems by poets as different as John Ashbery, Theodore Roethke, Robert Duncan, Elizabeth Bishop, Marianne Moore, Adrienne Rich, Wallace Stevens, Robert Frost, and Mark Strand. He dedicates poems to Susan Stewart, Harold Bloom, and Robert Dash—a poet, a literary critic, and a painter. He loves jazz and writes beautifully about Ornette Coleman. He is unafraid of declaring his enthusiasms or entering territory that could easily devolve into the sentimental but never does. His mood changes, often in the same poem. He can be mordant, bleak, anguished, humorous, tender, and even sweet. He has no axe to grind, a rarity in this day and age.

In Koethe's best poems—and there are many more than I can list—one feels a pressure to get to the core of understanding time. Where does it go? What have we done with it? How does it persist? Even at his most grim, he refuses to ask for sympathy and, to my mind, there is a dignity and beauty in that: "I'm sixty-two. That's all I am." He can begin his poem, "La Durée," with "Proust read Bergson, then he wrote his poem." More than 150 lines later, after bringing in the philosophers Ludwig "Wittgenstein" and David "Hume," the writer F. Scott "Fitzgerald," and standing in a "Kmart / Parking lot" in "Milwaukee," he can end with: "I'm hungry. I think I will get a hamburger at Dr. Dawg." This is what Koethe does so well: he does not seem driven by the desire to discover who and what he is, how he came to be the person he is—a retired professor of philosophy, a man who for a long time lived alone. For all of the movies, stories and books, philosophers and paintings, places and foods he has in his poems, I don't feel like what I have gotten are revelatory descriptions and anecdotes. The feelings he gets to are a nuanced *cri de coeur* of "what is difficult to say."

Douglas Crase, Literary Subversive

Douglas Crase is an American poet, essayist, critic, and biographer who writes luminously about a range of subjects. Since 1981, he has published five books, two of which are poetry. None of his books is longer than 300 pages.

For those who do not know his work, the recently published *Lines from London Terrace: Essays and Addresses* (Pressed Wafer, 2018) is a good place to start.

The book encompasses work written between 1977 and 2016: it consists of essays and reviews that originally appeared in *The Nation, Seneca Review, Art & Antiques, Raritan, Poetry, Poetry Pilot, Tether*, and exhibition catalogs. It also incorporates an address he made at the Rochester Public Library in honor of John Ashbery in 1977, and statements and papers he delivered at various seminars and panel discussions. Crase has lots of intelligent things to say about the poems of Ashbery, Elizabeth Bishop, Robert Frost, Amy Gerstler, John Koethe, Lorine Neidecker, James Schuyler, and Marjorie Welish; the prose of Marianne Moore; the essays of Ralph Waldo Emerson; the garden of the painter Robert Dash; and the philosophy of Richard Poirier. There is a section on the origins of the New York School which every aspiring poet and budding critic should read.

In his review, "The Poet's So-Called Prose," about *The Complete Prose of Marianne Moore* (1986), edited by Patricia Willis, Crase traces the concept that poetry and criticism are inseparable back to Moore, a seemingly unlikely source for such a postmodern view:

> But Moore, joyously quoting Eliot quoting Pound, actively believed that criticism and poetry were not exclusive ("'they proceed as two feet of one biped'"). Perhaps they were not even separable.

Criticism, she wrote, inspires creation. More than that, "a genuine achievement in criticism is an achievement in creation"–her own prose being the case that proved her point, if not quite in the way she meant.

Crase's view—one of many that he carefully develops in this necessary book—challenges the received wisdom that the "bricoleur" impulse was imported to America from Europe, that we needed the writing of European intellectuals to understand what we were up to. Another point that Crase advances in this review is that reading and writing might also be inseparable.

The reason I am braiding these different kinds of writing (poetry, criticism, and quotation) together is because I think that the entire body of Crase's work invites the kind of close attention that is usually reserved for poetry.

Crase, who published a book of poems, *The Revisionist* (1981), to great acclaim, did not publish another book until 1997, when *AMERIFIL.TXT: A Commonplace Book* was issued by the University of Michigan Press in its series, "Poets on Poetry," edited by David Lehman. The book is a collection of quotations by twenty-three writers, from the colonial activist and Congregationalist minister John Wise to the American poets James Schuyler and John Ashbery. Other writers and thinkers that Crase cites include Rachel Carson, Emily Dickinson, W. E. B. Dubois, Ralph Waldo Emerson, Langston Hughes, Charles Ives, William James, Robinson Jeffers, Gertrude Stein, Wallace Stevens, and William Carlos Williams. The citations are arranged under categorical headings listed in alphabetical order, from "Anxiety of Influence" to "Wild Blue Yonder." This is the entry under "Equal Protection":

> And in this country one sees that there is always margin enough in the statute for a liberal judge to read one way and a servile judge another.
>
> —*Ralph Waldo Emerson*

In his use and arrangement of found (or read) texts, Crase's *AMERIFIL.TXT* shares something with the conceptual writings of Robert Fitterman, Kenneth Goldsmith and Vanessa Place. However, living as we do in a ghettoized literary culture, it would not occur to many critics to see what is front of their eyes—most likely because they would associate Crase with a late generation of the New York School and, flaunting their biases, not bother to read him, especially since, by their lights, he has published one book of poems in 1981, supplemented by a thin book of thirteen poems in 2017, hardly enough production to merit attention.

Crase's writing occupies an expansive, complex space that needs to be recognized. He does not teach in an English literature or creative writing department: he is not an academic worried about maintaining his or her position or accruing power, both of which are anathema to him. He is not interested in the hierarchical thinking and privileged constructs that so many literary critics delight in, what Charles North calls "papier-mâché."

Crase is that rare figure in American letters: a subversive who challenges the received wisdom promulgated in English and American literature departments from sea to shining sea. His essays about Ralph Waldo Emerson are central to his thinking:

> You're wondering if I'm really serious, if it matters that an ill-managed president broadcasts a piece of mimetic vandalism grabbed up by a speechwriter. But tropes that make the earth unlovely make humans that do not love the earth. If theirs is the species that also has the bombs, or just the subdevelopment rights, then I think poetry has quite a lot to do with salvation.

Writing about James Schuyler, he makes this statement:

> To a poet like that, reality would be the one thing that is not commonplace, and it would stand to reason that life cannot fully be lived until the reality is faced without embarrassment or flinch.

In an essay about Ashbery, he states:

> It is remarkable that a poem so periphrastic and evasive can be so frankly chilling at the same time.

Don't Crase's descriptions evoke the dilemma of our everyday life, with its intersection of changing weather, scientific discoveries, and constantly alarming news? What Crase shows by the example of his lines and sentences is that a writer need not be "cowed into euphemism."

In 2004, Crase published *Both: A Portrait in Two Parts,* a book that melds the biographies of the botanist Rupert Barneby and the aesthete Dwight Ripley, who was the financial backer of the Tibor de Nagy Gallery. Crase's double biography recovers an important story about "the poets of the New York School [...] and their own romance with the painters of their time, notably the painters of the Tibor de Nagy Gallery." Ripley was more than just the gallery's financial "angel": he was a polymath who published poetry in Catalan and Polish, exhibited his drawings, made important contributions as a botanist. He and Barneby, working collaboratively, discovered a number of rare plants, one of which was named after him—*Cymopteru ripleyi.* Barneby and Ripley had what Barneby called a "lifetime partnership."

Their fascinating story is one that chroniclers of the New York School of poets and the Second Generation of New York School artists have left out until Crase came along. The footnotes are just as fascinating and replete with detail. Crase's biography is the story of two men who met at a premier English boarding school when they were teenagers, and began a "sudden boyhood romance" that lasted a half-century, until Ripley's death.

In the first pages of *Both: A Portrait in Two Parts,* Crase recounts how his partner, Frank Polach, brought him to meet Barneby shortly after Ripley's death: this opening turns the biography into a memoir detailing Crase's discovery of the lives these two men led. In writing about Barneby whom he grew to know personally, and Ripley, whom he set out to understand, Crase's biography is about the domestic life of two men, as well as his own relationship with Polach, who, at the time, worked "as a plant information officer at the New York Botanical Garden." On that first visit meeting with Barneby, he sees an oil painting by Joan Miró and two drawings by Jackson Pollock, piquing our interest and his. The book ends with Crase and Polach burying Barneby's ashes in Honesdale, Pennsylvania, where they live, following Barneby's suggestion. Next to his interment, they buried the ashes of one of "Dwight's unfinished drawings," and marked it with a headstone.

If Guy Davenport is the geographer of the imagination, Crase is most certainly the geographer of places and histories that are folded deeply into what is called America: "Poems […] made of land and air and rock," as he writes in his superb essay on Lorine Neidecker, "Neidecker and the Devotional Sublime," included in this collection. Crase's essay is about Neidecker's poem, "Lake Superior," which he characterizes as "that spare ferropastoral of a poem in honor of the rock and mineral wealth […]."

Crase also states: "As far as the commonwealth is concerned, every one of us must know it would be better if we had never arrived." But we did arrive or were brought here, and what followed is a chain of events that bring us to the present, which Crase never turns away from and never becomes genteel in the face of.

In his "Afterword" to Donald Britton's book of poems *In the Empire of the Air* (2016), Crase begins with this statement:

> The appearance in print of the selected poems of Donald Britton is an affront to cynicism and a triumph over fate.

Britton (1951–1994) was one of the many thousands of individuals who died of AIDs in the 1980s. This is how Crase puts it in his "Afterword:"

> We had heard of a mysterious illness among gay men in May 1981, only two months after *Italy* [Britton's first and only book of poems published in his lifetime] appeared, but the first friend Donald or I knew to actually die was Larry Stanton, the painter, in 1984. After that, one lived with the certain apprehension that the friends who defined your life might suddenly wither, suffer, and disappear.

> The critic David Kalstone, a source of wisdom and encouragement to many of us, was hospitalized the next year and died at home on West Twenty-Second Street in 1986. Tim [Dlugos] tested positive

in 1987 and Donald the month after he moved to Los Angeles in 1988. Howard Brookner, who stopped taking the debilitating drug AZT so he could complete his first feature-length film (*Bloodhounds of Broadway;* it stars Madonna), was moved into an apartment in Frank's and my building and died there in 1989. Tim and Chris Cox died in 1990; Joe Brainard, then Donald, in 1994. We say "died," but of course they were killed, by a threat they never could have foreseen.

When Crase, in an essay I cited earlier, asks the reader if he or she is wondering whether he is serious about an "ill-managed president" reciting a phony poem, you know that he is. This is the same president who deliberately ignored the AIDS epidemic until May 31, 1987, six years after the first cases had been reported, essentially sanctioning suffering and death with a folksy smile.

In all of his writing, Crase gently places himself (and his mortality) into the words: he and Frank take a 50-minute subway ride to "the unfamiliar Bronx" to have dinner with Dr. Rupert C. Barneby; Howard Brookner moves into the building where he and Frank still live. Crase and Polach's wedding is reported in *The New York Times* (May 13, 2011). Their domestic relationship is one of the foundations upon which Crase's writing is built. The dead and living are everywhere.

In *AMERIFIL.TXT,* under the category "Sons and Lovers," Crase cited the following:

> Be an opener of doors for such as come after thee, and do not try to make the universe a blind alley.
>
> —*Ralph Waldo Emerson*

Whoever or whatever he is writing about, in whatever form he explores—from poems to essays to biography to memoir—Crase shows us something about ourselves in the constant commotion of what we inhabit.

Charles North Shows Us How to Read without Relying on Theories

I missed *States of the Art: Selected Essays, Interviews, and Other Prose 1975–2014* (Pressed Wafer, 2017) by Charles North when it first came out, but—unlike certain movies—I was able to get my hands on a copy. North's book is a miscellany of the different forms he has practiced over the past 40 years: art reviews done for *Art in America;* book reviews that appeared in little magazines and periodicals; introductions at poetry readings he has hosted; a letter to the *New York Review of Books* in which he takes issue with "Helen Vendler's positive review of James Schuyler's *Selected Poems*"; an interview with the poet Angie Mlinko; seven journal entries; a note on how he came to write his "first baseball lineup poem," a form he invented; and eulogies made at memorials.

States of the Art is divided into five sections. The first three were originally collected in *No Other Way: Selected Prose* (Hanging Loose, 1998), which has long been out of print. This book reprints that earlier selection as well as includes about 100 pages of pieces North has written between 1999 and 2014. An occasional writer of criticism and related forms, it is good to have all the critical writing that North wishes to save gathered in one place. The book is around 250 pages—not hefty, weight-wise—and definitely something to keep nearby. There are so many pieces that I liked in this collection that I cannot name a definitive favorite; what I have is more like a top ten list.

North might be an occasional writer of critical prose, but he takes each situation seriously, as if his life depended on it, which it does. He can be anecdotal and analytical, effortlessly moving from one mode to another, as he does in his piece on Jim Brodey, which he read at the poet's memorial in 1993. It reminded me of how good Brodey could be, prompting me to move his books from the shelf to the ever-shifting, sprawling pile on the table near my desk, which is one thing criticism is supposed to do: get you to read, look, and think.

North's review of F. T. Prince's *Collected Poems,* which was "cavalierly dismissed by the *New York Times* reviewer," is a model of a nuanced response based on close reading:

> Prince's extraordinary gifts create extravagant expectations. Which brings up the continuing, fascinating (at least to me) issue of clarity vs. reticence. Can repression be good for the poet, as opposed to the patient? Marianne Moore's advice to be clear as your natural reticence allows you is only partly helpful here. The difficulty in letting feeling out, explicit in the "Memoirs" and implicit in his exiled heroes and virtual obsession with isolation and loss, underlies the earlier poems' emotional charge. Once feeling makes it out into the open, no disguises, the scholar appears to gain the upper hand: decorum overrides passion. I can't think of a happier find, for anyone, than this poet's hitting upon the dramatic monologue with its built-in distancing and licensing, post-Browning and post-Pound. It let him produce the sinewy, sensual (actually quite sexy) poems he should be famous for.

This is criticism at its best: a passionate, sympathetic reading that acknowledges the poet's limitations while clarifying the particular strengths. You are not apt to read criticism this sensitive and analytical by well-known academic critics such as Helen Vendler or Marjorie Perloff, who can seem to be unduly motivated by a desire to control the narrative of what gets read and what gets ignored. Instead of trying to attain and consolidate power (and becoming a reliable commodity in the process), North is engaged with something more elusive and humbling: what happens when he reads a poem.

This is how he begins his letter "To *The New York Review of Books*":

> This is occasioned by Helen Vendler's positive review of James Schuyler's *Selected Poems* (*NYR,* September 29, 1988), toward

which anyone in his right mind, at least anyone who cares about modern poetry, ought to feel gratitude. The review accounts for some of Schuyler's aesthetic waywardness, his position apart, not only from well-known mainstreams historical and contemporary, but also from those New York School poets with whom he is often associated. It places him in a context of important forerunners–Hopkins, Whitman, Stein, and Stevens, to name a few. And it takes Schuyler's life's work seriously, as few critics have done, and makes useful points about his embracing of the banal and homespun along with the extraordinary. I respect Helen Vendler and her continuing efforts to come to terms with those who are writing at the same time she is, by no means an easy task in the postmodern world, if it ever was. What leaves me uneasy is her approach.

By the time the reader reaches the last sentence of this extraordinarily precise, subtly gradated paragraph–exemplary of the writer's close, sympathetic reading—you know that what is going to follow will be revelatory and useful, which it is.

While North recognizes that "Vendler is one of the few intelligent and knowledgeable writers to tackle the difficult business of contemporary poetry without using up that poetry as part of some theoretical program," he questions her assumptions:

> […] but must we ride the same horses time and again, as if the unspoken principle were to plunge a poet into an American mainstream, with familiar American landmarks dotting the shore (in or counter to the mainstream, it amounts to the same thing), [in order] to proclaim the writer worth attention–while leaving out all, or at least a good deal of it, that really makes him worth attention [?] Schuyler has written some of the most beautiful poems of the last thirty years, including poems that fit on half a page, and it's hard to imagine a reader gaining a sense of that from this review.

This is what North does in his readings of John Wheelwright, Joe Ceravolo, Tony Towle, Barbara Guest, Frank Lima, Paul Violi, and others: he shows what really makes their work "worth attention." His essay on Frank O'Hara's relationship to the Russian experimental poet and playwright, Vladimir Mayakovsky, is brilliant, as is everything he says about Schuyler and his poems.

While I have concentrated mostly on his reading of poetry, there is much else to recommend in this book. Many writers grow into their reviews over time: they become better at it. North was very good from the start. His review of Richard Tuttle's controversial retrospective at the Whitney Museum of American Art in 1975, which likely led to the firing of the curator Marcia Tucker, never gets caught up in the hoopla of its "champions and its detractors." Rather, as with his reading of poetry, North pays close attention to what is in front of him, never resorting to what he calls, in another context, a "theoretical program." His review of Aristodemis Kaldis has one of the best opening sentences: "A Kaldis landscape is like an overloaded closet, but the pleasures of what is likely to topple on you more than make up for the blow." You keep reading because you want to know where North is going take you. This is true of the entire book, even in pieces that are not as good as the best ones he has written (his 1977 review of Alma Thomas's paintings is the weakest thing in the book, and it is still better than most reviews of her work at the time) are worth reading. The very first essay announces North's impulse throughout the collection. It is a response to Harold Bloom's "highly laudatory article on John Ashbery (*Salmagundi*, Spring–Summer 1973), which left [him] unexpectedly dismayed." Here is one reason for his consternation:

> However interesting his theory may be to structuralists or other combatants of criticism, he's not really dealing with the work of art. As idolatrous as his praise is at times, it hides its reason for being so.

As North goes on to state, in response to Bloom's theory of poetry, which he fleshed out in *The Anxiety of Influence* (1973):

> The point is that criticism has shaky ground to operate on but better shaky than papier-mâché, better to fumble around and dig out possibilities and be aware they're that, than to be content with systems.

The underappreciated belletrist tradition in America, which dates back at least to Edgar Allan Poe, and includes such modern examples as Sadakichi Hartmann's writings on photography, Edwin Denby's dance reviews, John Ashbery's art criticism, James Baldwin's essays on race, Susan Stewart's essays on art, and James Agee's film criticism, is alive and well, and North's *States of the Art: Selected Essays, Interviews, and Other Prose 1975–2014* proves it.

The Many Pleasures of Reading Donald Britton's Poems

This slim volume of poetry might stir up the tears you have been keeping inside you, especially if, like me, you are old enough to remember the 1980s and the AIDS epidemic, the seemingly endless roll call of people you knew and didn't know who died horribly. It was one of the many black holes in American history from which a few bright lights emerged. One of them is the publication of *In the Empire of the Air: The Poems of Donald Britton,* edited by Reginald Shepherd and Philip Clark.

Clark co-edited *Persistent Voices: Poetry by Writers Lost to AIDS* (2010), with David Groff. As he tells us in his modestly written "Preface," when Shepherd, who first thought of putting together a volume of Britton's poems, heard about the anthology that Clark was in the process of assembling, he contacted him to make sure Britton's work was included. When Shepherd died, Clark finished the project. Along with their essays, there is an "Afterword" by Douglas Crase in which he writes movingly about the New York poetry circles that he and Britton moved in during the '80s. Crase is right when he opens his "Afterword" with:

> The appearance in print of the selected poems of Donald Britton is an affront to cynicism and a triumph over fate.

Often, it is poets who save other poets' works, at least until the writings are published. In this case, Nightboat is to be commended for publishing *In The Empire of the Air: The Poems of Donald Britton,* and *A Fast Life: The Collected Poems of Tim Dlugos* (2011), a friend of Britton's who also died of AIDS.

In the Empire of the Air was the title Britton chose for his second, never-published book of poems. The current volume gathers together "uncollected and unpublished poems" as well as all the poems from *Italy* (1981), his only published book, which was put out by Dennis Cooper's long defunct press, Little Caesar. Although the collection is less than 100 pages of poetry, it adds up to a remarkable body of work; having negotiated his way through the Language poets and the poets connected with the New York School (who, under the spell of Frank O'Hara, practiced what Eileen Myles called "exalted mundanity"), Britton arrived at a place all his own by the time he was in his late twenties. He writes about himself with the detachment of a scientist who is looking at his subject through a microscope, or the wrong end of a telescope. This is the poem "A Real Life" in its entirety:

> I awaken–
> a clam between
> cool sheets
> A nude bather
> like Cezanne's
> And showering
> in the dark
> I imagine
> my body.

This is not a variation of O'Hara's "I do this, I do that," because nothing happens in the poem. The poet is alone. He gets up and showers in the dark. Britton's subject is a state of awareness that underscores his sense of displacement from himself. He neither inhabits his body nor is he cut off from it. The writing is terse and quick. Everything has been pared down, "I awaken," he writes, and then becomes "a clam between / cool sheets." One hears "happy as a clam" and "clammy" reverberating through Britton's line. He may have been inspired by John Ashbery's attention to clichés and banal chatter, but he's the one who wrote/heard it where he did.

Britton can write erotically charged poems. This is the last stanza of "Hart Crane Saved from Drowning (Pines 1926)":

> But the naked Cubano all testicles and rod
> laving amid ripe tendril of the water ridges
> trumped fate with desire: so he postponed his resolve
> for six years and a boat and a woman

In its momentary strangeness, "laving" carries the sonic traces of three other words: loving, living and laughing. The elemental scene of a naked man washing himself persuades Crane to change his mind about drowning himself. In his precise attention to sound, Britton is also responding to the many critics who find Crane's writing problematic because it emphasizes sound over sense.

He can write with a cool, sympathetic detachment. This how the poem "Amorous Day" begins:

> An amorous day and not to be denied:
> toothpaste coffee toast portend
> the cold sea-swell of my urges.
> Aromatic whisker parted,
> raw and swollen testicle tamed, incognito–
> and every pustule in its place.

Everything—from the "toothpaste" to the "cold sea-swell of [his] urges" to "every pustule in its place"—is treated with the same amount of attention and emotional reserve. It is like a painting by Alex Katz with a Francis Bacon painting lurking inside. One's private moments and inner life meld with one's presentation of the self in public. The point is to keep everything in its place without denying the "urges."

Britton's sympathetic detachment comes out of necessity. Even in his coolest, most measured takes, there is an urgency that infuses his poems with an emotional charge. Still, it is emotion experienced from a self-protective distance. This is how the poem, "My Mother's Afternoon Nap" ends:

> She feels the pillow crease her cheek,
> uncertain in the ache of waking.
> No gloss of love dispels

John Yau

> the image of those angels she attends,
> bow-tied detectives who take her away

These four works appear in the section of "Uncollected and Unpublished Poems," the section that opens the book. The middle section is Italy, which came out when Britton was thirty and clearly a masterful poet, able to begin the poem, "November" with this stanza:

> Tonight you are privy
> To the stars' most intimate
> Thoughts about you. Under
> Their menace, edges of furniture
> Seem like old news
> As tears fall single file.

The poems he selected for his second, unpublished collection close out what amounts to a selected poems. Britton's poems are condensed and expansive. Attentive to line breaks, he is able to move from perception to perception in a blink.

> Above and beyond this aimlessness
> Light in fistfuls
> Scores the upside-down window on a blond floor
> The skywriting's reflected backwards in
> And red buildings lop off the sky
> Somewhere down near where the canal starts
> Ringing like glass
> To be near the flower you think is dead.
>   ("Four Poems" p. 43)

I cannot do better than Crase in describing Britton's accomplishment: "The language Donald achieved in his poems was frequently so ravishing that one could feel the pleasure of his mind as it coursed over the emerging syntax, a kind of pleasure he identified indelibly in "Winter Garden" as 'the ever-skating decimals' joy.'" It is this pleasure that the patient reader encounters in Britton's poems, his discovery of what can be done with language as well as what it can reveal ("as a mirror / Hides its feelings, or a photograph / Is respected for holding no opinion."). He didn't use words to write a poem. He wrote from inside language—as from inside a mirror or photograph—because he lived there as much as he inhabited the world. Many of the poems are haunted by Britton's awareness that he lived on the cusp of eternity ("sadness surges in, / a passing-windshield light-effect / on the ceiling"). Little did he know that it would grab him so soon.

Recounting all the friends of his who died, starting in 1984 and culminating with Britton's death in 1994, Crase writes: "We say 'died,' but of course they were killed, by a threat they could never have foreseen." This is the fate and government policy (the "Reagan Years") over which Britton's poems accord a belated triumph and affront.

Killed by the State

A few weeks ago, while I was reading *In the Empire of the Air: The Poems of Donald Britton,* edited by Reginald Shepherd and Philip Clark, I was reminded of *A Fast Life: The Collected Poems of Tim Dlugos* (2011), edited by David Trinidad. This happens with poetry—one poem or book leads to another, like a chain letter. Britton and Dlugos were friends, but their writing could not be more different. For one thing, Britton's selection amounts to less than 100 pages, while Dlugos's is over 600. Ted Berrigan called Dlugos "The Frank O'Hara of his generation." The comparison is both apt and beside the point. Dlugos's poems need to be read for what they are, indispensable testimony of an age and time.

Without dwelling on the biography, which can be gotten from Trinidad's "Introduction" and "Chronology," it is enough to say here that Dlugos (1950–1990) and Britton (1951–1994) were good friends, and that Dlugos dedicated the poem "Qum" to Britton. Both died of AIDS or, as Douglas Crase correctly writes in his "Afterword" to Britton's *In the Empire of the Air:*

> We say 'died,' but of course they were killed, by a threat they could never have foreseen.

Trinidad usefully divides the poems into the cities where Dlugos lived: Philadelphia, 1970–1973; Washington, D.C., 1973–1976; Manhattan and Brooklyn, 1976–1988; New Haven and Manhattan, 1988–1990. In twenty years, the reader goes from the exuberant disclosures of a young poet absorbing Frank O'Hara's dictum, "I do this, I do that" to the poems written after he tested positive for HIV (November 1987) and began studying at Yale Divinity School, with the intention of becoming a priest in the Episcopal Church.

According to Trinidad's useful chronology of Dlugos's life, after two years writing "sporadically" from 1985 until 1987, he began writing "regularly" in 1988.

Dlugos's last poems amount to a diary of a man who learns that he is under a death sentence. For all of their personal revelations and close observation of his life and those around him, Dlugos's poems are on the opposite end of the spectrum from the so-called confessional mode of Robert Lowell, Anne Sexton and Sylvia Plath. The poem "Powerless," which is about going to his first AA meeting and much else, begins:

> I was a mess. I felt like crying
> all the time.

At no point does Dlugos ask for our sympathy. In fact, despite hitting bottom, there is a warmth and humor to the poem:

> I made a call and went to my first
> meeting a few blocks away. I'd been wondering
> where all the healthy, handsome people
> in West Hollywood had disappeared to.
> I found out. An old guy
> with a shaven head and twenty years
> spoke first.

If Dlugos ever steps out of the poem, it is to recollect passion not in tranquility but in a lucid fever that ought to burn through any aesthetic objection you might have ("Too New York School" or "Not experimental enough") unless, of course, you need to cling to those ideals to get through the day. Dlugos learned to let go of everything. In the poem "No Voice," we read:

> You made pissing away
> your gifts look like an art form,
> but striking a profile
> with your arm akimbo

> on the moving sidewalk headed
> toward the precipice cheapens
> every death, not just your own.

Dlugos uses the vernacular to apprehend the figure he is describing. There is no reliance on metaphor, no extravagant gesture or knowing aside. Such directness comes from William Carlos Williams. It looks easy, but it isn't. What's not apparent is how much Dlugos has cut away as he moves smoothly from one perception to another. "No Voice" ends:

> Scarecrow, genius, major
> minor artist and the keenest
> critic of your brief day: it's no faux pas
> to want to stay.

Dlugos did not romanticize suffering or death. He was a poet, a homosexual, and a political and social activist. But he did not consider himself to be a special case and would never compare himself to a Jew being sent to "to Dachau, Auschwitz, Belsen" as Plath did. In the poems he writes in the last two years of his life the reader will come across "Radiant Child," which was written on February 16, 1990, the day Keith Haring died of AIDS at the age of thirty-one.

> A baby in a desert
> boom town wears a T-shirt
> on which is an image
> of the Radiant Child.
> The infant is no larger
> than a young man's hand,
> the generous hand of the artist
> who died this afternoon.
> By the time she's old enough
> to crawl like the child
> in the drawing, his hand
> will wear a coat of dust,
> or long ago have been

> reduced to ash. Ashley
> Noel Snow, my lover's niece,
> a brand-new life in a T-shirt
> from the Pop Shop, in a snapshot
> he would have loved to see.

The pared-down vernacular that Dlugos got from O'Hara and Williams is always linked to immediate, everyday perceptions filtered through a particular consciousness; it is evidence of his engagement with the present, fully aware that he has little time left in this world. Present in his work from the beginning, it is this directness that remains fresh. We read the poem and hear him speaking. The poet is in the room with us, talking gently in a soft, unprotected voice. There are no rhetorical flourishes, no attempts to impress us with his knowledge or experience.

In "Signs of Madness," Dlugos writes:

> Recognizing strings
> of coincidence as having
> baleful or hermetic meaning,
> e.g. the fact that each
> of Ronald Wilson
> Reagan's three names has
> six letters, Mark of
> the Apocalyptic Beast,
> languorous and toothless
> though it would have to be
> to fit that application.

This is how Dlugos characterizes Reagan, who did not acknowledge the AIDS epidemic until May 31, 1987, six years after the first cases had been reported. He may be the Apocalyptic Beast, but he is also lazy and toothless.

In the late '80s, after Dlugos was diagnosed HIV positive, he remembers the literary critic David Kalstone, whose apartment on West 22nd Street he visited "on a winter day / in 1976" and a book he borrowed and never returned. Ten years later, in 1986, Kalstone died of AIDS at the age of fifty-three. In his masterpiece—what else to call it?—"G-9," Dlugos writes:

> My first time here on G-9,
> the AIDS ward, the cheery
> D & D building intentionality
> of the décor that made me feel
> like jumping out the window.

No matter the situation, Dlugos remains open to his feelings of vulnerability and never tries to step away from them. "D.O.A.," the last poem Dlugos wrote before dying of AIDS three months later, and the last poem in the book, should be required reading in every literature class.

A Forensic Poet for Our Time

What do you do, if you are a poet who has never " been comfortable with autobiographical material?" Monica Youn's poems brim with answers to this question that a younger poet might do well to notice. In her recent book, *Blackacre: Poems,* she refracts the particulars of her life through different prisms: Francois Villon's "Ballade des Pendus" ("Ballad of the Hanged Men"), in which a group of hanged men speak in a collective voice; the next-to-last shot in Michelangelo Antonioni's *The Passenger* (1975), starring Jack Nicholson and Maria Schneider; John Milton's "Sonnet 19 (*On his Blindness*)."

Executed by hanging, assuming a dead man's identity, or going blind—many of the figures Youn focuses on exist in an extreme state, fundamentally cut off from others. For the most part, Youn does not turn her extreme figures into occasions for a dramatic monologue. Rather, she approaches the subject from different perspectives. The three-line poem "Portrait of a Hanged Man" is further inflected by her reading of "St. Julian" (1455) by Piero della Francesca. It opens with this line:

> The eyes / as if / pinned in / place tacked / up at / the corners / then pulled / taut then

Another poem in the series, "Exhibition of the Hanged Man," opens with these lines:

> To *spectate*
> is a verb

> that does not
> mean *to watch*.
>
> It is
> intransitive.
>
> Although
> the Latin root
>
> *spectare*
> means to watch;
>
> nonetheless,
> it is wrong
>
> to say
> *you spectate me;*
>
> but not wrong
> to say
>
> *you watch me.*

Youn recognizes that whoever or whatever we are, our existence and how we might understand that contingent condition takes place in language. What connects one pronoun to another? What is looking? What is seeing? What happens when these acts occur?

> I become
>
> temporal; bounded
> in time. I am
>
> an event now,
> a kind of show.

> I entertain
> visitors.

Who are the "visitors?" What is being an "event" akin to? What connections and resonances might the reader make of this in our media-saturated world? Youn's poems arise out of close reading and close looking. Her approach is forensic—measured and detailed. When she does approach the explicitly autobiographical, we don't read "I," but "you," as in: "But what is it you want? For example, you are in a high-school parking lot." The very different and distinct angles through which Youn pulls the precise elements of her life seem to become more specific, even as they become more distanced from the transparent "I" long associated with the autobiographical: this is a compelling paradox (or Gordian knot) animating her poetry. We stop thinking about whether or not the poem is about the author, and begin thinking about language and how it works, what being conscious of being on the cusp of infinity stirs up.

Blackacre is practically a handbook on poetics. The reader should delight in the way Youn breaks up her lines horizontally, how she groups words into phrases at once sonorous and mineral-like ("red mullions flaunting"), the shifts in tonal registers, the cool surfaces she achieves and the intense heat they evoke. There are long skinny poems, prose poems, a poem where every section begins with the conditional "as if." She goes from the documentarian mode to the mythic. In addition to Latin etymology, movies, and Piero della Francesca, she brings in urban legends and slang—the high and low, or what Clement Greenberg called "avant-garde and kitsch," without ever devolving into the latter. Youn speaks to the reader in a tone that is simultaneously confidential and dispassionate; it is a voice that has traveled a long distance across many different kinds of territory.

There are many standout poems in this dazzling collection. What strikes me each time I read these poems—and some I have read many times—is that I never feel as if the poet is showing off. Youn never comes across as trying to impress the reader with her knowledge, which is considerable. No matter how steeped in etymology, art history, history, literature, and law—branches of knowledge Youn clearly knows—each poem feels urgent and necessary.

In the prose poem "Blueacre," Youn isolates and measures the penultimate shot of Antonioni's *The Passenger*, when the camera looks through a hotel window, "a seven-minute-long, single-take tracking shot in which the camera adopts the perspective of David Locke (Jack Nicholson), and is positioned to look out of his hotel window," the poet tells us in the "Notes" at the back of the book. It is an incrementally built catalogue of heightened details that slows down our sense of time. The window becomes a stage—people move across it. Different sounds are registered. The camera (poem) is a state of consciousness, but to what end is never stated.

Narrative offers resolution or revelation, conditions that have become conventional in many poems. We know how it will all end long before we finish the last line. This never happens in a Youn poem. And yet, as in Antonioni's film, we cannot turn our eyes away, cannot stop reading. We soak up the details, realizing surely how often we are not present. The desire to be present is what drives Youn's poems. Like Antonioni's camera, she doesn't flinch.

In Youn's "Notes," we learn that:

> The term 'Blackacre' is a legal fiction first used by the great English legal scholar Sir Edward Coke in a 1628 treatise. In Anglo-American legal parlance, "Blackacre" is a standard placeholder used to denote a fictional piece of land, often a bequest, much as the term "John Doe" is used to indicate a fictional or anonymous individual.

Writing about the title poem, "Blackacre," on *Harriet,* the Poetry Foundation's online blog, Youn also describes her poetics:

> We never start with a blank slate—each acre has been previously tenanted, enriched and depleted, built up and demolished. What are the limits of the imagination's ability to transform what is given?

In these two sentences Youn defines a position that rejects the conceptualist "uncreative" stance that one "massages" the found (or "tenanted") text, but cannot otherwise do anything to it, as well as distances herself from those poets for whom the lyric "I" is central. Her poem "Brownacre" offers many pleasures, including the way she stands the familiar operating procedure of a confessional poem on its head. Instead of focusing on a traumatic event and the bruised (damaged, broken) feelings that result, Youn writes:

> I wasn't paying attention: I was watching the thing
> you had just said to me still hanging in the air between us,

We never learn what "you" said, and we don't have to, do we? Not when we read hallucinatory lines like these, as the poet's attention focuses on the "thing [...] [still hanging in the air between us:"

> the molecules of concrete coalescing grain by grain
> into a corrugated pillar topped by a cloud–a tree form:

In the masterful "Blackacre," the book's title poem, Youn reads Milton's famous sonnet on being blind. "Blackacre" consists of fourteen numbered sections in prose; it is both a reading of poem and, as Youn writes on *Harriet:*

> [...] about my "barrenness," my desire to have a child who would be genetically "mine," my increasingly irrational pursuit of that desire, its long-drawn-out failure, the fallout of recriminations and regrets, and my eventual decision to have a child by other means.

Through her close reading of Milton's poem, she discovers an affinity between her state and Milton's:

> My mistake was similar. I came to consider my body–its tug-of-war tautnesses and slacknesses–to be entirely my own, an appliance for generating various textures and temperatures of friction.

Youn's use of "appliance" brings us back into the mediation from an unexpected angle. An "appliance" is a utensil used to perform a specific task, which is typically domestic. How many different and distinct ways might we consider her use of "appliance?"

Each of the fourteen sections of "Blackacre" is a prose poem, which corresponds, improvises upon, dances with some part of Milton's fourteen- line, dense, rhyming sonnet. Youn is fearless throughout the poem, bringing the reader to disturbing, intriguing states that she points to but never explains:

> [...] Does the wideness of the wide-legged girl evoke a kind of blindness, a dark room where one might blunder into strangers, the way two men once met each other in me.

Youn examines the body, language, and the language used to describe the female body. The tone can, by turns, be interrogatory, tender, coldly scientific, analytical, allegorical, plain and painful, all without ever asking for sympathy or singling herself out. In every generation there are a handful of poets who challenge the way we think about language and how it is used. Youn is part of that distinguished company.

The Confessional Poem Made New

More than thirty years have passed between Bill Zavatsky's first full-length book, *Theories of Rain and Other Poems* (1975) and his second full-length book, *X Marks the Spot* (2006). And yet, while Zavatsky wasn't gaining a reputation as a poet in the interim, he certainly has been in the thick of things. In the 1970s, Zavatsky, who was in his early thirties, was the director of the important small press SUN and *SUN* magazine.

Under his direction, SUN published translations of *Sens Plastique* by the Mauritanian writer and aphorist Malcolm de Chazal, *The Dice Cup: Selected Prose Poems* by Max Jacob, *The Sun Placed in the Abyss and Other Texts* by Francis Ponge, and *How I Wrote Certain of My Books* by Raymond Roussel. The translators included John Ashbery, David Ball, Michael Brownstein, Serge Gavronsky, Ron Padgett, Zack Rogow, Trevor Winkfield, and Zavatsky himself.

In addition to the translations, SUN published books by George Economou, Jaimy Gordon, Michael Heller, Bill Knott, Philip Lopate, Michael O'Brien, Ron Padgett, Peter Scheldahl, James Schuyler, Harvey Shapiro, Tony Towle, Paul Violi, and Marjorie Welish—an electic list guided by sensibility rather than ideology.

Zavatsky's generosity alone constitutes a major contribution to American literature. For one thing, the translations introduced a younger generation of writers (myself included) to the work of little-known foreign authors (de Chazal and Jacob), as well as little-known texts by Ponge and Roussel. And, if this was not enough, Zavatsky was the first to publish books by Lopate and Welish, as well as reprint Schuyler's *Freely Espousing*.

Along with publishing books by others, he and Padgett co-translated *The Poems of A. O. Barnabooth* by Valery Larbaud, and with Zack Rogow he co-translated *Earthlight: Poems by Andre Breton*. Published in *SUN*, his translations of Robert Desnos remain among the best.

Given Zavatsky's first book of poems, and the considerable time he has devoted to publishing poets who are associated with the New York School, as well as his own beautiful translations of Breton and Jacob, among others, the reader might reasonably expect the poems in *X Marks the Spot* to show traces of his love for Surrealism, the hermetic and aphoristic. The fact is that Zavatsky has done the one thing that we least expect of others, but often secretly desire for ourselves; he has reinvented himself and, in the process of doing so, he has reinvigorated a form of poetry that can be characterized as transparent, autobiographical, and confessional.

Zavatsky has not only transformed the predictability of the confessional poem into a capacious form capable of being simultaneously funny and horrifying, but he has also revealed that mode's most obvious avoidance, which is both exposing and owning one's familiar acts of self-pity (aka self-loathing). This is the demon Sylvia Plath, Robert Lowell, Anne Sexton and their heirs rigorously avoid, perhaps because it cuts much too close to the bone. Better to put the blame on father, daddy, or Satan than to look at yourself with a magnifying glass.

Zavatsky does something close to the opposite of what the confessional poets do with self-pity. He replaces its claustrophobic subjectivity with a cool objectivity that is as heartbreaking and lyrical as the music of jazz pianist Bill Evans (there is a wonderful poem for him in the book).In the book's title poem, "Where X Marks the Spot," the reader comes across these lines about 50 lines into the poem:

> I felt life fall away from me. Again I felt
> that I would never be happy. I felt the words
> that I wanted to say to you leaving me, rushing
> out of my chest like dead air, until I had no more words
> to say. I seemed to cut and swallow my food
> as if it were me myself that stuck in pieces

> on the end of the fork I had raised to my mouth.
> Had I been chewing on my own flesh?
> Self-Pity the Devourer took me by the hand
> that held the fork, and once again I feasted
> on all that was dark and hopeless in myself,
> in lieu of all that was beautiful, desirable,
> and unattainable in you.

A longtime jazz pianist, Zavatsky never devolves into that declarative insistence that often gets confused with sincerity. His language shifts seamlessly from the transparent ("I seemed to cut and swallow my food ...") to the darkly comic ("Had I been chewing on my own flesh?"), to an allegorical personification at once medieval and contemporary ("Self-Pity the Devourer took me by the hand / that held the fork"), while also establishing a resonant juxtaposition. A suddenly dislocated being, the narrator is both inside and outside himself.

Zavatsky's ability to shift perspective is one of the things that distinguish his work from the confessional poets, the majority of whom are stuck in their "I." For the most part, they inhabit a landscape that is decidedly 19th-century, which is to say a place unaffected by the innovative perceptions that characterize Cubism, Futurism, and Surrealism. Zavatsky has transformed his knowledge of Surrealism's surprising juxtapositions and Cubism's dislocations into a mode of perception that is both open to the world and vulnerable to the mind's wandering. His poems are not made up of surface gestures. They are layered and sinuous, the direction of the narrative thrust turning, twisting, and jumping in ways that catches us up.

> But I remember Danny:
> ugly string tie below thick eyeglasses,
> forehead shining under greasy wedge of hair.
> The lights were down, he could see everything.
> Tonight, as leader, he called the shots. No more
> crummy houses to paint, no more used-car hustles–
> Danny had recently filed for bankruptcy.

John Yau

> I had spotted it in the paper.
> Of course, I never mentioned it; besides,
> Danny seemed untouched by this swipe of Fate,
> a man who picked himself up, said "Fuck you!"
> to the heavens with his hands, and went his way.

Zavatsky's description of a sleazy. small-time musician is both biblical and cinematic, sad and comical. It is only a small part of the poem, "THE WOMAN WHO DANCED AND TOOK OFF HER CLOTHES, THE WOMAN WHO SANG AND CRIED," one of the many poignant poems in this extraordinary book.

"104 Bus Uptown"—the title of the first poem in the book begins: "How bad can it be / dear wacky New York City, / when the first twelve lines / of *The Love Song of J. Alfred Prufrock* / blink down at me / from a poster on this bus...." As Zavatsky knows, each day of our lives can be a roller coaster ride, rising to that sense of urban camaraderie when you see that you are sitting on the same bus as "the beautiful actress Beverly D'Angelo," and just as quickly and unexpectedly descending, as he does in "X Marks the Spot," to depths of isolation and loneliness that each of us knows all too well:

> ... I caught a glimpse of your
> face as we put our arms around each other,
> and your face said everything to me about
> how you wasted the afternoon, how eager
> you were to speed away in your car, a mixture
> of disgust and relief that the thing would soon
> be over, that I would be crossed out forever
> from your life–and everything that I hated
> about myself, my stupid chin, my ugly nose,
> my hopeless balded head, my stuck-out ears,
> my wreck of a heart, crashed over me,
> spinning me into the vortex of self-hate
> that I have only ever let myself feel
> a little bit at a time, though it is always there.

A Thriver in the Muck

Sometimes, it is hard to remember that Social Media came along years after the rise of the personal computer and the Internet, which Al Gore called the "Information Superhighway." But like the highway in Jean-Luc Godard's apocalyptic comedy, *Weekend* (1967), the internet is littered with refuse and ugliness of all kinds: overturned vehicles and violence.

The number of places on the internet hosting manifestos, mutterings, rants, complaints, confessions, conspiracy theories and declarations of undying love has proliferated so much in the past thirty-five years that no one can keep track of them all. And with this exponential breeding—like rabbits, you might say—comes what some see as the inevitable decay and dilution of language, a further step in its entropic spiral.

The cataclysmic change that language is undergoing stems from universal access to what Marx called the means of production. More people than ever before can write down what they think, from foot fetishes to flower arranging, and post it online, knowing someone else will read it. One consequence of this is that the space between the writer and reader has gotten smaller, even as book sales continue to diminish. Are we entering the Post-Book age? To know how to spell or write a grammatically correct sentence is not required. Proofreading is a dying art. This makes a messy situation even more chaotic.

2500 Random Things about Me Too (Los Angeles: Les Figues, 2012), which has an "Introduction" by Kevin Killian, is a collection of short autobiographical ruminations that Matias Viegener posted on Facebook over a period of one hundred days. The book is divided into one hundred sections, each containing twenty-five statements, corresponding to the number of posts he made each day. According to his article, "How I Wrote a Book on Facebook" (*Huffington Post*, 9/25/2012):

> I gave myself a couple of constraints right away: The list had to be composed that day, on the spot, usually as I was online on Facebook. My goal was to be random and never repeat myself, but I also decided that I'd never re-read an old list. At first I sat by my laptop and waited for things to pop up, but after two days I started keeping a piece of paper with me and making "random" notes. What if I came up with more than 25 things that day—did I have to dump the extras? That seemed pointless, so I started a little savings account of randomness.

Despite Viegener's desire for randomness, certain preoccupations recur throughout: the death of his friend, Kathy Acker; the coming death of his dog, Peggy, who dies near the end of his 100 days; memories and fantasies having to do with sex; his childhood, which is laced with feelings of dislocation, all of which are haunted by an awareness of time passing, which is understandable given his daily routine of writing—performing and, in some sense, exposing himself—online.

The book is full of all kinds of tidbits, ranging from intimate memories to discreet gossip:

> Adam slept over a few times, and once we went to the Zen Center in the Bronx with his father, Armand, a poet, who treated me very sweetly even though I was his seventeen-year old son's legally adult boyfriend.

Elsewhere, he posts:

> And last week, another friend who hates his success. Everyone watches you, he says, and waits for one misstep. All the ones who stood in the way now suck up to you, and all your old supporters can't wait to see you stumble.

The list also includes all kinds of unclassifiable information:

> There is another thing going around online where you find your

porn name by combining the name of your first pet with the street you lived on as a kid, which makes my porn name Fluffy City.

And there are many instances of what Willem de Kooning referred to as "slippery glimpse[s]."

> The teacher asked them what was going on. They just got up and walked away, their pants covered in mud.

At one point, Viegener goes to Colombia and posts a number of entries about his trip, which lasts ten days (sections xxxix–xlix). In section lxxvii, he alternates posts about his aging dog Peggy and his friend Kathy Acker: "I've been visiting Kathy's death." In section xlv, he posts: "I remember seeing a stray dog rotting by the side of the road in Tijuana, while Kathy was dying in a hospital nearby."

It seems to me that when Viegener was making his daily post, he wasn't thinking about what he would write the next day or the day after—that the very form of the writing and its being made instantly public counteracted any ability to step outside of time and think about what to do in the next chapter. In this sense, his public ritual of diaristic short entries made it difficult to be self-reflective. At the same time, while *2500 Random Things about Me Too* is comprised largely of surfaces, the veneer of impenetrability—something we associate with the work of Andy Warhol—isn't to be found in Viegener's posts, where he often writes about his doubts:

> I am using the most obvious devices here: mixing genres or styles, for example pairing the sentimental with the obscene.

2500 Random Things about Me Too is a list that wanders all over the place, a collection of statements, phrases, contradictions, disclosures, one-word entries. At points, the author seems to be thinking out loud (or in print). He turns things over, changes his mind, makes assertions and hesitates. At other times he seems almost to be stammering. Every now and then, a narrative begins to emerge only to abruptly shift into a completely different direction. It is, one might say, a form of free association as long as we acknowledge no association is completely free.

The reader learns a lot about the author, but also, in some ways, nearly nothing, which is true of everyone: "I love movies that make me cry. I loved *Beaches*." Viegener is artful about his artlessness and knows what he is up to, writing-wise. One entry reads: "It's like a combination of John Cage and Joe Brainard, writing yourself out in bits and pieces." He follows this entry with: "Both of them were gay too. Can a gay man's life only be told in random fragments?"

He also writes these two consecutive entries:

The list is a bastard form, meant to compartmentalize the wildness of things.

The list is the instrumentalization of language.

I have only one small quibble with this marvelous book. I don't think fragmentation is only true for gay men. It is a condition that we all experience, but which experimental writers are more likely to find ways to deal with, while conventional writers continue to think that their lives add up, finding solace in narrative.

Jennifer Reeves, Writer and Artist

Prepare to be completely disarmed by Jennifer Wynn Reeves's honesty, tenderness, humor, and intensity, her sexual focus, her thoughts about art and artists, and her unembarrassed chronicle of her fatal illness. Dashing from precise outward observations to inward reflections and flights of the imagination without ever pausing to catch her breath, Reeves's writing dissolves all kinds of boundaries, particularly those separating private life from public presence. She is a writer and artist who transports us to a world brimming with wonder.

Reeves's writing is compressed and graceful, stripped down, always chugging along. This is how her entry for "May 13, 2010" begins:

> He died first. She died second. He was an early riser. She was a night owl. He'd slather mile-high slabs of butter on his toast, would bring her breakfast in bed, called her "honey". He wore a bag on his gut. She was infertile and wickedly sarcastic. She put lemon zest in raisin pie. He had a horse named Dan. She had four poodles. Ahab, Anthony, Anita, Allegra. She wore her glasses around her neck.

This is only about half the entry. Once you begin, you don't want to stop. Everything in this passage is necessary and tight: all the sentences miraculously fit together without ever becoming predictable. We never learn why every poodle's name begins with "A" nor does the author comment on her deadpan observation that "She was infertile and wickedly sarcastic." The writing is particular and rhythmic. I was not surprised to learn that Reeves took "ballet, piano, singing, violin, swimming, golf and tennis lessons" when she was a child and started out as a "music major" in college. No matter how harrowing or personal the material might be, Reeves never seems to falter or lose her balance.

A figure-skater in prose, Reeves makes impossible leaps and sudden switches feel inevitable. She speaks to her readers in an intimate, personable tone about all kinds of subjects. And yet, even after you've become familiar with her voice, she will surprise you and make the hair on your arms stand up. This is what Reeves has accomplished: she creates a palpable world and brings you, the reader, completely into it. Her writings leave you with an indefinable taste, touch, smell, and much, much more. She is one of those rare writers whose work you cannot get enough of, which makes the publication of *Jennifer's Book* a reason for joy, as it is likely that new readers will discover the work of someone they had not known before.

Like her art, which resists categorization, this book will occupy a singular place on your shelf and—dare I say it—in your heart. To be a fan of Reeves is to wish that fate had given her more time. In 2008, Reeves became a dynamic presence on Facebook, where she paired her sharply compressed observations with images that ranged from her artwork to family photographs to objects from her life. Her juxtapositions of text and image quickly gained a large and loyal following, as well as generated an outpouring of comments and reflections.

Reeves's postings struck a chord. She was unafraid of exploring every corner of her life and her art, which she believed were inseparable. Readers were moved by her candor, vulnerability, and tact: she had no axe to grind, no agenda to put forth. She was not interested in gaining followers, but in the revelations unearthed in the process of creation. She wanted to be astonished and she wanted to chronicle her amazement at being alive. This, more than anything else, is what she wanted to share with others: an enduring joy of life no matter what cards fate deals you. For Reeves, as her readers learned in real time, those cards included an abusive marriage, bulimia, an ovariectomy when she was forty-seven, a schizophrenic mother, a murdered father, who was shot in the head, leaving her to be raised by her grandmother, and her diagnosis of terminal brain cancer. At no point did she bemoan her fate, even with death galloping toward her. Her gentleness, humor, and grace are present in everything she did.

Jennifer's Book brings together a generous selection of her postings, dating from March 31, 2010, to May 9, 2014, six weeks before she died at the age of fifty-one. She wrote movingly and beautifully about art and artists, from Charles Burchfield, Anselm Kiefer, and Jonathan Lasker to Pablo Picasso and Henri Matisse. The passages she writes about artists, art, and art-making are as deep and smart and heartfelt as anything I have read, and that is a lot. She imagines Clyfford Still and Arthur Dove talking in heaven. She brings you into the domain of her erotic life and imagination without embarrassment. She writes about the difficulties of her childhood without a trace of rancor. She steps back and comments on her own writing. "Grace to be born and live as variously as possible," wrote Frank O'Hara. That grace is in everything that Reeves wrote and lived. We are lucky to have had her with us as long as we did. Read this book and celebrate her memory. Take a walk with her the only way you can.

Ann Lauterbach Expands the Possibilities of Poetry

Spell is Ann Lauterbach's tenth book of poetry. On the front cover is a silhouette of a crow's head, which William Kentridge has drawn on a page from a dictionary, using a brush loaded with dense black ink. By bringing image and word into inseparable proximity, Kentridge's drawing calls up the question: what is the relation between word and thing? (Lauterbach and Kentridge are friends, so the cover came from them rather than the publisher's designer. It should also noted—and this becomes evident in *Spell*—that Lauterbach has had a long and deep engagement with art, and written beautifully about different artists and art works.)

Visually, the crow's silhouette sits between the title above and the author's name below, with the profile of their hand-drawn letters echoing stencils and typeface. Turn the book over and you see that the crow extends to the back cover. In fact, you could say that the front cover (crow's head) is figurative and the back cover (crow's tail feathers) is abstract. Other than Kentridge's striking image, there are no blurbs beckoning the reader to discover what truths lie between the covers. Either you begin reading and fall under its spell, or you don't.

The first line of the opening poem, "Pause," reads: "The arc of distance is partial." The last line of the last poem, "The Poet," reads: "The basket marked the poem rides out into the encrypted, unreadable sea." Between these two lines, between the "distance [that] is partial" and the "encrypted, unreadable sea," the poem and poet must make their way, knowing that whatever is expressed is partial in every sense of the word. How do you get outside of yourself and your own views? This is one of the questions Lauterbach returns to in *Spell*.

The book, which contains around 135 pages of poetry, consists of 55 poems, nearly half of which are less than a page. There are poems after works by W. G. Sebald, Lucretius, and Ovid; responses to Balthus's painting, *La Chambre* (1954); Verdi's penultimate opera *Otello,* based on Shakespeare's play, *Othello;* and Claudia Rankine's books *Don't Let Me Be Lonely* and "her acclaimed 2014 *Citizen,*" as Lauterbach notes in her poem, "Wounded Evidence"; as well as a "Hymn," a "Partita," a "Spell" and an "Invocation."

Interspersed among the poems are 13 prose dialogs between "Evening" and an unnamed "I," which is clearly both the poet and not the poet. "Fact," the first dialog, begins:

—Hello, Evening.

—Hello, What's up?

—Just now a jet streamed across the sky, making a high, loud whine; my hands tingled with dread.

—It's a sound that causes alarm in many. Your experience on 9/11, living near Ground Zero, will always make this ripping roar one of terror for you. I have it, too, from time to time, with thunderstorms. It's as if all the beating hearts of the dead have gathered.

Later, in response to the poet, "Evening" declares: "Nobody mourns me. I come and I go, I do not age, or get sick, or die." Among other things, "Evening" represents change and the indefinable, akin to the "unreadable sea" upon which the poem is placed in a basket.

The poet's response opens up a paradoxical space in which this and the other dialogs unfold: "And yet, you mark time, day after day." Within this space, in which time has collapsed, "Evening" and the poet discuss many diverse subjects as well as veer off in unexpected directions.

The subjects of the dialogs include "a small still-life painting by

Chardin, *Seville Orange, Silver Goblet, Apples, Pear, and Two Bottles* (1750), that [she] saw a few days ago [...]"; the writings of Hannah Arendt, whom Lauterbach views as a touchstone, "a frequent voice for those of us who are trying to find a way from the past to the future"; memories of childhood and the different associations that can be stirred up by a word, event, or thing.

There is an easygoing banter between "Evening" and the poet, as if they are old friends, which in a sense they are. As defined by Lauterbach, the dialog can go anywhere at any time, with one voice leading and the other following or changing direction. Each of the dialogs ends with a dictionary entry for the word or words used in the title:

("fact (n.) 1530s, 'action, anything done,' especially evil deed, from Latin factum, 'an event, occurrence, deed, achievement,' [...]").

Lauterbach is fascinated by a word's etymology, and how traces of its history remain in its current usage.

What should be clear by now is that Lauterbach wants to bring every kind of writing into her work: dialog, essay, letter, diary, lyric, prose, list, philosophical investigation, dictionary entry, memory, fiction, dream, and citation. In her determined expansion of the field of poetry, she stands apart from other poets engaged in avant-garde writing, for a number of reasons. First, she rejects irony as a framing device in the exploration of the limits of language and its capacity for representation. There is never a flippant moment, which could be seen as coming from a privileged position. Second, she rejects literalism ("Facts aren't the same as persons.")

In her dialog, "Paradigm," Lauterbach writes: "to know how or if thought, when it is expressed in written language, bears a relation to the activity of worldness, or being in the world." Wary of naming, she investigates the relation of word to world and dream. The dichotomy of transparency and opacity that is often applied to poetry crumbles when it comes to Lauterbach's work: she is interested instead in what connections can be established between divergent discourses—between levels of transparency and opacity, and the contexts that can arise out of these proximities.

As she writes, in "Paradigm," of her reading of the French philosopher Jacques Rancière:

> I think he wants to suggest or possibly create links between politics and aesthetics, to insert or assert our capacity to imagine and create into our sense of politics.

The relationship between politics and aesthetics has long been a preoccupation for poets.

As Lauterbach sees it, one problem is that there are "young artists [who] are beginning to think like bean counters and rationalists," when "these realities can be addressed only by immersion in an entwined animation of knowledge with imagination." She opens her dialog, "Phenomenon," with this: "Why does it take so long for knowledge to inform behavior?"

One can read the 13 dialogs as a running commentary on the poems and on poetry. They form the book's spine. By allowing different points of view to be expressed in each of these staged encounters, Lauterbach is able to turn a subject over, examine it closely as well as speculate wildly. She introduces quotes from books she is reading, remembers moments from earlier in her life, as well as ruminates on the relation of word to phenomenon (changing reality). It seems to me that Lauterbach's dialogs, which have precedents in the dialogs between self and soul of Andrew Marvell and William Butler Yeats, is something she has invented out of necessity: she wants to expand the possibilities of poetry so that it can embrace every kind of connotative and denotative discourse, while being about language itself.

Lauterbach's poems are "entwined animation[s] of knowledge with imagination." On one hand, she is continuing, enlarging, and examining Samuel Taylor Coleridge's belief that poetry is the imagination working on the objects of life and nature. At the same time, she disagrees with his assertion that: "A poem is that species of composition which is opposed to works of science, by proposing for its immediate object pleasure, not truth [...]." In an age dominated by literalism and an insistence on facts, what possibilities can the "imagination" summon into words?

This is the complicated spatial construct that Lauterbach's poems define and inhabit. It is a space that is both mental and physical, made of all manner of stuff, from memories of childhood to what happens when you don't know where the words will take you. This is a book of misgivings, spells, invocations, dialogs, commentaries, songs, and ruminations on philosophy, poetry, art, and politics. It embraces the abstruse and the transparent, often in the same work. The language is sinuous and dazzling. There is so much going on in *Spell* that I have not processed it all. I am still mulling it over. That seems to me the strongest kind of work, the kind you don't get to the bottom of in two sittings.

The Rise and Fall of Three Actresses

At the glamorous Press Ball in Berlin, which took place on New Year's Eve 1928 and lasted well past midnight, Alfred Eisenstadt, a young photographer, took a series of photographs of three young women arm-in-arm, almost like old friends. One of the photographs, reprinted many times, has achieved an iconic status. The women were Marlene Dietrich, Anna Way Wong, and Leni Riefenstahl, and all of them were on the brink of achieving international fame and varying degrees of infamy. Wong is in the center, flanked by Riefenstahl on the right and Dietrich on the left. Dietrich clenches a cigarette holder between her teeth, her lips slightly parted. The women were modern, full of confidence and hope.

Since their deaths, all three women have been the subjects of numerous biographies, studies, and essays. Dietrich and Riefenstahl wrote memoirs, which were full of evasions and exaggerations. In Karin Weiland's double biography, *Dietrich & Riefenstahl: Hollywood, Berlin and a Century in Two Lives* (2011) and other tomes, their biographers write about Dietrich's bisexuality, which she projected onscreen, Wong negotiation of Hollywood's racism and China's outrage at the roles she took, and Riefenstahl's troubling relationship with the Nazis and her groundbreaking, controversial film, *Triumph of the Will* (1935), glorifying Adolph Hitler at the Nazis' Nuremburg Rally.

Eisenstadt's photograph shows the first Asian woman to become a Hollywood star, flanked by a German actress and singer who transformed herself over a career that lasted from the 1910 to the early 1980s, and a German filmmaker, actress, and photographer whose films Hitler, admired, championed, and supported.

Between this remarkable chance meeting and their deaths, the world has undergone convulsive events and changes pertaining to racism in Hollywood and America, anti-Semitism, displacement and migration, once-forbidden love, and patriarchal oppression of women. The lives of Dietrich, Wong, and Reifenstahl are intertwined with these changes and with one another. They give anyone interested in examining history, women's rights, racism, and much else, having to do women's personal relationships and the glass ceilings they encountered, a lot to think about.

Giving readers a lot to think about, while writing an entertaining, episodic narrative is precisely what Amanda Lee Koe has done in her marvelous debut novel, *Delayed Rays of a Star* (Nan. A. Talese/Doubleday, 2019), which centers on the three women. In the acknowledgements, Koe writes: "[...] I was waylaid instead by one faithful Alfred Eisenstadt monograph containing the curious picture (and its kinetic twin) that would begin (and end) this all."

Koe's narrative moves back and forth across time and jumps from one locale to another. It is clear from the episodes and set pieces that she has read a lot of background material, absorbed what she has read, and, and selected both major and minor incidents to fictionalize, usually by adding an array of diverse and wildly interesting characters—bit players, to use Hollywood parlance—that achieve star status. By establishing multiple view points within each episode, she is able to go down different, overlapping, and parallel paths.

In one episode, Koe effortlessly switches from Reifenstahl considering all the obstacles to making a film in the mountains, far from the war and Berlin, to a crew member, Hans Haas, recalling his service in the Afrika Korps and being hopelessly in love with fellow soldier. Like a film camera changing its focus and frame, Koe is able to draw a rich parade of characters within a historical framework created with a dense tapestry of details and feelings.

In another episode, the reader is inside Wong's head as she prepares to drive to Las Vegas to see Dietrich, now long past her prime, perform a nostalgic version of her nightclub act. Wong has not been a star in years, since she was turned down for the lead role in the 1937 film version of Pearl S. Buck's *The Good Earth* (1931). The reason she was denied the role, which went to Luise Rainer, was because she failed the screen test: "Too Chinese to play a Chinese. Does not fit my conception of what Chinese people look like. Recommend to use as atmosphere and not principal characters." Jealous and insecure, she and Dietrich have a revealing encounter, which takes place over a few hours. This is just one of the many wonderful, extended scenes in this terrific book.

Koe understands her subjects—their vanities and vulnerabilities—well enough to invent scenes that are simultaneously believable and fantastical. This is what makes the book riveting. Along with exploring their complicated feelings about each other, Koe muses on their relationships to Joseph von Sternburg, Ernest Hemingway, Erich Maria Remarque, Walter Benjamin, Joseph Goebbels, and Adolph Hitler, all of whom appear in the book (though it should be noted that Hitler is referred to as "H").

Mixing together fact and fiction, Koe has woven in material that builds upon decades of gossip and speculation. Were Dietrich and Wong lovers? Did Dietrich see or talk to anyone in the last 10 years of her life, when she lived in Paris, bedridden and alone. Koe's invented maid, Bébé, a Chinese immigrant, offers another view of Dietrich, at once tender, tough, and sympathetic. More importantly, Koe gives Bébé her own rich life and biography.

Did Riefenstahl know what would happen to the Roma and Sintli extras she had in her movie after they were sent back to the camp? Koe's nuanced handling of this well-known incident in Reifenstahl's life could stand alone as a piece of fiction, as could many of the other chapters.

My only quibble with the book is that I thought Koe could have built upon some incidents rather than changed them. In one chapter, she recounts Walter Benjamin's interview with Anna May Wong, who was in Berlin to act in Peter Eichenberg's films. Eichenberg became a Nazi sympathizer, which may be one reason why these films are not better known (and seemingly difficult to obtain).

Koe's description of the films and Wong's major roles in them are right on the money, from what I've read. Yet in the book the interview is in English, not German, as it actually was. Within a short amount of time, Wong had learned German well enough to converse with Benjamin, which both surprised and delighted him. It should also be noted that very few Chinese women were in Berlin at the time, and Wong and her sister, who accompanied her to Europe and the interview, were likely the only Asian women Benjamin ever spoke with.

By changing the language to English and including her adaption of Pauline Fran's translation of the interview, with its famous description of Wong's loose long hair as resembling "a dragon frolicking in water," I think Koe misses an opportunity to consider Wong's mastery of different languages, which gave her a certain advantage in the Berlin film world and elsewhere. In this alone, one senses the voracious depth of Wong's determination and genius.

However, my quibble is the kind you can only have with a nearly perfect novel. *Delayed Rays of a Star* is the strongest debut novel I have read in a very, very long time. Like the figures she writes about, Koe will soon become a star.

Dissolving the Boundaries of Asian American Fiction

The porous border between nature and humans has become even more so in the 12 stories in *Our Colony Beyond the City of Ruins* (Subito Press, 2018) by Janalyn Guo. None of the characters seems at all surprised by the perilous world in which they live: in the story, "Night Floats," for example, sand dunes divide a city and various inhabitants, known as "levitators" can hover high up in the air, where there are no boundaries, and dream of "circumnavigating the world on rollerblades and sailboats, hiking from Alaska to Chile, living remotely in the mountains and backcountry skiing, exploring the last of the wilderness." No matter how odd and challenging the world has become, Guo's characters have adjusted to the situation, even if they find it difficult to establish bonds with others.

In "Bloom," the collection's first story, the narrator's aunt runs "a small gua sha parlor in Fushun, China." Gua sha, also known as "coining," is an ancient Chinese practice in which someone scrapes your skin with a sharp tool. The belief is that the scraping helps the blood flow to areas of the body that are tired, stiff, and even injured. It is an extreme form of massage therapy that most likely originated in a time of debilitating manual labor.

Guo's story begins in a realist vein:

> [The gua sha parlor] was a converted storage space, squeezed tightly between an arcade and a bathhouse. If you held your ear against one wall, you could hear the plinky electronic music coming out of the gaming cabinets. If you held your ear up to the other wall, you

could hear water gurgling through the pipes and the shouting of men in the midst of their bathhouse conversations.

This is life in one of the industrial cities that have sprung up in the last 25 years in China, like the ones you see in Jia Zhangke's films, such as *24 City* (2008) and *A Touch of Sin* (2013). What is immediately clear is Guo has an eye for the telling detail. Each sentence is smooth and precise, conveying texture, smells, and sights. The writing is sensuous, and that in itself quickly pulled me in: I became an avid reader, curious to learn what happens next. And what happens next in this story starts out innocuous enough: "An abundance of motes, spores, and seedpods rained down on us that spring."

From that sentence the narrator effortlessly pivots to a conversation she is having with her aunt as they take a walk:

> She told me about a small batch of customers she had every spring whose pores opened up especially big. She called them "men in bloom." They returned to the parlor, angry and fearful, to show her that their backs were sprouting flowers or vegetables or bay trees. My aunt took them into a private room where she assured them that there was nothing to worry about. She sat them down and asked them: Well, isn't this what you wanted.

Guo might as well be talking about the reader because isn't that what you want, to be brought by words to a place where anything can happen? It is certainly what this reader wants. If you regularly read fiction and watch movies, at a certain point you pretty much know what is going to happen next. Can the writer or filmmaker surprise, interest, or excite you? Can he or she keep you eager?

This is what Guo does in *Our Colony Beyond the City of Ruins,* her debut collection. She elaborates a self-sufficient world that runs according to its own inner logic. In "Bloom," the narrator "[performs] gua sha on [her] life" and wonders how it will change her. The ending leaves us in a world still open to our curiosity, one that is not neat, and this is true of all the stories in this marvelous collection.

I say *marvelous* because each of Guo's stories is packed with strange and spectacular events, which she renders with enough explicit detail to keep this reader hungering for more. She can shift registers in the blink of an eye. After a character in "Night Floats" describes the liquid diet he must subsist on after he has his jaw wired shut, he finishes with this flourish: "In fact, along with my shake, I ate a plump marshmallow shredded into small pieces."

In the story "The Sea Captain's Ghost," the reader encounters three characters: the Sea Captain's Ghost, as well as the Sea Captain, who is not dead yet, and the Sea Captain's Daughter, Daphne, who lives in the "Starfish Villa," which is colored "light pink" and has "five arms that convene at the center [...] like a starfish." The fabulist side of Guo's stories never overwhelms the emotional. She never explains away the inchoate feelings bubbling in her characters.

No matter what happens, Guo's characters adjust to their new circumstances. "Acting Lessons" begins: "When our men came down with a strange sickness, my mother and I took over watching the frog pond." This is followed in the very next sentence by, "We wore their clothes." How can you not want to go on, not be curious to see what will happen next, or how Guo will fill in the space she just opened up by placing these sentences together. Not only does the author fill in the space, but she opens up more spaces: "Not accustomed to being still, I continued to perform for my mother as the leading lady of her night-vision diorama."

Guo goes down multiple tracks simultaneously. There is the "strange sickness"; and the narrator's mother, who was "not an actor anymore"; and the father, who was a "renowned director" famous for staging Henrik Ibsen's *A Doll's House* in village after village along the Yellow River. Once the narrator gets these balls in the air, she adds more as she moves forward in time and space. And for all the strangeness of this world—its sense of nature gone out of control, confronting its inhabitants with threatening circumstances—what drives the stories are the relationship of a daughter and her parents, a worker and her co-worker, a girl of 11, and a boy who lives "two pools" down from her "[in] the island town of Crow, [where] only hearts were planted in the ground to conserve space."

John Yau

Guo's stories take place in China's cities and countryside, in Paris, and in made up places. New diseases and weather patterns are mixed together with ancient remedies and rituals. Her concoctions do many things. For one, they imagine a preternatural world that people have gracefully adjusted to. They also do something that I think needs to be said: they take Asian American fiction to a new place, where categories that may once have been used to separate realist narratives, science fiction, fabulist concoctions, and folktales no longer apply. That is a major accomplishment.

Acknowledgments

"What Is a Poet?" first appeared in *Hyperallergic Weekend* (September 2, 2018).

"Rudy Burckhardt and Edwin Denby, Flâneurs of Astoria" first appeared in *Hyperallergic Weekend* (October 22, 2017).

"The Flickering Grace of Rudy Burckhardt" first appeared in *Hyperallergic Weekend* (December 28, 2014)

"Frank O'Hara and the Practice of Everyday Life" first appeared in *Lovers of My Orchards: Writers and Artists on Frank O'Hara* (Montepellier: Presses universitaires de la Méditerranée—PULM, 2017), edited by Olivier Brossard.

"Kanemitsu in California in the 1960s and '70s" first appeared in *The Brooklyn Rail* (May, 2008).

"On the Poems of John Godfrey" first appeared in *Hyperallergic Weekend* (January 27, 2013).

"Stranded with Rick Snyder" first appeared in *The Brooklyn Rail* (November 2009).

"Asians in Hollywood" first appeared in *Hyperallergic Weekend* (July 15, 2018).

"Patty Chang: *The Product of Love*" first appeared in *The Brooklyn Rail* (July–August, 2009).

"What Happens After Eric Baus's Pharmacy Fills with Sand?" first appeared in *Hyperallergic Weekend* (August 3, 2014).

"In Death, Licked by a Dog" first appeared in *The Brooklyn Rail* (June 2009).

"On *Haute Surveillance* by Johannes Göransson" first appeared in *Hyperallergic Weekend* (May 12, 2013).

"Staying Up with Suzanne Buffam's *Pillow Book*" first appeared in *Hyperallergic Weekend* (May 14, 2017).

"When a Poet Becomes Invisible" first appeared in *Hyperallergic Weekend* (September 7, 2019).

"Nicolas Hundley's Heretical Machinery" first appeared in *Hyperallergic Weekend* (May 29, 2016).

"Will Alexander's Celebration of the Possible" first appeared in *Hyperallergic Weekend* (August 13, 2017).

"China's Buried Past and Submerged Future" first appeared in *Hyperallergic Weekend* (July 6, 2014).

"The Five-Star Delight of Driving Across America with Ron Padgett" first appeared in *Hyperallergic Weekend* (May 7, 2017).

"At Play in The Fields of Language: The Poetry of Cathy Park Hong" first appeared as a two-part review in *Hyperallergic Weekend* (December 1 and December 2, 2012).

"Donna Stonecipher, Global Flâneur" first appeared in *Hyperallergic Weekend* (August 5, 2018).

"Ai Weiwei: *New York Photographs 1983–1993*" first appeared in *The Brooklyn Rail* (September 2011).

"John Ashbery—A Prince of the Clouds" first appeared in *Hyperallergic Weekend* (October 7, 2018).

"An Artist Conjures the Ghosts of Displacement" first appeared in *Hyperallergic Weekend* (May 13, 2018).

"The Earth Before the End of the Earth" first appeared in an earlier version on the Poetry Foundation website (July 13, 2011). The essay was revised in mid-December 2018.

"The Great Kenward" first appeared in *Hyperallergic Weekend* (November 6, 2016).

"Language Is Not Colorless: The Amazing Writing of Sawako Nakayasu" first appeared in *Hyperallergic Weekend* (April 26, 2015).

"Introduction to *New Generation: Poems from China Today*" first appeared as the introduction to *New Generation: Poems from China Today* (Brooklyn: Hanging Loose Press, 1999).

"The Need for Opaque Identities" first appeared in *Hyperallergic Weekend* (November 3, 2018).

"Trevor Winkfield's Undomesticated Imagination" first appeared in *Hyperallergic Weekend* (February 25, 2018).

"An Arcadian Moment in New York's Lower East Side, circa 1969" first appeared in *Hyperallergic Weekend* (June 8, 2014).

"George Schneeman, Quietly Radical" first appeared in *Hyperallergic Weekend* (November 4, 2017).

"Why I am a Member of the Ron Padgett Fan Club" first appeared in *Hyperallergic Weekend* (November 24, 2013).

"Ian Hamilton Finlay's Philosophical Gardening" first appeared in *Hyperallergic Weekend* (September 30, 2018).

"When Capri Was the Place to Be" first appeared in *Hyperallergic Weekend* (April 7, 2019).

"How Frederic Tuten Became a Writer" first appeared in *Hyperallergic Weekend* (March 10, 2019).

"Wallace Berman's Magical World" first appeared in *Hyperallergic Weekend* (April 21, 2019).

"'Purity' and the 'Avant-Garde'" first appeared in an earlier version in *Boston Review* (April 29, 2015).

"Marilyn Chin: Poet, Translator, Provocateur" first appeared in *Hyperallergic Weekend* (July 27, 2014).

"Foreign Sounds or Sounds Foreign" first appeared in *Hyperallergic Weekend* (August 28, 2016).

"The Meme After the Fall of The Tower of Babel" first appeared in *Hyperallergic Weekend* (November 11, 2012).

"Nicholas Moore, Touched by Poetic Genius" first appeared in *Hyperallergic Weekend* (January 11, 2015).

"Why I Am a Member of the Christopher Middleton Fan Club" first appeared in *The Brooklyn Rail* (October 2010).

"Christopher Middleton's Prose" first appeared in *Hyperallergic Weekend* (October 26, 2014).

"One More Thing I Want to Say About Christopher Middleton" first appeared in *Hyperallergic Weekend* (July 1, 2018).

"Why I am a Member of the Lee Harwood Fan Club" first appeared in *Hyperallergic Weekend* (November 9, 2014).

"Digging into Time and Memory with John Koethe" first appeared in *Hyperallergic Weekend* (January 4, 2019).

"Douglas Crase, Literary Subversive" first appeared in *Hyperallergic Weekend* (March 4, 2018).

"Charles North Shows Us How to Read without Relying on Theories" first appeared in *Hyperallergic Weekend* (February 25, 2018).

"The Many Pleasures of Reading Donald Britton's Poems" first appeared in *Hyperallergic Weekend* (June 26, 2016).

"Killed by the State" first appeared in *Hyperallergic Weekend* (July 10, 2016).

"A Forensic Poet for Our Time" first appeared in *Hyperallergic Weekend* (September 11, 2016).

"The Confessional Poem Made New" first appeared as an earlier version in *The Brooklyn Rail* (June 2006).

"A Thriver in the Muck" first appeared in *Hyperallergic Weekend* (May 26, 2013).

"Jennifer Reeves, Writer and Artist" first appeared as "Introduction" to *Jennifer W. Reeves on Facebook: insightful on a blank page scratch by scratch* (2018)

"Ann Lauterbach Expands the Possibilities of Poetry" first appeared in *Hyperallergic Weekend* (February 10, 2019).

"The Rise and Fall of Three Actresses" first appeared in *Hyperallergic Weekend* (August 31, 2019).

"Dissolving the Boundaries of Asian American Fiction" first appeared in *Hyperallergic Weekend* (January 13, 2019).

About the Author

JOHN YAU is the author of many books of poetry, fiction, and criticism. His poetry books include *Radiant Silhouette: New & Selected Work 1974–1988* (1989) *Borrowed Love Poems* (2002) *Ing Grish* (2005) and *Bijoux in the Dark* (2018). His fiction includes *Hawaiian Cowboys* (1995) and *My Symptoms* (1998). His books about art include *Wifredo Lam: Catalogue Raisonné of the Painted Work: 1961–1982* (2002); *A Thing Among Things: The Art of Jasper Johns* (2008); *Joan Mitchell: Trees* (2014); *Catherine Murphy* (2016); *Thomas Nozkowski* (2017); and *Philip Taaffe* (2018). He has previously published two collections of criticism: *The Passionate Spectator: Essays on Art and Poetry* (2006) and *The Wild Children of William Blake* (2017). He has received awards and fellowships from the John Simon Guggenheim Memorial Foundation, National Endowment of the Arts, Academy of American Poets, New York Foundation of the Arts, and the Foundation for Contemporary Arts. He has been named a Chevalier in the Order of Arts and Letters by the French government, and been given the Distinguished Alumni Award from Brooklyn College (Class of 1978) and an honorary doctorate from the College of Creative Studies in Detroit. In 2018, he was awarded the Jackson Poetry Prize, which is awarded annually by *Poets & Writers* to "an American poet of exceptional talent who deserves wider recognition." He is Professor of Critical Studies at Mason Gross School of the Arts (Rutgers University) and lives in New York.

www.ingramcontent.com/pod-product-compliance
Lightning Source LLC
Chambersburg PA
CBHW020323170426
43200CB00006B/255